BROTHERS IN BLOOD
The Rise of the Criminal Brotherhoods

BROTHERS IN BLOOD

The Rise of the Criminal Brotherhoods

DAVID LEON CHANDLER

E. P. DUTTON & CO., INC.   NEW YORK 1975

Library of Congress Cataloging in Publication Data

Chandler, David Leon.
  Brothers in blood.

1. Organized crime—History. 2. Mafia. I. Title.
HV6441.C43 1975   364.1'06   74-22033
            ISBN 0-525-07185-7

Copyright © 1975 by David Leon Chandler
All rights reserved. Printed in the U.S.A.

First Edition

10 9 8 7 6 5 4 3 2 1

No part of this publication may be reproduced or transmitted in any form or by any means, electronic or mechanical, including photocopy, recording, or any information storage and retrieval system now known or to be invented, without permission in writing from the publisher, except by a reviewer who wishes to quote brief passages in connection with a review written for inclusion in a magazine, newspaper, or broadcast.

Published simultaneously in Canada by Clarke, Irwin & Company Limited, Toronto and Vancouver

Designed by The Etheredges

CONTENTS

INTRODUCTION: THE BROTHERHOOD ORGANISM   1

BOOK ONE: ORIGINS   3

COMPAGNIA DELLA GARDUNA   5
MAZZINI   14

BOOK TWO: THE SICILIANS   33

WHAT IS MAFFIA?   35
THE MAFIA IN SICILY   52

BOOK THREE: TRAVELS IN AMERICA 65

THE BLACK HAND 67
THE BIRTH OF THE AMERICAN MAFIA 73
SAN FRANCISCO, 1878 99
NEW YORK, 1878–1918 105

BOOK FOUR: COSA NOSTRA 127

COSA NOSTRA: RIVALRY AND CONSOLIDATION 129
THE MAKING OF THE SYNDICATE 158
LOUISIANA IN THE TWENTIETH CENTURY 172

BOOK FIVE: UNIONE CORSE 195

CONTEMPORARY OPERATIONS 197
THE NARCOTICS SERVICE 208
UNIONE CORSE 218
CONCLUSION 226
APPENDIX A: EARLIER SOCIETIES 230
APPENDIX B: MINOR BROTHERHOODS OF THE NINETEENTH CENTURY 236
INDEX 241

ACKNOWLEDGMENTS

My thanks to Paul Mahon of New York City and Russell Sackett of Washington, D.C.; and to Richard Angelico, Jim Bell, Anne Coyle, Tom Flaherty, Connie Griffith, Colin Hamer, Lucy Kelly, Aaron Kohn, Leigh Morin, Janice Pikey, Sandy Smith, Ted Swift, Greg Walter, Candy Weiss, Jack Weiss, John Zwick, and to several confidential correspondents in the United States, France, and Italy.

INTRODUCTION: THE BROTHERHOOD ORGANISM

The men you will meet in this book will be unknown to you for the most part, yet they have shaped some history. They are the dons, capos, and soldiers of a criminal collective that has evolved over the past five hundred years. They have formed organizations known as the Spanish Garduna, the Neapolitan Camorra, the Sicilian Mafia, the American Cosa Nostra, and the Unione Corse.

The brotherhood began as a freak offshoot of fifteenth-century humanism. It was a century when Western authority, secular and religious, was breaking down. Throughout Europe people were seeking a new order. Some, like Joan of Arc, chose a path of reform Christianity. Others, like her friend the young marshal Gilles des Rais, chose Satanism. In Castile, Ferdinand executed a complex twenty-year offensive to conquer Muslim

Granada and unify Spain under one government. And also in Spain, somewhere in the hills above Seville, a group of propertyless outcasts, men and families who had become hill bandits, came together to form a criminal collective. It was the first brotherhood society.

Nothing like the brotherhood existed prior to the fifteenth century. There had been earlier "criminal societies," most notably the Assassins of eleventh-century Persia; the Thugs, founded in thirteenth-century India; and the Chauffeurs, founded in thirteenth-century France. But each of those claimed noncriminal motives to justify their existence. The Assassins were political terrorists. The Thugs and Chauffeurs were religious cults.

The men of the Spanish brotherhood did not lean on such rationales. Their conceptual innovation was to provide their services for church, state, criminals, or virtually any client with the required fee. They conducted themselves as a business, investing some of their revenues in police and political protection, setting some aside for pensions, and sharing the rest as profit. A rigorous code of conduct was imposed and secrecy and discipline were strict.

Their most inflexible law was the application of the death penalty for those who violated either secrecy or discipline. The brotherhood's adherence to that law has subsequently caused a relative absence of historical treatment. Journalists, sociologists, and governmental agencies have written histories on some of the individual societies, particularly the Mafia and the Cosa Nostra. But such efforts have examined only sections of the overall organism, an arm here, a leg there.

It is the intention here to survey the origins of the brotherhood and its constituent societies, tracing its development from the original society, the Garduna, to the now-evolving Unione Corse. Along the way some questions will be finally laid to rest, such as what is the Mafia and where did it come from?

BOOK ONE
ORIGINS

COMPAGNIA DELLA GARDUNA

In Seville there is said to be a brotherhood of thieves with a chief magistrate and captains who sell services; it has a depository for stolen goods and a chest with three keys in which the loot is kept; from this chest they take what they need to defray expenses and to bribe those who are in a position to help them when they are in trouble. They are very careful to accept only men who are strong and active and old Christians,* their membership being limited to the servants of powerful and high-placed individuals such as agents of the law; and the first oath to which they swear is that, even though they may be drawn and quartered, they will endure it and will not inform on their companions. And so, when something is missing from the home of a respectable citizen and

---

*Old Christians as opposed to "new" Christians. The latter were Muslim or Jewish converts to Christianity, and it was felt they were not to be trusted.

> *people say that the devil has taken it, the truth of the matter is that it is not the devil but one of these. That they have a brotherhood is certain, and it has lasted longer than the principality of Venice; for although the law has caught a few unfortunate ones, it has never been able to run down the leader of the gang.*
> —MISCELANEA, BY LUIS ZAPATA, WRITTEN CA. 1598

Luis Zapata was one of the earliest writers to mention a criminal society which had laws, a secret oath, a hierarchy of authority, selective membership, and services for sale. The leader, whom the law had "never been able to run down," was well known to another writer of the era, Miguel Cervantes. And four years after Zapata's account, Cervantes wrote a profile of the leader which launched Cervantes' reputation as a popular novelist and set the stage for the *Don Quixote* novels.

The brotherhood described by Zapata and Cervantes was the parent society of the Sicilian Mafia and the American Cosa Nostra. More enduring than "the principality of Venice," it was created sometime in the early fifteenth century. Nineteenth-century scholars, investigating the folklore, established a traditional date of origin as A.D. 1417.

The age was as morally fluid as our own and its inhabitants as uncertain as ourselves. A feeling of doom extended over the planet. Writers and artists, whether Korean, Aztec, Inca, English, or French, warned of disintegration of the social fabric. Astrology, sorcery, and occult practices thrived. Violence flourished. Commoners and governors alike were open to bribes. Murderers, thieves, and drunkards owned the streets and highways. Sodomy was frequent, prostitution was general, adultery was universal. Nudist sects abounded. Obscene pictures were widely marketed and were sold even in churches.

The symbol of the age was the dance of death in which cavorting skeletons led men, women, and children step by merry step to hell. The theme was a constant one in plays, public entertainments, poetry, and the paintings of Dürer, Holbein, and Bosch. The world was viewed as evil and it was a popular belief that no one had entered paradise in the first

COMPAGNIA DELLA GARDUNA 7

thirty years of the century. In two-thirds of the world, order was drowning in waves of dissent and revolt; all authority was questioned, and people felt capable of challenging a social and religious authority that was beginning to collapse.

Nowhere was that authority in more turmoil than in the Iberian peninsula on the fringe of Europe. At the beginning of the century Iberia was divided among the rival Christian kingdoms of Navarre, Aragon, and Castile, and the Muslim nation of Granada which held the southeast corner of modern Spain. Commerce languished, hampered by debased currencies, royal monopolies, diverse weights and measures, highway bandits, Mediterranean pirates, and taxes levied by the Roman Catholic Church and others. Life was difficult for everyone. For the lower social orders it was nearly impossible.

By the end of the fifteenth century, everything had improved. The Moors were expelled. Spain was consolidated under one government. Weights and measures and currencies were standardized. Social order was imposed and trade flourished. With an empire extending from Sicily in the east to the newly discovered Americas in the west, Spain was the most powerful state in the world.

The sweeping changes did not occur peacefully. They were brought about over a period of years by the determination of Ferdinand, king of Sicily and Aragon, and of his queen, Isabella of Castile. Their marriage in 1469 was the first step toward the unification of Spain. Step two was the subjugation of Moorish Granada, an enterprise in which Ferdinand employed a number of tools. A primary tool was the Office of the Holy Inquisition. A secondary tool was the Garduna, the brotherhood described by Cervantes and Zapata.

The Spanish Inquisition was established by Ferdinand in 1478 to strengthen his governmental control over the peninsula. Ostensibly organized to discover whether Spanish Jews were sincere in their conversion to Christianity, it was popularly received by the general Christian population. From the beginning, however, it functioned as a secret police and a trial court answerable only to Ferdinand. Unlike the earlier medieval inquisitions in other nations, the Spanish Inquisition was under full control of the king rather than the pope. Ferdinand used it to conduct espionage among his subjects and to punish and intimidate political dissent. Held in the ever-tightening grip of the Inquisition, the commerce, arms, and population of Spain were welded into a single weapon powerful enough to crush Granada.

The Inquisition was particularly active along the borders of Granada and it was there that the priests apparently came into contact with the Garduna, probably around the year 1480. If the traditional date of origin of 1417 is correct, the Garduna had already been in existence for some sixty years. No written account of the Garduna's first sixty years has been found, but it can be inferred that it had evolved beyond the hill bandit stage and had become city oriented.

This city orientation was in itself an unusual phenomenon. In that era, most communities were too small and population movement, monitored at city gates, too controlled for gangs to survive without detection. Instead outlaw bands traditionally cut out a geographic territory for themselves in the countryside and levied tariffs on travelers. The members of the Garduna, however, were known not as highway predators but as "martens," highly intelligent animals with gorgeous fur that raid chicken houses without a sound from the chickens. The marten was a master burglar and so were the members of the Garduna, operating in the villages, towns, and cities.

Around the year 1480, shortly after the Inquisition was introduced to Spain, the Garduna hired out its services. It was a significant union, for it brought the proletarian Garduna into alliance with high officers of government, an advantage it would enjoy in Spain for the next 340 years.

The Garduna made commando raids inside the borders of Granada. Their harassment of villages and large estates caused tension among the Moors. Moorish troops were detached from the main army to provide garrison defenses. This guerrilla activity was of substantial assistance when Ferdinand began his military campaign against Granada in 1482. When the conquest was completed ten years later, the Garduna switched from its sanctioned raids on Moors and Jews to more stealthy predations against the entire Spanish population. It felt secure in doing this because of the liaisons built up over the ten-year period with priests, inquisitors, and royal officers. During the war, the Garduna had been employees. After the war, the Garduna became in effect employers, buying protection from members of the government.

It also continued to sell its services, and beginning in the year 1520 the Garduna commenced to keep written records of its crimes, clients, and fees. These records would be referred to by Cervantes in 1602 and actually produced at a trial in Seville in 1822. They showed that the most frequent clients were the priests and officers of the Spanish Inquisition, who accounted for nearly one-fifth of all the commissioned crimes. Over the 147-year period covered by the record, the priests had ordered and paid for slightly more than two thousand felonies, an average of one per month. The fees charged were regular rates—so much per murder, so much per abduction. Of the priest-commissioned crimes, the carrying off of women made up about one-third. Assassinations formed another third. The balance was taken up by lesser crimes—robbery, false testimony, denunciation, and maiming. The usual financial arrangements were that one-half the price of the crime was paid in advance and the remainder upon completion.

By 1602 the Garduna was a venerable institution in southern Spain. Its headquarters was Seville, a city with a large population representing virtually every culture, be it European, African, Muslim, American, or Oriental. The municipal administration was exceedingly lax and corrupt and the city was filled with thieves, bandits, pickpockets, and lawbreakers of every sort. One chronicler, Luis de Peraza, reports that even small boys went armed in imitation of their elders—armed with knives, not toys—and thieves' argot was almost a common speech.

The writer Miguel de Cervantes Saavedra was serving time in the Seville prison, having been convicted of embezzlement. While in prison he wrote a story called *Rinconete and Cortadillo*, which was his first popular work. The story is best known as the literary parent of the *Don Quixote* novels, but it is also the world's earliest profile of a brotherhood boss, a man named Monipodio.

The story concerns the adventures of two vagabond boys, Pedro Rincon and Diego Cortado. Pedro is a practiced cardsharp and Diego an equally skilled pickpocket. Both are younger than sixteen years. They journey to Seville, where they promptly seek out the main marketplace and steal a man's purse. Shortly afterward they are approached by another teenaged boy who says he witnessed the theft. He asks if they have registered in the "bad book of Señor Monipodio's customs house." Pedro and Diego have never heard of such a thing and are told that all thieves in Seville must register with the boss, Monipodio, who is "the father, teacher, and protector" of all criminals.

They are led to Monipodio's large, sprawling house. A variety of criminals lounge about in the courtyard, including two dandyish *ponteadores*, professional killers in the Garduna. These are elite technicians and Cervantes describes them as "swaggering young ruffians with large mustaches, broadbrimmed hats, Walloon ruffs, colored stockings and showy garters. Their swords exceeded the length allowed by law and each carried a brace of pistols."

The boss, Monipodio, was a huge dark-complexioned man with a thick black beard. He wore "an expensive shirt open at the throat to show his hairy chest, wide linen breeches, no shoes, and a swordbelt draped across his chest from which hung a broadsword made by the finest swordmaker in Spain."

The boys are questioned about their skills and backgrounds and, as a literary convenience, Monipodio waives a customary one-year tryout for novices and inducts them into the Garduna. They are given the secret oath, violation of which is punishable by death, and told that all loot must be turned over to the boss for division.

Part of the spoils, Monipodio explains, will go to benefactors of the brotherhood, including "the constable who tips us off; the executioner who shows us mercy; the one who defends us in court . . . and the court clerk who, if things go as they should, sees to it that there is no crime that is not a misdemeanor and no misdemeanor that gets much punishment." In short, the Fix is in, from the lowly constable on the street to the very bowels of justice, the records clerk.

As the story unfolds, we learn that the Garduna not only protects its members from the law but also schools them in new techniques. As one proves his skills and loyalties, one advances in rank and each promotion brings more prestige, more profit, and more authority. The Garduna is a bureaucracy of specialists presided over by a paternal dictator who gives advice, settles disputes, protects his people, and allocates rewards. His authority rests on respect for his office, his personal wisdom, and force. Violation of the boss's discipline is punished by the deadly ponteadores.

Details of the specialization are plentifully supplied by Cervantes. In one instance, two elderly and dignified men visit the house. The boys are surprised to see such unromantic figures in Monipodio's company. They are told, however, that the men are "hornets," who roam the city by day spying out houses to be robbed at night. Because of their social position the "hornets" have access to the better houses and to the Bank of India, where they watch to see who withdraws money and where the money is taken. The old men are "quite as useful as any other member of the brotherhood, if not more so, and receive a fifth of whatever is stolen as a result of their efforts, just as His Majesty gets a fifth of any treasure that is found."

Detailed, too, is the businesslike way in which respectable citizens commission crimes. Cervantes compares it to ordering a suit from the tailor. The citizen places his order, makes a 50-percent down payment, and the job and the fee are entered by Monipodio in a logbook.

After a series of successful adventures involving the boys and Monipodio, Cervantes leaves the story open ended. The boss is still prosperous and uncaught and the boys are working for him. Cervantes tells the reader he will write a sequel of their further adventures.

The work was a popular sensation, Cervantes' first. But despite his later pattern of writing sequels using successful characters, such as Sancho Panza, no sequel to the story of the Garduna boss is known to exist.

Perhaps Cervantes was cautioned against a sequel. *Rinconete and Cortadillo* most likely outraged the municipal authorities and possibly the Garduna itself. For it is an outright satirical exposé rather than a piece of fiction. The details have proved quite accurate in every respect, down to the location of houses and the names of streets. A nineteenth-century scholar even pinpointed the house of Monipodio, it being a residence and courtyard at number four, calle de la Cruz in modern Seville.

The mention of a logbook, "Señor Monipodio's bad book," is further proof of Cervantes' accuracy. Identical logbooks, perhaps the same ones, were produced in Seville more than two hundred years later at a trial of Garduna leaders.

The trial was held in 1822, a few months after the Spanish government had finally expelled the Inquisition from Spain. After the Inquisition priests left, the government dispatched a troop of mountain chasseurs to exterminate the Garduna. In a surprise raid, they seized the house of the grand master of the society, one Francisco Cortina, a powerful and wealthy Spaniard and frequent guest at the royal court. In his house were found logbooks dating from 1520 to 1821.

The ledgers showed that the Garduna had main branches in Seville, Toledo, Barcelona, and Cordova, with subsidiary organizations in many smaller towns. Entries relating to the Spanish Inquisition spanned 147 years, from 1520 to 1667, when written references to Inquisition-commissioned crimes ceased without explanation. The government, however, demonstrated in the 1822 trial that the Garduna's special relationship with the clergy was continuing even at that time.

Testimony at the trial showed that the grand master had control of all profits and would divide the proceeds into three parts. One went into the general fund, to pay for bribes to judges, magistrates, governors of prisons, and other officials. Another third was reserved for contingencies such as pensions for the wives of dead or imprisoned members. The final third was turned back to the members who had committed the crime, after the boss had taken his share.

These special funds were the same as those described by Cervantes in 1602. An identical system was used by the American Cosa Nostra in the 1960s, according to U.S. Senate committee investigations.

Indeed, many features developed by the Garduna have survived into the twentieth century. One of these was the Garduna model for a hierarchy. At the top was a boss, a grand master. Beneath him were chiefs of various localities, captains called *capatazes* (or in the Cosa Nostra, *capos*). Beneath them were a layer of specialists—commercial spies, financial technicians, expert killers. At the bottom were the soldiers, the rank-and-file membership who acted as foremen to oversee particular crimes. The crimes themselves were usually done by nonmembers, either novice applicants to the society or common criminals hired for a particular job.

Also surviving into the twentieth century without change were an oath of secrecy with direct consequences for disobedience, a law against the molestation of women associated with fellow members, and the institution of service-for-hire, whether that service be murder, robbery, gambling, correction of an injustice, or movement of contraband.

The ledger book seized in 1822 provided the basis for conviction of the grand master and sixteen of his chief captains. They were hanged in the marketplace of Seville on November 25, 1822. The mass hangings provided a final sequel to Cervantes' book.

There is no indication that the Garduna was a factor in Spanish cities after that time. In 1872 the historian C. W. Heckethorn reported in *Secret Societies of All Ages* that the Garduna had emigrated to the New World: "The Garduna was reorganized in South America, where it existed in 1846 in Brazil, Peru, the Argentine Republic, and Mexico, and where for a few dollars a hired assassin will rid you of an enemy."

No further reports of the society have been uncovered. The Garduna effectively vanished in the nineteenth century. Long before it expired, however, its vigor and its institutions were passed on to a direct descendant—the Camorra of Naples.

MAZZINI

> In a Naples prison in 1906 a duel took place in which the honor of the Neapolitan Camorrists and the Sicilian Mafiosi were at stake. A most deadly challenge was given and twelve Neapolitan champions were chosen to fight twelve Sicilians. In the ensuing combat two Sicilians rolled dead upon the floor and three Neapolitans were mortally wounded. It was necessary for soldiers to pull down the roofs of the room and point their guns against the strugglers in order to pacify those wild beasts.
>
> OUTLOOK MAGAZINE, July 29, 1911

Spanish kings ruled Naples and Sicily from 1504 to 1707 and from 1738 to 1860. In the first Spanish reign, a criminal society was founded in Naples called the "Camorra," a Spanish word meaning "fight" or "quarrel."

The infant Camorra was a direct offshoot of the Garduna, and very probably was composed of Spanish Gardunists and native Neapolitans.* During the second Spanish reign, the Camorra gave birth to a new society, the Sicilian Mafia. The connecting link between the Camorra and the Mafia seems to have been the Italian revolutionary hero Giuseppe Mazzini.

The Camorra of Naples was the most powerful criminal society of the eighteenth and nineteenth centuries. In the Camorra we find the contemporary godfather—fully recognizable, fully grown—not an ancient museum relic with bare feet, clanking sword, and paralyzing breath, but a silk-suited, swaggering, knowledgeable solver of problems.

The Cammorist was a man of the big city, savvy and streetwise. It was to him that businessmen went for enforcement of contracts, or to whom fathers of compromised girls applied for marriage or revenge. He was a broker, though not always an honest one, operating between and among elements in an unstable social system.

The earliest investigation of the origins of the Camorra was published in 1862 by the French historian Marc Monnier. He concluded that the Camorra was an offshoot of the Garduna and noted that the two societies had much in common. Both were based on hierarchical government, both had the same laws, both existed to sell criminal services. The Camorra, however, went a step beyond the Garduna operation. Whereas the Garduna sold services to individual clients, the Camorra sold on a mass-market basis, providing law and order and merchants' licenses to entire sections of Naples and taxing the population accordingly. The Camorra was a second government.

Researching the files of the Spanish viceroys, Monnier found that the earliest reference to a Camorra-like gang in Naples was made in a Spanish rescript in the year 1529: "A certain Giulio Monti was hanged as a chief of plebeian bandits

---

*The assumption is based on the pattern of subsequent brotherhood societies such as the Sicilian Mafia, the American Mafia, and the American Cosa Nostra. In each of these, a cadre of immigrant members from the parent society collaborated with native criminals to form a new society.

who, in the heart of the city and in full day, subjected to the payment of taxes all defenceless persons." Slightly more detailed but equally brief reports to the Spanish king were filed by viceroys during the period 1568–1610. Monnier discovered six of these rescripts and each referred to a "secret society of criminals" which monopolized crime in sections of Naples and levied taxes for services.

One of the features of the early Camorra was the kiss of death, a ritual kiss on the cheek of a prospective assassination victim. The rank-and-file were organized into brigades or families. Each brigade *(brigata)* was presided over by a captain *(capo)*. All the captains of Naples collectively formed a Grand Council, which functioned both as a supreme court and as a legislature. Normally, the Grand Council was the final authority in the Camorra, but occasionally an exceptionally strong captain could impose his authority on the council and emerge as a grand master or, in modern terms, a boss of bosses.

Monnier's findings were confirmed in the 1870s by another researcher, Cesare Lombroso, known as the father of modern criminology. Lombroso paid less attention to historical research and instead concentrated on personal interviews with two hundred imprisoned Camorrists. He arrived at conclusions similar to those of Monnier. Lombroso believed that the Camorra dated from at least the sixteenth century and possibly as early as the reign of Ferdinand of Spain, who died in 1516.

Lombroso was impressed with the Camorra's well-developed social structure. It had an argot (language) of its own and an oral history. He classified the Camorra's organizational structure as "feudal." Territory was allocated to families on a vassalage basis, and the Grand Council or Grand Master granted licenses to do business within the territory. In return, each family owed the governing body a portion of its revenues, as well as homage and obedience.

In its earliest years, the Camorra's chief source of recruits was the prisons. Among documents Monnier turned up was a rescript of September 27, 1573, in which the viceroy stated: "It has come to our knowledge that extortions occur among the prisoners in the prisons of the Gran Corte della Vicaria, certain prisoners creating themselves as magistrates, and forcing others to pay them." The Camorra levied a tax on all new arrivals, and taxed all gambling in the jail. By the time the prisoners were set at liberty, they were willing recruits for this powerful organization.

"When a man of rank was thrown into prison," said Monnier, "he often received a special permit from the Camorra to carry arms. Thus, Signor Michele Persico, afterward a well-known member of the Italian parliament and a friend of Gladstone, and the Baron Carlo Peorio, two famous political prisoners of the Bourbons, on entering the Castel Capuano were accosted by a companion who made them a profound bow and presenting them with two stilletoes said: 'Take these, your excellencies, we authorize you to carry these arms.' " By such means, the Camorra courted the favor of powerful persons and when the Bourbons were overthrown by the Republicans the Camorra did not suffer.

As in the Garduna, the Camorra had a trial period for its recruits. Novices, called *garzone di mala vita,* served a probationary term of at least one year before graduating to *picciotto di sgarro* ("beginning member"). Until the mid-nineteenth century, the *picciotto* could only become a full-fledged Camorrist by committing a murder ordered by the society. This requirement was later eliminated.* Once the murder was done, the picciotto swore an oath on crossed swords with his hands immersed in his own blood that he would be faithful to his associates, that he would have no secret relation with the police, that he would never denounce a companion, that he would never have recourse to the law.

Once initiated into full membership, each man took his place in the lower ranks of the family structure. Families were divided into subgroups called *paranze.* Bosses of *paranze* had the title of *caporegima.* The capo supervised the everyday details of robbery, murder for hire, protection, blackmail, loan-

---

*The tradition, however, carried on. In the American Cosa Nostra it is a mark of distinction for a member to have "got his bones"; that is, to have murdered someone on the orders of a superior.

sharking, and the taxing of gambling halls. He levied a franchise tax on cabdrivers, boatmen, auctioneers, and dealers at state fairs headquartered in his district.

The revenues were turned over to the boss of the family. An amount was set aside to corrupt the police. Another fund was set aside to pension widows of deceased or imprisoned members. The third share was divided as profits. This was identical to the Garduna fund allocations described by Cervantes.

If a Camorrist was arrested, the man next on the list in the hierarchy automatically took over his place and duties, at least on a temporary basis until his promotion was confirmed by a formal meeting of either the family or the Grand Council.

Members judged guilty of offenses against the society could expect severe punishment. Testimony at the trial of sixty-six Camorrists in 1911 revealed that in bygone days there was a single penalty for disobedience or other infractions. The penalty was death. "However, at the present day," said the *Edinburgh Review's* account of the trial, "the penal code has grown milder. The following offences, however, still incur the death penalty: the revelation of secrets of the society, defrauding the society of its gains, and adultery with the wife of a member."

The findings of Camorra researchers in the nineteenth century had been made nearly four hundred years earlier by Cervantes in his story of the Garduna. The criminal services, the division of funds, the laws, and to a certain extent the organizational structure were identical and unchanged. Equally striking is testimony before the U.S. Senate in 1964 which shows the Cosa Nostra to be the same creature as that described by Cervantes, Monnier, and Lombroso.

For instance, Cosa Nostra member Joe Valachi testified that when he was initiated into the society he was told by his boss: "Here are the two most important things you have to remember. Drill them into your head. The first is that to betray the secret of Cosa Nostra means death without trial. Second, to violate any member's wife means death without trial."

The initiation rites of the Camorra and the Cosa Nostra are identical. Heckethorn, in *Secret Societies of All Ages,* described a nineteenth-century Camorra initiation: "On the reception of a picciotto into the degree of camorrist, the sectaries assembled around a table on which were placed a dagger, a loaded pistol, a glass of water or wine, and a lancet. The picciotto was introduced, accompanied by a barber who opened one of the candidate's veins. He dipped his hand in the blood and extending it towards the camorristi, he swore for ever to keep the secrets of the society and faithfully to carry out its orders."

Joe Valachi testified in 1964: "I sit down at the table. There is wine. Someone put a gun and a knife in front of me. The gun was a .38 and the knife was what we call a dagger. Maranzano [the boss] motions us up and we say some words in Italian. Then Joe Bonanno pricks my finger with a pin and squeezes until the blood comes out. What then happens, Mr. Maranzano says, 'This blood means that we are now one Family. You live by the gun and the knife and you die by the gun and the knife.'"

Another feature common to both the Camorra and Cosa Nostra is the Grand Council. In 1967, the Presidential Commission on Law Enforcement reported: "The highest ruling body in Cosa Nostra is the Commission, sometimes called the Grand Council . . . it is not a recent invention."*

A profile of an average Camorrist was published in 1890 by the Italian sociologist Alongi who had conducted interviews and physical examinations of more than two hundred members. According to Alongi, "The majority have naturally great physical strength, though many become syphilitic through habitual intercourse with prostitutes. The courage with which they endure physical pain is so extraordinary as to suggest a profound insensibility; they betray no signs of suffering under the most

---

*The earliest public report of an American Grand Council was published in the *Cleveland Plain Dealer* on December 6 and 7, 1928. Underworld sources described a meeting in that city of a national "Mafia Grand Council." In 1940, a confidential U.S. Narcotics Bureau report stated that a "Grand Council of nine men" ruled the American organized crime families. Investigations begun in 1959 by the Department of Justice concluded that American organized crime was coordinated by a "Commission or Grand Council" made up of nine to twelve men.

painful operations, and laugh while they sew up their own wounds. Not a few have epileptic tendencies, which they endeavour for some unknown reason to conceal. Many are, apart from their criminality, strange in character, and have occasional fits of apparent mania, not a few having been actually confined or having relatives who have been confined for insanity.

" . . . They are incapable of any work requiring perseverance and are devoted, during the leisure afforded them by the business of the society, to games of all kinds. Their affections are demonstrative but unstable. Religious feeling is general among them, taking the form of a love of ecclesiastical ceremonies and some peculiar superstitions. They are particularly devout to Our Lady of Mount Carmel, whom they regard as their special patron, and to the Souls in Purgatory, who in return for masses said for their repose render their clients invisible to the carabinieri. They have no political feelings, except a detestation of the police, although they are ready in their own interests to serve any political party."

Among the Camorrists studied by Alongi was Tobia Basile, who spent thirty years, from 1860 to 1890, in Italian prisons. Basile was more than fifty years old when he first entered prison in 1860 and while an inmate he established a school to teach the traditions and practices of the Camorra.

"His numerous pupils," wrote Alongi, "used to go to his lessons regularly to listen to his advice, to learn from him the science of 'prudence in crime' for he was a walking encyclopedia on the art of the *mala vita*. His long stay in the penitentiary, his cold and reflective temperament, his cleverness, and his venerable age made him a much-heeded master. For a few cents he would teach the art of stealing from a puppet entirely covered with numberless tiny bells that would jingle at the slightest touch; he taught the tradition of the Honorable Society and the chief rules to be observed in order to conform to its spirit, the art of dealing a straight or a treacherous blow, the way of slipping along the floor without making any noise, the secrets of the Camorristic jargon, a quantity of methods successful in diverting the attention of the police, the way of behaving in the courts, and all the numberless swindles committed against the emigrant who, coming from the provinces, stops a few days in Naples on his way to America. This extraordinary man was in possession of a complete outfit of false keys, files, and picklocks, and taught the aspirants all that it was necessary to know before being initiated into the Honorable Society."

While in prison, Basile came to value his silent and contemplative life, which suddenly became impossible upon his release and reunion with his wife. She unloaded conversations which had built up principal and interest for thirty years. Basile suffered it for ten years. Then on May 7, 1900, she disappeared. Basile, who had become something of a celebrity because of the Alongi reports, told newspaper reporters she had been abducted "for a ransom which a poor man like me doesn't have." Neighbors noted that as the months and then years passed he became more and more distraught and manic. Basile walked around in a daze, muttering about ghosts and spirits. One day he was seen packing his belongings in a cart, and was gone.

In 1910, the house was demolished by a new owner. In Basile's bedroom, workers discovered a shrine to Our Lady of Mount Carmel festooned with pieces of paper on which were written cabalistic signs. The shrine was reverently removed. Behind it was a false wall. Behind the wall was the skeleton of Mrs. Basile. From the condition of things, it was apparent that she had been walled up alive and had spent days screaming and trying to claw her way through the brick and plaster with her nails. The head of Basile's bed was approximately two feet from her tomb.

The Camorra virtually ruled Naples during the reign of the Spanish Bourbons, from 1738 to 1860. During the 122-year Bourbon rule, the Camorra expanded into nearly every field of economic enterprise including the stock market, food warehouses, manufacturing, and the licensing of retail shops. The Camorra's expansion into "legitimate business" was a turning point in the philosophy of the brotherhood, which had previously confined itself to out-and-out crime. This widening of interests was caused by a difference in quality of government. In Spain the regime reserved police powers to itself and provided services to meet at least the minimal needs of the population. That limited the Garduna's opportunities for growth. In the Kingdom of the Two Sicilies, however, the Spanish rulers offered virtually no services, being content simply to collect taxes. The Camorra, an existing and disciplined bureaucracy, moved in to fill the vacuum, first to control crime as the paid agent of the Bourbon police, and afterward as the de facto preserver of law, order, and commerce in the cities and towns of southern Italy.

In *Secret Societies of All Ages,* Heckethorn wrote that "the police being very badly organized under the Bourbon regime, leading merchants were glad to engage the Camorra to superintend the loading and unloading of merchandise. Camorristi were found at every town gate, the offices of the tax collector, the customs house, and the stations of coachmen and porters to impose their tax. Nurserymen bringing fruit into the town were mulcted for one sou the basket." Camorra protection was encouraged by the police; by paying a small sum every month, the private householder received protection against crime which the regular police were unable or unwilling to give.

In 1859, a year before the Italian revolution, the Bourbon police discovered that the Camorra was conducting espionage for the revolutionary alliance headed by King Victor Emmanuel II of Sardinia and the republicans Garibaldi and Mazzini. Some three hundred of the Camorra rank and file were rounded up and put into prison. In June 1860, when the revolution succeeded, the Camorrists were freed.

"Their first act," according to Heckethorn, "was to attack the commissaries of police, to burn their papers, and to beat the gendarmes to death with cudgels." The surviving police force hid its uniforms and fled. "The Camorra then encouraged the general population of Naples to riot and loot, and many neighborhoods even commandeered warehouses to store their contraband. Don Liborio, the new Prefect of Police, threw himself into the arms of the Camorristi to save Naples from pillage. And they prevented it. They were formed into a civic guard which kept order."

For the next several months, the society functioned as the police, judges, and tax collectors of Naples. During their administration, the crime rate dropped dramatically. Smuggling, for instance, had been the most widespread crime in Naples. It vanished entirely. The reason was that the Camorra had been the chief practitioner of smuggling. The society now forbade it and instead embezzled the duty taxes it collected on all goods entering Naples.

This proved to be a mistake. In the beginning, the society turned over nominal amounts of taxes to the government, but very quickly the amounts became too nominal. In the early months of 1861 the public treasury was receiving an average of twenty-five sous, approximately $1.10, in daily import duties for the entire port of Naples.

The regime responded with a surprise nighttime raid, arresting ninety Camorrists. The following day, import duties turned over to the government increased to approximately $4,200. But their compliance came too late. The Camorra's reign as an officially authorized government agency had ended.

The general public probably didn't mind if taxes were collected by the Camorra instead of the government. Indeed, during the society's brief rule the people had enjoyed certain advantages. Civil liberties, of course, were not much in evidence, but the war-weary people did receive order and security. The people of Naples viewed the conflict between the Camorra and the legal government as something not involving them.

The government followed up its first raid with a second nighttime raid. Conducted by the army, it bagged four hundred Camorrists in a six-hour period. The captives were dispatched to prisons throughout Italy to remove them from the Naples area. The Camorrists responded fiercely.

"Many of them," said Heckethorn, "returned to Naples and raised tumults in the streets. As the months passed, they became powerful at elections and with their cudgels directed the politics of the electors. Peaceful citizens were nightly assaulted and robbed in the streets of Naples. Burglaries became quite common. This state of things lasted till 1862," when the southern provinces were declared to be in a state of siege and martial law was imposed.

The Royal Italian Army was put into the field against the Camorra. Commencing in Naples and sweeping down into Sicily, between five and ten thousand troops were engaged for more than a year in the civil war. In 1863, the commanding officer told newspaper reporters that the "Camorra society and its branches in Sicily have been exterminated."

The battle with the army did not exterminate the Camorra but did mark the end of its power. The "branches in Sicily" were replaced by a new society, called the Mafia. By the end of the century, the Camorra had returned to its original state of four hundred years earlier—a local Neapolitan organization with no power beyond the borders of the province.

In 1911 even its power in Naples was shattered. In that year thirty-five Camorra leaders, including the Grand Master, Enrico Alfano, were tried for murder, convicted, and given long prison terms. The 1911 trial was the official obituary of the Camorra. In America a remnant of the society held on until 1918 when it was destroyed in New York by the American Mafia.

The successor to the Camorra was the Sicilian Mafia. And while the origins of the Garduna and the Camorra are relatively hazy, it can almost definitely be stated that the Sicilian Mafia was created by one man in Palermo in the year 1860. That man was Giuseppe Mazzini, the scholar and republican who was one of the primary shapers of nineteenth-century liberalism.

Mazzini was a complex, learned, and adventurous man. He was socially nimble, able to charm aristocracy, bourgeoisie, and proletariat. William Lloyd Garrison, the fierce American abolitionist, was a close friend and for twenty years nagged Mazzini to cease smoking. Other intimates included Dante Gabriel Rossetti, Algernon Swinburne, and the Brownings, whom Mazzini introduced to George Sand. He exchanged letters and complicated schemes with both Abraham Lincoln and Karl Marx.*
Mazzini fought on the side of kings and royal armies and he

---

*In a letter to Lincoln in 1863, Mazzini proposed that once the Civil War was won by the Union, Lincoln should subtly provoke a misunderstanding with Mexico and thereby unite North and South against a common foe. Lincoln's fought against them. He personally led at least three revolutions which failed dismally and two revolutions which temporarily succeeded.

Born in 1805 near Genoa, Mazzini spent his youth studying literature and philosophy. In his twenties, outraged by the various foreign occupations of Italy, he joined the Carbonari, a secret revolutionary group newly founded in Naples. Headed by two Corsicans, Francesco Passano and Raimondo Doria, the Carbonari was a mix of professional criminals, liberal aristocrats, and adventurous intellectuals. Mazzini was imprisoned by the French in 1830 for his Carbonari activities. In prison he sorted out his thoughts and established values by which he would guide his life.

His basic belief was that "life is a mission," a journey with a purpose, and he chose for himself the goal of unifying his native land, Italy. "The means by which to free Italy," he wrote, "is insurrection by guerrilla bands—the true method of warfare for all nations." These prophetic words would lead to his establishment of the Mafia.

Freed from prison in 1831, Mazzini promptly organized "The Young Italy Society." It differed from the Carbonari in that it emphasized youth (no person over forty was eligible), it was unabashedly committed to terrorism and assassination, and its members were to be loyal to a single leader—Mazzini.

No direct evidence exists, in the form of a memoir, statement, or letter signed by Mazzini, that conclusively proves he was the father of the Mafia. But the articles of organization which Mazzini drew up for Young Italy show that he and the brotherhood societies had certain common attitudes. For instance, Article 30 states: "Those who refuse obedience to the orders of this secret society, or reveal its mysteries, die by the dagger without mercy."

Articles 31 and 34 provide a judicial process identical to that of the Camorra: "The Secret tribunal [of Young Italy] pronounces sentence and appoints affiliated members for its execu-

---

reply indicated he found merit in the idea (*Mazzini*, by Bolton King, New York: E. P. Dutton & Company, 1902).

tion." The secret tribunal consisted of Mazzini and his chief captains. In the Camorra the tribunal consisted of the Grand Master and the family bosses.

There are six other articles of Young Italy, including a prohibition about members' wives, that relate to the oral code of the Camorra, the Mafia, and the Cosa Nostra. These similarities do not necessarily indicate that Mazzini used the Camorra as a model for the Articles of Young Italy, although that is not beyond possibility. But it does indicate that he and the brotherhood shared certain viewpoints on secret and illegal societies. Going a step further, one might ask if Mazzini were himself capable of murder, or of authorizing murder. The answer is yes.

The proof of it, however, is complicated by the political passions that surrounded Mazzini. His enemies were so determined to bring him down that, in several instances, they forged evidence linking him to assassinations. But it is fairly well established that Mazzini launched an attempt to kill King Charles Albert of Piedmont, and personally handed travel documents and a dagger to the would-be assassin, Antonio Gallenga. (Gallenga, a Corsican, backed out at the last moment and later became a correspondent for the London *Times*.) A more successful attempt was made against a police informer named Emiliani, who was stabbed to death near Toulouse. French police discovered an assassination order signed by Mazzini. And in 1848, Mazzini is believed to have presided over a secret tribunal which ordered the execution of Count Pellegrino Rossi, head of the ministries of police, finance, and the interior in Rome. Following Rossi's death, Mazzini replaced him as the most powerful man in Rome and for a brief reign relished his popular title of "The Dictator of Rome."

During the 1840s, Mazzini seems to have had close relations with the Camorra, and several friendly biographers report that he was assisted by the Camorra in a brief revolution in Naples in 1846. In the same revolution, Mazzini created an elite murder society, whose name is unknown. He gave written orders stating:

"At the first sortie each band should attack and kill the known Centurions [i.e., the auxiliary papal police] in the locality and all the known enemies of the Federation should be killed. It will not be a bad plan for every congregation to make a list of those enemies. . . . Our men will respect religion; but they will kill without pity priests whom they find at the head of the Centurions. The houses of the Centurions and of such seditious priests will be set on fire."*

Finally, in a series of letters and interviews published throughout the 1850s Mazzini personally defended a general policy of assassination. His argument was called "The Theory of the Dagger," and he put the theory into practice in the revolution of 1860.

Mazzini was not particularly welcome in the 1860 revolt. The leader was Garibaldi, who hoped to unify Italy under the monarchy of King Victor Emmanuel II of Piedmont. Garibaldi feared that the presence of the popular republican hero Mazzini would alarm the king and cause him to withdraw his money and troops. Nevertheless, Mazzini did have a substantial following, an enormous public reputation, and he wanted to participate. Garibaldi solved the problem by discreetly asking Mazzini to take a low profile and help organize Sicily, where the revolution was to begin.

Mazzini was residing in London and for about a year he communicated with Sicily via an agent. This agent was Rosalino Pino, a young Sicilian nobleman, who was authorized in Mazzini's name to establish secret revolutionary groups in the Palermo area. On April 3, 1860, the Mazzini groups in Palermo rose up and overthrew the Bourbons. Within days, Mazzini arrived to take command. A month later, Garibaldi and his Red Shirts landed in Sicily and the drive north into Italy began.

Mazzini remained in Palermo, gathering new recruits and sending them north to join Garibaldi. A *New York Times* account of August 2, 1860, reports that "picciotti by the hundreds are coming to Palermo to join Mazzini." A pogrom, of the kind Mazzini recommended in the 1846 revolt, commenced in Palermo province. Former officials and police were lynched

---

Joseph Mazzini by E. A. Venturi. London: Henry King, 1877.

daily by the picciotti and their houses burned. The terrorism of the Mazzinists created a huge scandal in the European and American press. Garibaldi, in the field with his army, decreed the death penalty "against anyone rising against the former police."

This Mazzini pogrom seems to have been the work of the original Mafia.

By September 1860, Palermo had settled into a semblance of order. In November the word "Mafia" appeared for the first time in public print.* The occasion was a play entitled "La Mafia," produced in Palermo by the Sicilian dramatist Giuseppe Rizzoti. It was a comedy of prison life in which the author humorously described an alliance between the jailers and the strongest of the prisoners. The prisoners stole and the jailers shared in the profits. Asked what the title signified, Rizzoti replied, "It is a bit of prison slang. I heard it while visiting the jail. It expresses the covenant made between warders and prisoners." He added that the system of bribery his play described referred not to the political situation in Palermo, but to Naples and the Camorra. He conceded, however, that a Camorra system had been transplanted to Palermo.† The play was highly successful and was followed in 1863 by a sequel produced under the title "I Mafiosi di la Vicaria" ("The Mafiosi of the Prison").

The sudden appearance of Mafia titles and themes suggests that the public had become intrigued by a new and exciting phenomenon. The date of the production is crucial. The Mafia was not a subject of public discussion prior to 1860; afterward it was. The fact that the play was a comedy suggests that the Mafia in 1860 wasn't yet dangerous enough to prevent playwrights from exploiting it or audiences from laughing at it.

---

*There exists a "Mafia" island off the coast of Tanzania which was given the name "Maffyah" by the Portuguese in the sixteenth century. The spelling was changed to "Mafia" by Richard Burton, probably around 1880. Neither "Maffyah" nor "Mafia" exist in Portuguese and the origin of the word is unknown.
†The date of the Rizzoti interview is unknown. The above version was reported in the November 8, 1890, *Illustrated American*. The author has been unable to discover the original source.

Significantly, from about 1870 until Mussolini's purge in 1928, little writing was published in Sicily on the subject of the Mafia.

Another contemporary source linking the Mafia to the 1860 revolution was a notorious Camorrist named Crocco Donatelli. In 1872 Donatelli was tried for seventy-four murders. In his own defense he described himself as a product of a violent environment and began recounting his life's history. He said that in 1859 he and other Camorrists had joined "the troops of Garibaldi and Mazzini." The revolutionary army included "42 criminal bands, each captained by a brigand chief." About a third of these criminal companies, he said, were organized by Mazzini in Sicily.

A less ambiguous account of the Mafia's role was given by another participant in the revolution, Giulio Lecca, an official of the Italian foreign ministry. In an 1888 interview he said, "The Mafia originally—that is thirty or forty years ago—was a political organization hostile to the Pope of Rome and the King of Naples. At that time some of the most respectable names in Italy were to be found among the members of the Mafia. But it degenerated from its high political purpose into an association of the lowest kind, whose leaders lived in luxury by levying tribute on working men, and through whom it was possible to get a personal enemy removed."*

Contemporary sources, then, provide two important pieces for the Mafia puzzle. First, it originally was associated with revolutionary activity. Second, it burst into public notice about the year 1860, and the name is not known to have appeared in any document prior to that year.

The word *Mafia* first appeared in a dictionary in 1868 when Traina's Sicilian-Italian dictionary defined it as a "neologism," a newly coined word denoting "any sign of bravado, a bold show." Montillaro's dictionary of 1876 was the next to include *Mafia*, defining it as a "word of Piedmontese origin . . . equivalent to Camorra." Mazzini was a native of Piedmont.

The first authority to connect Mazzini directly with the

---

*Lecca was interviewed in *The New York Times* October 16, 1888, and October 22, 1888. He was acting consul in New York City at the time.

founding of the Mafia was A. Vizzini in his book *La Mafia*, published in Rome in 1880. The Vizzini theory was picked up and expanded upon a few years later by Heckethorn, who asked:

"What is the meaning of the word Mafia? And whence comes it? The invention is attributed to Mazzini; it certainly was unknown before 1859 or 1860, the time when that agitator made his appearance in Sicily. It is well known that he had no faith in any class of society except its very dregs, and his having formed the vagabonds and thieves, who then swarmed all over Sicily, into a secret society of his own, seems well borne out by facts. The allegation is that he first formed a secret society called the *Oblonica* which word was coined by Mazzini from the two Latin words *obelus*, a spit, and *nico*, I beckon, which being joined and contracted became *oblonica*, meaning 'I beckon with a spit.' . . . Within this sect he formed an interior, more deeply initiated one, the members of which were called *Mafiusi*, from *Mafia*, composed of the initials of the five following words: *Mazzini, Autorizza, Furti, Incendi, Avvelenamenti*. 'Mazzini authorizes thefts, arsons, poisoning.' And the *Mafiusi* were accustomed to call these crimes their pani, or bread, since it was by them they lived."

Heckethorn's account is open to some criticism. His dislike for Mazzini is unabashed, and unfortunately he failed to give his sources for the "allegations" which he considered to be borne out by the facts.

In addition, there are numerous other theories of Mafia origin, none of which mention Mazzini. The most widely accepted version gives the society a patriotic birth. According to this theory the society was formed in 1282 as part of the Sicilian Vespers revolution against the French. The first mention of this theory, however, doesn't occur until 1890, six hundred years after the alleged origin. There is not the least evidence to support this claim, nor any other which antedates 1860.

For the Mazzini theory there is a preponderance of evidence. In his lifetime he created a number of secret societies, the earliest of which, Young Italy, resembles the Camorra (and the later Mafia) in its laws and judicial process. The unnamed society he formed in 1846 was specifically authorized to commit murder and arson. His association with Camorrists in the 1846 revolution and with Sicilian picciotti in the 1860 revolution is undisputed. Furthermore, there was a tradition in the Mafia that Mazzini was its creator.

In New Orleans in 1890, an imprisoned Mafioso named Joseph Polizi told many stories of the Mafia's history to a Pinkerton undercover agent, posing as a fellow prisoner. "The Mafia," Polizi said, "was begun by a great brigand named Giuseppe Mazzini."* Polizi, who was not only illiterate but had subnormal intelligence, could have had no source for the statement other than what he had been told by his Mafia colleagues in New Orleans—virtually all of whom were illiterate. It is fair to conclude that in 1890 Mazzini was part of the society's folklore.

Mazzini is in the same spot as a man caught at the scene of a burglarized safe. He has a history of safe-robbing. The jewels are in his pockets. And there are no other suspects. Mafia does indeed seem to mean "Mazzini authorizes thefts, arsons, poisonings." Using old-time Camorrists as his officers and sergeants, he created a guerrilla command of recruits from Palermo streets and the Sicilian countryside, an organization that would not die with him in 1871.

*The interview was reported in the New Orleans *Daily Picayune*, November 22, 1890.

BOOK TWO
THE SICILIANS

WHAT IS MAFFIA?

The English-speaking world first learned of the society's existence in 1874. In September of that year, the correspondent for *The Times* of London cabled a report from Perugia, an ancient university town in central Italy. He said that refugees were entering the city, their flight "occasioned by the exceptional state of the Island of Sicily" where a "new Camorra was organizing called the Sicilian Maffia."* He reported that a "large body of the Sicilian malefactors had been arrested in Palermo on the charge of robbing the Mont de Pieti, a government pawn-broking establishment of that city into which they had managed to effect their entrance by a regular series of underground engineering." After tunneling in, the Mafia had dragged out the

---

*In a story printed three weeks later the spelling was changed to "Mafia."

equivalent of about $200,000. They were eventually arrested, but when the government went to trial the jurors called wouldn't appear. The army was called in to eradicate the society and was promptly embarrassed when a Mafia chief known as Don Pasquale captured an entire cavalry troop in the hills outside Palermo. This original report tackled the question head-on: "What is the Maffia? It is the Sicilian form and name corresponding to what in Naples was so long and ominously known as the Camorra. The Maffia includes within its ranks members of all classes of society: the old Neapolitan Camorra could point to a Neapolitan Prince of the Blood as one of its members, and if the Sicilian Maffia is not quite so highly honored, it comprehends noblemen, judges, lawyers, merchants, agriculturists, every grade of life in short down to the pickpocket." The society, said the London *Times*, was a product of poverty and unemployment on the island and "has a code of silence" and "its own set of laws which replaces the legal authority." Mafiosi could often be identified by a sort of uniform they wore, which the *Times* described as "a curious cap with a tassel hanging in front."

A follow-up story, printed November 2, 1874, reported the government's view that the "Honorable Society, which they call themselves," had been crushed by "exceptional measures taken against the Sicilian Mafia." Military troops had been quartered in every large town "for the destruction of the longstanding secret organization called the Mafia." Three weeks later the government also announced the eradication of the Camorra.

Three years later the Mafia was in the news again. It had kidnapped an English banker, and the British government threatened to invade Sicily unless the society was dismantled. The kidnapping occurred on a bright November afternoon. At a rural railroad stop twenty miles south of Palermo, four men disembarked: John Forester Rose, a twenty-two-year-old English bank representative, his younger brother George, and two Sicilian clerks. They were met by a mule-drawn omnibus which was to transport them to some sulphur mines owned by the Rose family. At the first bend of the road, barely out of sight of the train, the omnibus was stopped by four Sicilians, "armed, splendidly mounted and dressed like country gentlemen."

The leader went up to the Englishmen, saluted, and asked, "Which of you is Mister John Rose?" Rose acknowledged himself by jumping down from the omnibus and running back toward the train. The others in his party quickly did the same. The bandits followed at a casual pace, letting their horses walk to the train slowly. They felt no need to rush, confident that there would be no help for John Rose from passengers or crew. At the train, the bandit leader politely pushed his horse through a cluster of excited people and found Rose in the center of the crowed. He saluted him again, motioned for a spare horse to be brought up, and led Rose off into the hills.

It took four hours for the news to reach Palermo. The city was only twenty miles away, but the telegraph wires running alongside the railroad had been cut, and a messenger sent by the train engineer chose not to hurry. When the news did arrive, the incident became an international sensation. John Forester Rose was the scion of an English banking family with large absentee interests in Sicily. His captor, according to *The New York Times,* was "none other than the renowned Leone himself."*

Leone was the most infamous bandit in Italy, a Robin Hood type, reputed to be the leader of all Sicilian Mafias. This rumor deserves some inspection, for it goes to the heart of the question of the structure of the islandwide Honorable Society.

The Palermo Mafia, with a membership ranging from barons to cavaliers to bankers to middle-class merchants to cutthroats, was the first Sicilian Mafia. In the 1860s its Mazzinist and Camorrist founders recruited the more promising hill bandits. Beginning about 1870, they added elements of another

---

*The story of Rose's kidnapping was resurrected fifteen years later by English and American newspapers, by which time the Robin Hood aspect, i.e., an absentee landlord kidnapped by a popular bandit, had been eliminated. In the later versions, Rose was a mild-mannered English curate picking wildflowers when he was grabbed up. Rose's transformation from landlord to curate was probably engineered by a pro-establishment editor.

existing criminal class. These new recruits were the guards of the latifundia, armed men who protected and sometimes managed the large manorial estates of absentee landlords. By 1870 these three categories—the original Palermo guerrilla revolutionaries, the elite of the hill bandits, and the latifundia guards—comprised the Palermo Mafia.

During that decade the society acquired a glamorous image. From all over Sicily, reported *The New York Times,* young men came to Palermo to "peer sideways and study these swaggering mafiosi, with their curt jargon of speech, rakish set of hat and long lock of hair." The term *mafiusa* came to mean something admirable, beautiful, and bold.

The visitors studied and made discreet inquiries. The boldest and most criminal of them returned to their own districts and established separate Mafias, patterned on the Palermo model but often altered to meet local conditions. Shortly after the Rose kidnapping *The New York Times* noted that "every one of the 360 communes in Sicily has its own Mafia. In one place their energies control political offices, in another the sale of real estate. The Palermo Mafia is the largest and therefore the most powerful. . . . These societies are criminal in aim, with regular constitutions, rules of admission and penal statutes . . . the so-called capi-mafia [that is, family bosses] are men of substance and education."

This loose organization of semiautonomous country Mafias made the Sicilian society different from the Camorra, whose branches always remained under strict control of the main office in Naples.

To believe that Leone headed all the Sicilian Mafias, one must believe that educated, well-to-do people like barons and bankers would take orders from an illiterate holdup man who hardly ever visited Palermo, the seat of Mafia power. This does, however, seem to be the case. Indeed, peasant leadership became a tradition of the Sicilian Honored Society. All three twentieth-century Mafia leaders were country men. They seldom visited Palermo, and two of them were illiterate. In the Sicilian Mafia, humble origin was a matter of pride, and leadership was based on character. Financial wealth, social standing, and education had little weight.

Leone held Rose prisoner in a cave outside Palermo. Details of his imprisonment do not exist, but they can be inferred from an account given by another hostage held at the same time by Leone's men. The second hostage was another banker, Alessandro Parisi. He had been grabbed on the streets of Palermo and taken to the same network of caves where Rose was held. Parisi's cave was carpeted and the walls and entrance were hung with rugs and curtains. His captors fed him an unvaried but filling menu of macaroni, meat, and soup, and on several occasions when Parisi complained he was without appetite, they put a knife to his throat and forced him to eat. They kept him in cigars and gave him the daily news, including, said Parisi, "an attempt at brigandage which had, unfortunately from their point of view, miscarried."

The bandits' favorite topic for conversation with Parisi was distribution of wealth. "The fault," they told their captive, "lies with the rich who show a tenacity anything but high-minded in holding onto their wealth ... many mafiosi, under other circumstances, would be decently honest people, *as the world goes.* They enroll for protection. It is a choice between hammer and anvil."* Parisi was freed a month later, after much haggling between the society and his family.

Meanwhile, a ransom note was mailed to Rose's wife demanding thirty thousand dollars. She replied by mail to Leone that she was unable personally to raise that much cash. The bankers of the Rose family offered her no financial help. Instead they privately asked the Disraeli government to send in troops.

Leone responded with a second letter, threatening to cut off the ears of the Englishman if the ransom wasn't promptly paid.† There was no reply. He sent a third letter, containing a shriveled human ear, and a fourth containing another. Frantic, Mrs. Rose went to the newspapers and they in turn stoked a

---

New York Times, February 23, 1878.
†In January 1974, nearly a century later, J. Paul Getty III was ransomed from Italian kidnappers who had engaged in similar haggling with the victim's family. They had cut off one of the ears of the seventeen-year-old boy and mailed it to a Rome newspaper. Police arrested three men whom they identified as members of "the mainland Mafia."

public clamor to send British troops to Sicily. Disraeli was reluctant.

A fifth letter arrived with a piece of Rose's nose. It advised that his body would be transmitted piece by piece until the ransom was met. Didn't Mrs. Rose love her husband? Leone asked. Newspaper appeals had by now raised $16,000 in ransom and this was transmitted to Leone. Finding the amount satisfactory, Leone delivered his hostage to a British representative in Palermo, and Rose was returned to England. And now Disraeli moved, sending the Italian government a veiled ultimatum. Unless the Italians tracked down and punished Leone and his band, a British expeditionary force would be landed in Sicily to do the job.

An Italian army corps embarked on a year-long sweep of Sicily, often hanging innocent citizens along with Mafiosi. For that full year, however, Leone, his lieutenant Giuseppe Esposito, and the bulk of the cadre managed to elude the troops.

Finally the noose was drawn. In return for amnesty and a reward, two captured Mafiosi betrayed the site of Leone's headquarters to the army. During the night, several thousand soldiers converged on a hill outside Palermo, and by dawn had surrounded it. At the top was Leone's camp, numbering about 160 men.

The army advanced, tightening its ring as it moved up the hill. Leone's men, firing from a natural citadel of rock, cut down line after line. Halfway up, the death toll became too high and the army encamped for a siege. Days passed, and the number of Mafiosi dwindled as army snipers found their mark in daytime and Mafia deserters sneaked through the lines at night. Finally there remained only Leone, Esposito, and twenty-one of their men. In the army's final charge on the summit, nine Mafiosi were killed and fourteen taken alive, including the two leaders. Their capture ended what is probably the only set-piece battle ever fought in the history of the brotherhood.

The Mafiosi were paraded in Palermo as trophies of war, and the plan was to transport them to Rome for public trial. Security arrangements were carefully planned, because King Victor Emmanuel II suspected that the Mafia had bribed certain members of Parliament and his own ministries. Accordingly, the fourteen survivors were divided into two prison vans, with Leone and six of his men traveling in one and Esposito and the remaining six in the other. Esposito and his group succeeded in bribing a guard on their van and escaped before they left Sicily. Leone, however, was delivered to Rome, where he was quickly tried and sentenced to life imprisonment. In 1879 he, too, escaped and fled to Algeria, where shortly afterward he was killed in unknown circumstances.

Energetic as they were, these efforts to crush the society were futile. In Sicily, Giuseppe Esposito formed a new organization and succeeded Leone as the most prestigious of Sicilian Mafiosi. Esposito's hilltop war and successful escape had made him a legend, and between May 1877 and August 1878 he added to his fame by murdering with his own hand eleven wealthy landowners, along with the chancellor and vice-chancellor of a Sicilian province. Esposito was captured in a Palermo cafe, but again escaped. He fled the country, eventually arriving in Marseilles where he took a boat to New York, accompanied by six other fugitives. This unit, the leader of the Sicilian Mafia and his cadre, arrived in New York unnoticed in November 1878.

Esposito and his men bought a bar at 95 Thompson Street and made it their New York headquarters. In the spring of 1879, however, they moved on to New Orleans, having spent less than six months in New York. Their reason for rejecting New York as a permanent residence may have been nothing more profound than Esposito's first exposure to a northern winter. But most likely there were other causes. The period 1878–79 marked the crest of the reform movement that had begun with the smashing of the Tweed Ring. The newspapers still had the blood up and were damning New York as "the Eden of Cut-Throats." An even more important consideration for Esposito was competition in the underworld. No Italian criminal organization existed. New York crime was controlled by politically protected Irish and Jewish gangs. Italians would not have competitive power of any significance until the end of the century. In this early period, rising Italian hoodlums such as the brothers Paul and Jim Kelly—whose real name was Vaccarelli—took on Irish colors.

The Kellys, who were basically gamblers, rose to eminence in the early 1870s as members of an Irish gang known as the Whyos. When Esposito came to New York, the leader of the Whyos was an aggressive and corrupt police inspector, Alexander S. Williams. As a policeman, Williams had been unleashed in the reform movement of the seventies, and his free use of the club so cowed the gangs that he "made a demonstration for the benefit of police reporters and citizens who had protested against his wholesale use of the nightstick. While a small group watched, Williams hung his watch and chain on a lamppost at Third Avenue and Thirty-Fifth Street. The party then walked around the block and when it returned to the post the jewelry had not been disturbed." During this same period he brought the Whyos under his control. Between them, the Tammany politicians and police inspectors or captains like Williams maintained a monopoly on crime. The Kelly brothers could participate because they were willing to accept subordinate roles. (By the turn of the century, however, Paul Kelly had become one of the foremost crime bosses of New York, and his Five Points gang, numbering an incredible fifteen hundred members, included such youthful trainees as the Neapolitans Johnny Torrio and Al Capone and the Sicilian Salvatore Luciania, who later called himself Lucky Luciano. Kelly rounded out his career by becoming vice-president of the International Longshoremen's Association, AFL.

Finding a place in the ranks was not Esposito's style, and he and his Sicilians took a boat to New Orleans, arriving in the spring of 1879. Like New York, the southern city had a large Sicilian community. As in New York, too, Irish and Germans constituted the most numerous immigrant groups. New Orleans had proportionately fewer Jews and many more French, Spanish, and blacks. In both cities, Anglo-Saxons were a minority. Crime levels were about the same. Juveniles in New Orleans stoned streetcars, wrecked grocery stores, broke gaslights, snatched purses, and heisted goods from the levees and lumberyards. Gamblers and swindlers on Royal Street enticed and cheated strangers. Drug addiction was a citywide problem. The *Daily Picayune* explained that opium dens were profuse and heavily attended by Chinese and native Americans, men and women. The city's four thousand Sicilians were crowded into a few blocks of Vieux Carré tenements, and their appalling living conditions were reported in *Frank Leslie's Popular Monthly:* "Old hags, drunken men, pale-faced young mothers, and ghastly, bold-eyed children huddled together in penury and filth. A common court, the receptacle for rotten vegetables and cast-off clothing, does service as a common dressing room. A rusty pipe plays muddy water in a slime-lined basin, where sleep-begrimed eyes and crisp pink radishes are washed for the early market stalls. From this court a dozen rickety stairways lead up to as many unwholesome rooms, about whose upper galleries, out of reach of molding damp and hungry children, hang festoons of macaroni, peppers and garlic."

In many ways, then, New York and New Orleans were similar, but from Esposito's viewpoint, the southern city was more suitable. He preferred New Orleans for its hot Mediterranean climate and, above all, its powerful Mafia, which was well wired-in to the political establishment and dominated criminal activities in the territory.

The effect of Esposito's arrival on New Orleans's depressed Italian community must have been dramatic. He was a young, vigorous bull who came to America not in fear and rags but with the buoyant confidence of strength and wealth. Always well dressed, he paraded the streets with an air of authority. His sole concession to his fugitive status was to adopt the alias "Vincenzo Rebello." Otherwise, he flaunted himself. He bought a lugger, named her *Leone*, and hoisted to the mast what he identified as the flag of the Sicilian Mafia. The flag and boat were indeed clever showmanship, for while they thrilled Esposito's fellow Italians they carried no risk. American authorities knew nothing of Leone, Esposito, or the flag, and had they known probably would not have cared.

Esposito lived up to his position as New Orleans boss. Generous with his charity and his services, he was at the same time judge, executioner, and lord to the community of southern Italians. He dined at the best restaurants and was obviously well supported by funds.

In New Orleans he took a wife, a strikingly attractive girl named Sarah Castagno, of ordinary but honorable Sicilian background. They were married in October 1879, and a year later she bore him a son named Joseph. This marriage was ill fated, for back in Sicily was another wife and five children. She was somehow informed of the new marriage and, jealous, provided American authorities with information that would cause Esposito's destruction. The instrument of her revenge was a New Orleans policeman named David Hennessey.

Hennessey was a detective of the rakish New Orleans police force, whose typical member was described by a visiting Englishman as "apt to be young and slim, and to be attired on the go-as-you-please principle. It is true that his clothes are blue and his buttons metallic and that he wears a black felt hat with a slouched brim, similar somewhat to the head gear affected by brigadier generals during the Civil War. Still it is the business of a policeman to inspire awe; and how can you expect to be awe-stricken by a personage who wears a turn-down collar and a Byron tie, who carries a gold watch and chain at his fob, and who smokes a cigar on duty?"

Hennessey was of this sort. Despite his casual exterior, however, he was a professional. His father was a Union soldier who had stayed on in New Orleans after the war, joined the police force, and in 1867 was shot to death while pursuing robbers. To support his mother David went to work as a messenger on the force and was trained from youth in police work. He worked up through the ranks, and his skill and dedication soon made him a detective. He soon managed to bring his cousin, Mike Hennessey, onto the detective force to work as his partner. They were among the few noncorrupt members of the force.

The careers of David Hennessey and Giuseppe Esposito were entwined from the moment the Sicilian settled in New Orleans until the lives of both men were ended. Hennessey's interest in the Mafia seems to have begun with Esposito. Sometime around 1880, reports *New York Detective Library*, he confided to a friend that he had been hearing rumors of a secret organization and "that when a murder was committed mafias from other cities were chosen to do it; thus to escape detection, the gangs were generally six in number and they were paid from $25 to $100 for the work they did." Hennessey's claim—that the Mafias of New York and New Orleans were in regular communication and cooperated on crimes—would be repeated by police officers for the next forty years.

The events that brought Hennessey and Esposito into direct conflict began in January 1881, when Police Chief Tom Boylan was surprised by an unannounced visit from the Italian consul in New Orleans. The consul handed over a dossier he had received by diplomatic pouch from the police chief of Rome. It contained a photograph of a bearded man, an envelope postmarked New Orleans and addressed to the police chief of Rome, and a letter. The letter identified the photograph as that of fugitive Mafia chief Giuseppe Esposito and stated that he was living in New Orleans and had married a young widow who was pregnant. Without disclosing the source of his information, the consul asked Chief Boylan if he would discreetly determine where in New Orleans the photograph had been taken. Chief Boylan later gave the New Orleans *Daily Picayune* an account of the preliminary steps he took.

"I promised to make the investigation, and located the photographer, who was named Simon, on Hospital Street near the French Market, and secured the picture. I had another interview with the Italian gentleman who was well pleased with the success achieved till then. He asked me to have [Esposito] located and his movements shadowed. He related the crimes for which Esposito was wanted, particularly the kidnaping of the Englishman Rose and his maiming and maltreatment. He enjoined that everything must be done with the utmost secrecy. Esposito was located. His description tallied with the photo and the picture and all the relevant facts were transmitted to the Italian government. . . .

"In the meantime, while the photograph had been sent to Italy through the Italian consul for identification, I sent for Dave Hennessey, informed him of the facts and told him to keep a sharp lookout on Esposito and to keep a constant watch on his movements." Hennessey executed his assignment by means of an ancient police technique—he created an informer, a man close to his target who was vulnerable to police coercion. Hennessey chose a low-level hoodlum named Tony Labruzzo, who had moved his mother over from Palermo only six months earlier. When Hennessey threatened to deport the mother, Labruzzo agreed to inform on Esposito's movements.

Meanwhile, the Italian government was pressing on a second front. The chargé d' affaires in New York hired two private detectives, James Mooney and Dan Boland, to go to New Orleans and arrest Esposito on New York warrants. One day in June 1881, Mooney and Boland showed up in the office of the Italian consul in New Orleans, dramatically dropped a pair of handcuffs on his desk, and produced the warrants for Esposito. The astonished consul referred them to Chief Boylan, who promptly shouldered them out of the case. Still unsure whether or not the prominent citizen known as Vincenzo Rebello was indeed an Italian fugitive, he called in David Hennessey and told him to take whatever steps he wished "on his own authority and without the approval of the authorities of the city."

The arrest took place on July 5, 1881, in front of St. Louis Cathedral, where Esposito made a daily 11:00 A.M. visit. Hennessey waited in the park across the street, sitting in the shadows of a curtained carriage. Esposito appeared on schedule, dandily turned out in a fawn-colored coat, pipe-legged gray trousers, and a Panama hat. Hennessey jumped out, jammed a pistol into Esposito's back, and ordered him into the carriage, where he relieved him of two pistols and a knife. He then took him to headquarters, where Boylan wired the New York police that Esposito had been captured by "Detectives David and Mike Hennessey." In the darkness of the following morning, David Hennessey sneaked Esposito, loaded down with forty pounds of chains, aboard the steamer *City of New Orleans* bound for New York. He signed Esposito over to the custody of private detectives Mooney and Boland, and returned ashore.

The arrest was executed so smoothly that the news was not known in the city until the next day. Five of Esposito's original six Mafiosi were still in New Orleans and when the news broke, three of them sailed the lugger *Leone* to the Gulf and from there to points unknown. The remaining two boarded a riverboat and disembarked in St. Louis. Later reports credited them with having begun a Mafia in that city.

New Orleans was electrified by the arrest. The *Daily Picayune* reported that "perhaps no event that has transpired for years affected the countrymen of Giuseppe Esposito, the bandit chieftain, more than his sudden disappearance from amongst them on Tuesday. . . . Numerous were his friends and it now appears that by the merest imaginable chance was it that the Aids [i.e., detectives] Hennesseys and their colleagues effected his capture without bloodshed, for willing hands could have been found in abundance that would have been raised in his defense; and the detectives, had they been victorious in the event of a fight, would only have taken his dead body, for it had long since been resolved that Esposito should not be taken alive. . . .

"Yesterday, in the haunts of Esposito's adherents, was a day long to be remembered. Groups assembled at the various fruit stands and coffee houses in the vicinity of the French Market and discussed the matter in all its bearings. What agitated them and surprised them most was the quiet manner in which the brigand had been captured. How so famous a bravo, so bloodthirsty a criminal and desperate a fugitive could be captured at all, filled them with consternation, and only one reasonable theory presented itself to their minds: Esposito had been betrayed. Suspicious glances were cast from one to another. It was as much as one of their lives was worth, almost, to have been seen talking to a policeman for a month previously, and not a few altercations took place. One in particular came very near resulting in bloodshed. It appears that a lemon peddler named Gardette was accused by Tony Labruzzo, a merchant, of having been instrumental in the capture of Esposito, which imputation the former resented. Labruzzo was known as an intimate of the brigand, and naturally enough he took upon himself the role of his avenger. A large crowd gathered around the two men, and threatening glances were darted at each other. Labruzzo drew a long, large-bore dueling pistol and a long knife. Gardette, who is a short, thick-set, powerful man, seized the hand grasping the knife, when his adversary struck him several times in the face with the butt end of the weapon. Releasing his hold, Gardette darted suddenly through the crowd and ran home where he armed himself with a large sized Remington cavalry revolver and returned in search of his adversary.

"About this time Officer Quillan of the Harbor Precinct arrived and regardless of personal danger made his way into the midst of the circle of men and made the belligerents prisoners."

Tony Labruzzo was, of course, Hennessey's informer. The identity of the original informer, the person who sent Esposito's photo to Rome, was never revealed, but it was rumored to be a New Orleans relative of the wife Esposito abandoned in Sicily.

Esposito's capture made a comparable sensation in New York, where he arrived on July 13, 1881. According to the account in the *New York Herald*, as soon as the steamer made fast, "the detectives hustled Esposito into a carriage, which was surrounded by throngs of his curious countrymen." Reporters had learned on board that "some of the passengers and crew believed Esposito's story, which was that he was never a brigand at all and that instead of having cut off the Englishman's ears in Italy and sent them as a delicate present to his wife, his far more harmless occupation had been that of a fruit vendor in New Orleans. His name, the people said, was not Esposito at all, but Vincenzo Rebello, and the detectives had made up a case against him in order to capture the reward of $3,000 which the Italian government had set upon Esposito's head. It was also said that Esposito had been treated with undue severity, having been unnecessarily kept manacled the greater part of the time, and not only manacled but also chained to a bolt in the floor; but these precautions were rather liked by certain of the passengers, who did not at all relish the idea of having such a renowned murderer on board."

Esposito was removed to the Ludlow Street jail and shortly thereafter arraigned before a United States commissioner. At the hearing, a habeas corpus writ was introduced on the basis of testimony by six New Yorkers that the defendant was indeed named Vincenzo Rebello, a merchant with whom they had done business since he first arrived in New York in 1878. Five Sicilians from New Orleans verified the story and said they had known Rebello the fruit merchant for many years. Even while a manacled prisoner at sea, Esposito had been able to create a defense, one of mistaken identity, and within days of his arrival in New York had come up with eleven witnesses to verify it under oath.* Mafia machinery, working in two cities, had put together a tight story. In view of the testimony, extradition proceedings were postponed pending further identification from Rome.

Meanwhile, Joe Macheca, boss of the New Orleans Mafia, went to David Hennessey and offered him an astounding $50,000 to go to New York and testify that the prisoner Rebello was not the man arrested in New Orleans, and that a substitution must have been made on the boat by detectives Mooney and Boland. At the same time, the New Orleans Mafia was pressing its search for Esposito's betrayer. It took them eleven days to zero in on Tony Labruzzo.

On July 16, 1881, Tony Labruzzo, a widower, kissed his two children and asked his mother to put them to bed because he would be late returning from a meeting of the Tiro el Bersaglio. The term in idiom means "shoot the target" and in this case referred to a committee newly organized by the New Orleans Mafia for the express purpose of finding and killing the informer. It had been meeting regularly in the upstairs room of a boarding house at 51 Bienville Street since two days after Esposito's arrest. On this night the landlady several times went up to complain of noise. When the meeting broke up, the members drifted out by ones and twos. Labruzzo, one of the last to go, left alone. He had walked only about fifty feet from the house when, from doorways on both sides of the street, men stepped out and riddled him with bullets.

In New York, Esposito continued to wait in jail for the

---

*Of the eleven witnesses, two can positively be identified as Mafiosi. They are Rocco Geraci and Giuseppe Provenzano, both of New Orleans. The others from New Orleans were Antonio Angelo, Antonio Pellegrini, and Salvatore Masana. The New York witnesses were Sal Cameino, Misolo Toranbino, John Caruso, Sal Gaetano, Angelo Cusimano, and Pascale Salomoni.

resumption of his extradition hearing. He was visited almost daily by his New Orleans wife and baby and gave out many interviews, in all of which he repeated the story of his innocence. In New Orleans, Macheca continued to work on the Hennessey cousins and added to his $50,000 bribe an impressive display of political leverage. In August of 1881, only one month after the arrest, he forced the city administration to reorganize the police department, remove the Hennesseys from the direct supervision of Chief Boylan, and simultaneously demote them in rank. Installed over them as chief of detectives was a Macheca nominee named Thomas Devereaux, a political hack without previous police experience. The Hennesseys bowed their necks and still refused to perjure themselves.

In mid-September the extradition hearings were reopened. Esposito's identity was fully established by Italian carabinieri who had known him in Sicily. On September 21 he was sneaked aboard a Europe-bound boat without any opportunity to say good-bye to his family. This summary removal, said *The New York Times*, was prompted by the authorities' fear that "a rescue attempt might be made by certain Italians in this city, Brooklyn, and New Jersey who had been attending the trial."

Although deported, Esposito still influenced events in New Orleans. On October 13, 1881, the Mafia appointee, Chief of Detectives Thomas Devereaux, was in a New Orleans brokerage house when Mike Hennessey entered. A quarrel, then a gunfight ensued, in which Devereaux was killed and Mike wounded. There were conflicting statements on David Hennessey's role. One witness said David came into the office and rescued Mike by killing Devereaux. Others said David simply loaded his wounded cousin into a carriage and took him to Charity Hospital. Both Hennesseys were charged and, although acquitted six months later, they were dismissed from the force. David became a private detective and Mike moved to Houston where, five years later, he was murdered by "an assassin sent from New Orleans," an assassination ordered, according to *The New York Times*, "by the Mafia."

Esposito was convicted in Rome of six murders and spent the rest of his life in prison, constantly in chains. The New

Orleans Mafia spent nearly the entire year of 1882 reducing Esposito's house to splinters in an effort to find his fortune, reputed to be worth several hundred thousand dollars in gold, jewels, and various currencies. It was never found. His young wife Sarah certainly didn't have it. She disappeared from the city and it wasn't until seven years later that a stark paragraph appeared on the back page of *Daily States*, a New Orleans newspaper. "Our Louisville correspondent reports an item which will cause some of us to remember the capture of an infamous brigand several years ago by our police chief, Mister Hennessey. Last week the unfortunate widow of the bandit Giuseppe Esposito applied to the Mayor of Louisville to have their son Joseph, and a younger child, placed in an orphan asylum. She stated that she had managed to care for them many years by taking in laundry but was no longer able to support them. They were granted admission."

THE MAFIA IN SICILY

The period 1870–1921 was one of growth for the Mafia. The society had crossed oceans to become an international organization, and had even established a family in Tunis to accommodate the flow of members passing through that port on their way to America and Australia. In Sicily the brotherhood held undisputed sway over the government. In mainland Italy it controlled key politicians, businesses, and banks. The Mafia also dealt effectively with its underworld rivals. In the thirty years before the turn of the century, at least nine other brotherhood societies sprang up in Sicily and the mainland, only to be stamped out by the Mafia.* The only rival to survive was a Sicilian group called the Stoppaglieri, which also made the

*See Appendix B.

crossing to America. But even the Stoppaglieri did not provide any real competition. The society's first successful foe was Benito Mussolini, a man who temporarily broke the Mafia.

In 1921, Mussolini, an expelled socialist party member, was elected to Parliament and founded the National Fascist Party. In 1922 Mussolini led his black-shirted Fascists in a march on Rome and was named premier. He quickly developed this position into a dictatorship, using an efficient secret police and the Fascist militia to put down all opposition.

One of Mussolini's chief agents of suppression was Cesare Mori, a native of Trapani, Sicily, who had been an officer of the artillery. It was Mori who was chosen to squash socialist unrest during Mussolini's political campaign in Bologna, and it was Mori who helped organize the march on Rome that elevated Mussolini to supreme power. For this he was rewarded with the post of prefect of Palermo, the most powerful position in Sicily.

Mori's assignment in Sicily was to root out the old corrupt administrators and replace them with loyal Fascists. As it so happened, these officials of the former regime were protected by the Mafia and it was on this issue of who would control Sicily that Mussolini and the Mafia clashed. In many cases Mori succeeded in deposing a Mafia-favored bureaucrat, only to see the society kill his Fascist successor. As a further demonstration of Mafia power, the Fascists were often murdered in downtown Palermo, at midday, before hundreds of people. No witnesses could ever be found.

Mussolini himself went down to inspect the situation, but according to several sources, he too was humiliated by the Mafia, in the town of Piana dei Greci. The community, an hour from Palermo, had an Albanian population which had preserved the Greek Orthodox religion, the language, and the customs of its homeland. But the town was controlled by a Mafia family, and the Mafia chief, Don Ciccio Cuccia, was mayor.

As Mussolini would learn, Don Ciccio was a man keen on adding to his prestige. He had demonstrated his ambitions on an earlier visit by King Victor Emmanuel II. To receive the king, Piana dei Greci put on an elaborate show complete with folk costumes, special foods, dances, and music. In the midst of the confusion, a group of Albanian dancers surrounded the king, on orders from Don Ciccio, and separated him from his entourage. The Mafia chief then led Victor Emmanuel into the church, where a Greek Orthodox ceremony, unfamiliar to the king, was about to begin. The king was led to the baptismal font, where he found himself being handed a bawling baby. A few moments later, the priest waved his hands and King Victor Emmanuel II was godfather to Don Ciccio's son.

To guard against similar surprises, Mori arranged for Don Ciccio to meet Mussolini outside the town. This was done, and Don Ciccio was then made to sit in Mussolini's open touring car and enter Piana dei Greci surrounded by Fascist motorcyclists. The angry Mafia mayor told Mussolini, "There is no need for so many police. Your Excellency has nothing to fear in this district when you are with me." The bolt found its mark and Mussolini was embarrassed. When the car entered the town square, Don Ciccio, encouraged by his success, stood up in the car and shouted for all to hear, "Let no one dare touch a hair of Mussolini's [bald] head. He is my friend and the best man in the world." It had been arranged for Mussolini to make a speech from a balcony overlooking the plaza. When the time came, Mussolini walked out and found himself facing an audience (according to one account) of some "twenty village idiots, one-legged beggars, bootblacks and lottery-ticket sellers." No one else.

On the return trip to Palermo, Mussolini ordered Cesare Mori to eradicate the Mafia. He gave the prefect extraordinary powers over all seven provinces of the island, and instructed him "not to err too often on the side of gentleness."

Mussolini could not have made a better choice. Mori had spent his prewar career as a *delegato,* the lowest grade of police official, in Trapani province. In that province, Mafia gangs made a practice of hamstringing cattle whose owners refused to pay their Mafia tax. There Mori had made a local name for himself, organizing bands of carabinieri and police officials to scour the hills for the cattle maimers.

Another of Mori's qualifications was that he personally knew the lower ranks of Mafiosi and was familiar with their peculiarities. In a book he later wrote, *The Last Struggle with the Mafia,* he described the Mafioso as "difficult to find at home after dark; if he is there, he is not in bed but underneath it. He prefers to sleep by day and to be awake at night, like the watch dogs by whose friendship, naturally, he sets great store. If he sees that he is being watched, he disappears completely for at least three days. If you send for him, he disappears for at least a week, and in his place comes somebody with whom you have nothing to do, in order to find out what is going on. Sometimes, however, when he is far from your thoughts, you may see him pass quite close to you with a deep bow. That is a bad sign. It means that he has been up to one of his little games. His meeting with you will serve as a proof of the alibi he has already arranged."

In spite of his familiarity with Mafia ways, Mori did not underestimate the difficulty of eradicating a criminal society that enjoyed strong popular support. "Everywhere we turned," he wrote in his book, "[the Mafiosi] were protected by the people. And why not? If a peasant lost his sheep and complained to the government, it would take a week of his time filling out reports and testifying, and it was still rare for him to get his sheep returned. If, instead, he complained to the Mafia, his property—minus the Mafia's portion—was returned to him promptly and he was unlikely to be bothered again. Naturally, the peasants preferred the Mafia to the government."

Because of the importance of the Mafia to the people, Mori felt that his attack would have to be both physical and psychological. "The secret of success, I felt sure, lay in the heart of the Sicilian. . . . It was not to be [just] a grand police campaign, but a reversal of the people's conscience."

He calculated that the government, represented in his own person, had to visibly demonstrate its power to eradicate and humiliate the Mafia. He therefore costumed himself in a fancy black uniform, complete with silver dagger. Despite his advanced years, he personally made captures and posed for photographs in which he stood triumphant over kneeling, handcuffed prisoners. In the Mafia-infested western provinces, the towns he visited were encouraged to welcome him with triumphal arches bearing the words "Ave Caesar."

During the purge, legal rights were nonexistent. Confessions were often obtained by the *cassetta* torture, which involved stretching out the suspect on his back across a wooden box, roughly the dimensions of a three-foot cube. With hands and feet wired to the sides of the box, the prisoner was drenched with brine and whipped. The brine caused the lashes to be more painful but to leave no mark. There were other tortures, too, including one of the earliest uses of electric shock on the genitals. A third favorite was to stick a funnel into the victim's mouth and force him to swallow salt water until his stomach swelled. Judges did not concern themselves with details. Sometimes two different gangs were tried and sentenced for the same crime by different courts. People were convicted of crimes that had never taken place.

The purge climaxed in 1929 with the arrest on framed-up charges of the most charismatic and powerful leader in the Mafia's history—Don Vito Cascio Ferro. Although Don Vito has been dead nearly half a century, in many parts of Sicily his name still invokes images of manly virtues, strength, dignity, compassion, and justice. When he went visiting, the mayors of the towns through which he passed met him at the town gates and kissed his hand in homage. He was a dashing dresser—frock coat, wide-brimmed fedora, pleated shirt, and flowered cravat—and in later years indulged himself in a long, flowing white beard. He was a favorite of salon society, played musical chairs with counts and countesses at fashionable balls, listened with reverence to poetry readings or to the latest phonograph cylinders, and was in demand to open art exhibitions.

But Don Vito had more practical talents. He invented *pizzu*, which translates as "wetting the beak," a system whereby the Mafia imposed a small tax on virtually every economic enterprise in Sicily. His innovation was to wet the beak moderately on a broad spectrum of the economy rather than impose heavy levies on a few businesses—with a great increase in income as a result.

Don Vito's career ended in 1932 when he died in prison. He had been prosecuted on a framed-up charge of smuggling. He had endured the trial in silent dignity and spoke his only words at its conclusion, when he told the court, "Gentlemen,

THE MAFIA IN SICILY

since you have been unable to find any evidence for the numerous crimes I did commit, you are reduced to condemning me for the only one I have not."

The purge ended in 1929, shortly after Don Vito's trial. By then, more than twelve hundred persons had been convicted as Mafiosi. Of these, maybe half, probably not that many, were members of the society. An unknown percentage of the remainder were innocent of any criminal offense but were victims of jealous neighbors or Fascist party members. Nevertheless, Mori counted his campaign a success. The Mafia, the Honored Society, would remain dormant and virtually powerless for more than a decade.

One important result of the purge was an escape route Don Vito established for his followers. He used a fleet of fishing boats to carry Mafiosi from Sicily to Tunis or Marseilles, where they could safely book passage to the United States, Argentina, or Australia. It is not known how many members came to America during that period of 1922 to 1929 but they probably numbered, at the very minimum, five hundred.* There were two routes to the United States, a southern route and a northern one. The former involved passage from Tunis to Cuba and from there to New Orleans, Tampa, Miami, or Norfolk. Mafiosi using the northern route were smuggled into Marseilles where they booked passage to New York directly or to Canada, from where they entered via Detroit and Buffalo. These immigrant fugitives were for the most part the cream of the Sicilian Mafia, young men in their twenties and thirties, and from them would come the nucleus of Cosa Nostra leadership. The youngest of these future bosses was Joe Bonanno, twenty years old when he entered the United States in 1924. Others who immigrated during this period were Carlo Gambino (two days before Christmas 1921); Mike Coppola, a Detroit and New York underboss (1926); and Vincent Mangano and Joe Magliocco, future New York bosses (1926). These men seem to have been sent as delegates of the Sicilian Mafia leader Don Vito Cascio Ferro. They arrived

---

*The figure is based on records seized from the New York office of Mafia-Cosa Nostra boss Salvatore Maranzano in 1931.

in America with his recommendation and stepped into positions of power with amazing quickness.

While these young men were cutting the brotherhood's losses and moving on to the New World, a few of the older dons were relying on their cleverness to escape the purge. The most important of these was Don Calo Vizzini, whose political acumen saved his life. Foreseeing Mussolini's rise to power, he had identified with the Fascists early and sent the party a handsome donation to help finance its march on Rome. In that same year, 1922, he protected a Fascist *squadrista* who had murdered a political opponent. This squadrista eventually became an undersecretary of state to Mussolini and, although Don Calo was too prominent not to be arrested and prosecuted by Mori, his sentence was light. He was ordered confined to his village for five years, and even that restriction was soon lifted by the friendly undersecretary.

Passing unscathed through the purge, Don Calo kept a low profile through the thirties and through most of World War II. With the Allied invasion of Sicily in 1943, however, he once again put his political acumen to use. It was Don Calo who presided over the resurrection of the Sicilian Mafia.

Nearly extinct in 1943, the Sicilian Mafia since then has become as large, fearsome, and powerful as at any time in its history. Its renaissance was due to the replacement of the Fascist regime by the friendlier presence of the American army.

Exactly how much friendlier the Americans were is a matter of dispute. One side, whose spokesmen range from Don Calo Vizzini and his villagers to journalists Norman Lewis and Michele Pantaleone, contends that the United States military enlisted the Mafia to help the Allied armies in Sicily. The American government flatly denies having done so. And since the United States Navy's secret file on the matter disappeared shortly after World War II, absolute corroboration one way or the other is impossible.

The writers Lewis and Pantaleone, however, argue convincingly in their books.* In the summer of 1942, their story

---

*The Honored Society by Norman Lewis; G.P. Putnam's Sons, 1964. And *The Mafia and Politics* by Michele Pantaleone; Coward, McCann, 1966.

THE MAFIA IN SICILY ○ 59

goes, United States naval intelligence officers began a series of secret talks with Lucky Luciano, who was at that time a prisoner at Dannemora in upstate New York. They wanted Luciano to use his influence with gangsters back in Sicily, and when Luciano showed some cautious cooperation, the navy had him transferred to a prison more convenient to New York City. The negotiations seem to have concluded satisfactorily. Luciano arranged for the American military to contact Mafia leaders in Sicily; in return he was paroled right after the war by Governor Thomas Dewey, the same man who, as district attorney, had sent him to prison. Luciano was then deported to Italy. The official reason for the parole was an unspecified "service" that Luciano had rendered the United States government.

The nature of this "service" is the subject of dispute. According to the navy intelligence agents who dealt with Luciano, he helped only to ease some New York dock problems, such as espionage, pilferage, and potential strikes. Lewis and Pantaleone claim he did more.

They report that on July 14, 1943, five days after the Allies launched the invasion of Sicily, an American plane flew over Villalba, Don Calo Vizzini's village, and dropped a yellow flag or handkerchief inscribed with a black letter *L*. This signal was picked up by a resident and taken to Don Calo. The next time the plane appeared it dropped a packet addressed to Don Calo. Michele Pantaleone, then a small boy, was a resident of that village and, ironically, a protégé of Don Calo. Two days after the packet was dropped Pantaleone saw American tanks roll into Villalba with replicas of Luciano's handkerchief tied to their turrets. Don Calo and his nephew, Domiano Lumia, boarded one of the tanks and roared off. The GIs quickly tagged Don Calo as "General Mafia," and General Mafia spent the next six days with the Seventh Army as it rolled up the Mafia-infested western flank of Sicily. They met virtually no opposition. When the time came for the army to pass out of Don Calo's district and into the adjoining territory of Giuseppe Genco Russo, Mafia boss of Mussomeli, Genco Russo simply took over the role of protector.

From that moment, claims Pantaleone, the Sicilian Mafia was back in power. In his book he wrote that "the reconstitution of the old groups was inaugurated by American gangster leaders, who were almost all ex-mafiosi of Sicilian origin and who got in touch with their old friends in the island before the Allied landing, in order to induce them to help the Allies. This they certainly did, but as a result the Allies imposed Mafia mayors on a number of towns."

The evidence given by Michele Pantaleone, one of the most respected journalists in Europe, is virtually unassailable. Pantaleone's eyewitness account, reinforced by stories told to him by Don Calo, is supported by Don Giuseppe Genco Russo, the man who in 1954 succeeded Don Calo as Mafia chief of Sicily. In 1960 Genco Russo told the Italian magazine *Tempo* that "in 1943 the Allied armies disembarked in Sicily and I arranged that the war should arrive at Mussomeli without horrors, useless cruelties or death." Two years later a Palermo newspaper interviewed a number of Villalba residents who also testified to seeing the airplane, the L-marked handkerchief, and General Mafia's departure aboard one of the American tanks.

Corroboration comes from other sources as well. In granting commutation of Luciano's sentence, Governor Dewey stated that "upon the entry of the United States into the war, Luciano's aid was sought by the armed services in inducing others to provide information concerning possible enemy attack. It appears that he cooperated in such effort though the actual value of the information procured is not clear." Three days later, *New York Times* crime reporter Meyer Berger gave this account: "It is understood that Luciano provided Army intelligence officers with the names of Sicilian and Neapolitan Camorra members and a list of Italians sent back to their native country after criminal conviction in the United States; that many of these men helped defeat the enemy in Italy."

Luciano also aided the Allies through his underboss, Vito Genovese, who had fled to Italy in 1937 to avoid prosecution for the murder of a fellow Mafioso. Armed with $750,000 in cash, Genovese was a well-to-do fugitive, and he earned the favor of the Fascist government by contributing a quarter of a million dollars to Mussolini's party. But by 1945, when he was arrested in the town of Nola, Italy, he had obviously been persuaded to switch his allegiance to the Allies: when captured he was in possession of a short wave radio, had numerous Allied credentials, and, although he had been arrested by an American military policeman, he was under the discreet protection of much higher ranking American officers. Fifteen years after the war, Department of Justice officials informally investigated Luciano's role in the invasion of Sicily and reached the conclusion that Genovese had been in contact with the United States during the war, acting as an agent for the Office of Strategic Services, the predecessor of the Central Intelligence Agency.

Whatever Luciano's behind-the-scenes role, by 1944 the Mafia was riding high in Italy, thanks to direct aid from the American army. Armed with pistols, rifles, machine guns, and explosives picked up from battlefields, enriched by black-market goods obtained from American supply depots, and protected by Mafia mayors installed by the United States army, the Mafia was the dominant civilian force. Don Calo Vizzini now became chief of all the Mafias. In 1946 Luciano went to Palermo and immediately paid a visit to Don Calo, who had taken a suite at the same hotel.

Don Calo showed his gratitude to the Americans in his own way. During the postwar period, the don energetically led a movement to make Sicily the forty-ninth American state. Bizarre as the scheme may seem today, the annexation movement was very popular in Sicily. The people's enthusiasm so alarmed the ruling Christian Democrat party that it hastened to make peace with the Mafia and invited Don Calo to be its advisor on Sicilian affairs. Don Calo accepted the offer and abandoned the forty-ninth-state movement, which soon died out.

The cooperation between Lucky Luciano and Don Calo in 1944 was just the beginning of close interaction between the Sicilian Mafia and its American offspring, the Cosa Nostra. After Luciano, a flood of top-ranking American deportees entered Italy, including Frank Coppola of New York and Sylvester Carolla of New Orleans, both of whom were named in Italian government investigations into political corruption and narcotics smuggling. A 1972 study conducted by the Italian Parliament noted the Americans' growing influence, reporting that "with the arrival of Luciano, the [Sicilian] Mafia passed en bloc to the handling of [international] contraband," Luciano's specialty. The study also pointed out that Frank Coppola, who arranged passports for many of his fellow deportees, did so in "a manner that meant he was the regulator of the archives of the interior ministries."

Not all members of the brotherhood appreciated the infiltration of the Americans and their techniques, and the result was the Old-New Mafia wars of the fifties. Typical of the wars was the conflict in Corleone, where Luciano Liggio opposed the established boss, Dr. Michele Navarra, over whether to introduce American methods of construction racketeering at the cost of old-time Mafia monopolies. The "Old Mafia" preferred meager water supplies, which it could monopolize and tax. The "New Mafia," as represented by Liggio, supported dam construction and large water supplies, on the theory that more profits could be earned from construction shakedowns than from maintaining the old-style Mafia monopoly. The "New Mafia" won and since 1964 the Sicilian Mafia has operated in the business-oriented style of the American Cosa Nostra.

One episode in the Old-New Mafia wars reveals a final, important link in the chain of Mafia-Cosa Nostra relations. In 1963 Cesare Manzella, a prominent member of the Luciano-Coppola drug syndicate, was killed by a bomb planted in his car. After the bombing, Italian police investigators seized papers which revealed that a Grand Council had ordered a truce between all families. At the same time that it declared a truce, this council (which was itself an innovation) appointed a standing committee to which future disputes would be submitted for arbitration. These features—a commission and a council of *consiglieri*—had been copied directly from the American Cosa Nostra. Before the 1960s no such institutions had ever existed in the Sicilian Mafia.

The Sicilian Mafia began the 1970s stronger than it had ever been before. According to a report issued by Senator McClellan's committee of the U.S. Senate, the society had "expanded activities to include, aside from trafficking in narcotics, the creation of powerful monopolies for controlling the produce and foodstuff market throughout Italy; the controlling of buildings and roads, the sale and purchase of real estate in Sicily, the obtaining of concessions of special water supply points, and for exercising influence on an assortment of public works projects both in Sicily and elsewhere in Italy. [They have] expanded their spheres of influence much as has their counterpart underworld organization in the United States."

But while the Mafia has flourished, its birthplace has suffered. Sicily is a dramatic example of a brotherhood society's parasitic nature. For more than a century, the Mafia has repressed the Sicilian population, blocked socialist reforms, exploited land reform to its own advantage, and preyed on individual and cooperative economic initiative. Throughout the rest of Italy, even in the southern provinces, living standards have risen dramatically, but in Sicily the people are worse off than they were in 1860. The island has been raped ecologically; its working male population has dwindled to the critical point; the future seems without hope. The royalty, the landed aristocracy, the Fascists, the bourgeoisie have all collapsed. The only class that has prospered is a small section of the proletariat, the Mafia.

BOOK THREE
TRAVELS IN AMERICA

THE BLACK HAND

The earliest report of an Italian criminal society in America was in 1855, twenty years before Giuseppe Esposito galvanized the New Orleans Mafia. In that year several citizens of New Orleans were victims of extortion. The threatening letters they received were signed "the Black Hand." For nearly a century thereafter the Black Hand's simple technique did not vary. The victim was notified that if he did not pay a certain amount of money, he or his family would be killed. The note often bore the inky imprint of a hand and was signed "the Black Hand" "Mano Negra," "Company of Death" or, in later years, "the Mafia." By 1900 the Black Hand had become synonymous with "Mafia," but it was an erroneous identification. Not all members of the American Black Hand were Italian, nor was it a formal organization. "The Black Hand" was simply a name used by various free-lance criminals who considered the combination of words to be high sounding and terror inspiring. The Black Hand and the brotherhood were separate phenomena.

In nineteenth-century Spain, reports historian C. W. Heckethorn, a Black Hand society had existed. Called the Mano Negra, it was founded in 1835 by agricultural workers to agitate for socialism and agrarian reform. These laborers had been deprived of their communal rights by sharp village lawyers called *caciques*. The lands on which they had traditionally been allowed to cut timber and pasture livestock were taken from them when land reform in Spain broke up large estates and turned the property over to public sale. Ironically, says Heckethorn, "the caciques, though they bought the land, in many instances had not capital enough to cultivate it but nevertheless prevented the peasants from the free use of it. The agricultural laborer was left to starve, a condition which led to many disturbances. The members of the [Black Hand] society were bound by oath to punish their oppressors by steel, fire, or poison."

The association was strictly secret and, Heckethorn continues, "to reveal its doings by treachery or imprudence meant death to the offender. The society had a complete organization, with its chiefs, its centers, its funds, its secret tribunals, inflicting death and other penalties on their own members, and on landlords and usurers, such as the caciques. The members, to escape detection, often changed their names."

Around 1860 (approximately twenty-five years after its establishment) the society began to show signs of criminal degeneration. According to one American criminologist, the original Black Hand "consisted of missionaries who hoped to redress the balance between rich and poor; but it soon drew down to it many desperadoes who gladly accepted the openings it offered for carrying on their original trade. It became a very extensive and numerous society, existing in the provinces, each having its own center and out branches with a total of affiliated members exceeding 40,000."

From 1880 to 1883 the society was particularly active, especially in Andalusia. This provoked the government to take repressive measures. The chief leaders were imprisoned in 1883, and the society quickly deteriorated. But although the Mano Negra never passed beyond the borders of Spain, its symbol and its name almost certainly inspired the extortions later perpetrated by criminals in America, some of whom may even have been members of the original society.

The American Black Hand was traced back to the original Spanish society in an obscure *North American Review* article published in 1908. The author, Gaetano D'Amato, was prominent in the New York City Italian community, and he was writing to dispel the notion that the Black Hand and the Mafia were synonymous. It is a myth, he said, that "a terrible organization named the Black Hand Society exists in Italy and is sending its members to establish branches for the purposes of plundering the United States." D'Amato pointed out that "the Black Hand [had] scarcely ever been heard of in Italy. It was never heard of until long after the term had been used in the United States. . . . The term was first used in this city [New York] about ten years ago. . . . One or two crimes committed under the symbol gave it a vogue among the rapacious; and, as it looked well and attracted attention in the headlines, the newspapers finally applied it to all crimes committed by the Italian banditti in the United States."

D'Amato walked the streets among Mafiosi, Camorrists, and Black Handers, and is an excellent source for events he actually witnessed. His history, however, is partly inaccurate, for it was a group of criminals in New Orleans, not New York, that seems to have inspired the Black Hand extortion phenomenon in America.

On January 4, 1855, the New Orleans newspaper *The True Delta* reported that the body of a truck farmer named Francisco Domingo had been found on the Mississippi levee. He had been stabbed eighteen times and his throat slit savagely. Despite his Spanish name, Domingo was identified as a Sicilian, one of the three thousand Italians who had arrived in New Orleans since 1841.* His widow gave police a note Domingo

---

*Domingo's nationality remains open to question. Many Italian writers of the era complained that American officials automatically identified all dark-skinned Europeans as being one of two nationalities. If he wore a fez, he was a Turk; if not, he was Italian.

had received. He would die, the note said, unless he paid five hundred dollars. At the bottom appeared a large, inky, black hand. Mrs. Domingo said that in the past six months her husband had received several of these Black Hand notes. All had been delivered by strangers, some slipped into his palm, others into his pocket, and some left on his wagon. He had told her they were written by teen-agers who were stupid but not dangerous. The case was never solved.

In the next five years, six more murders occurred, each of them involving a note signed by an inky hand. Policemen were amazed to find that they were unable to beat, cajole, or purchase solutions. Witnesses refused to testify. Dying victims, fearing for their families, embraced their murderers and swore to their innocence. This lack of cooperation was much denounced by the police, who were mostly Irishmen. Neither the police records nor the newspapers mention or speculate about an extortion ring, so there is no estimate of the number of persons actually paying blackmail in New Orleans at that time.

Finally, in June 1861, two months after the opening of the American Civil War, *The True Delta* (ignoring police reluctance to follow up on the matter) directed suspicion to a building at One Twenty-nine Old Levee Street,* where resided an "organized gang of Spanish and Sicilian thieves and burglars who have long made their headquarters in the Second and Third Districts." The men, said the *Delta*, were probably the perpetrators of the extortions. Immediately following this public exposure the Spaniards vanished from the scene and only the Sicilians remained. Two weeks later, on July 9, 1861, *The True Delta* made another attempt to provoke official action, reporting on "an extensive colony of Sicilians [at the same address] who have earned for themselves an unenviable reputation" and had stolen two thousand dollars' worth of goods in the past week. Finally, on August 14, police raided the tenement,

---

*The structure and alleyway are still in use. By the present numbering system it is 917–923 Decatur Street, formerly Old Levee Street. It was the original headquarters of the Black Hand and in 1869 would become the first meeting place of the American Mafia.

caught several Sicilians in the act of counterfeiting coins, and led them away. Whether as a result of the arrests, the publicity, or the Civil War, Black Hand activity abruptly ceased in New Orleans.

Three years after the New Orleans gang dispersed, the second American Black Hand group appeared, in New York. On August 11, 1864, the torso of a young Italian man was found on the Brooklyn bank of the East River. He had been shot in the right temple by an "exceptionally large ball" and his body was sawed in half. In the dead man's pocket police found "an interesting note"; the contents were not made public. Two more bodies, killed in the same fashion, were found in Brooklyn before the year was out.

On May 29, 1865, a fourth body was found in a woods not far from the Coney Island railroad depot in Brooklyn. The victim was identified as a forty-year-old Italian gambler named Antonio Diodati. His corpse had been discovered by two young Germans who took the man they saw lying in the grass for a drunkard. When they rolled him over, his head fell off. He had been shot in the back of the head with a large ball. And this time there were cooperative witnesses. Women living nearby had seen Diodati enter the woods with three men and had seen the men leave the woods without him.

With the advantage of witnesses and identification, police took an interest in the case. In Diodati's boardinghouse they found a threatening letter, written in Italian, which, *The New York Times* reported, the police attributed to "some secret Italian society." Two days later, one Spaniard and two Italians were arrested at a residence on Sixteenth Street in Brooklyn and charged with the first and fourth murders. Among the contraband seized were plates, paper, a printing press, and $19,000 in counterfeit notes, plus five trunks of stolen goods.

After the arrests, Black Hand activity in New York ceased abruptly, just as it had in New Orleans in 1861. Perhaps the same gang that was arrested in New Orleans simply resumed operations in New York after their release from prison. In any case, the Black Hand did not appear again in either city until 1872, a year when Italian army purges sent many bandits and criminals of every type, including Mafiosi and Camorrists, fleeing to the United States. This second wave of Black Hand criminals was completely Italian and crisscrossed the country, following in the wake of Italian immigration. Isolated Black Hand crimes were reported in Philadelphia late in 1873, in San Francisco and Cincinnati in 1874, in Colorado mining camps in 1875, and in St. Louis in 1876.

By 1882 Black Hand extortion had occurred nationwide, and the press took notice. In August 1882, New York's Chief Inspector Thomas Byrnes, always alert to publicity, arrested three men he identified as "the Black Hand." He promised a wider investigation—"there is more to the case," he said—but never made good that promise. There was nothing more to say. The "organization" he had sworn to track down went no further than his three prisoners.

In the early part of the twentieth century, Black Hand free-lancers sometimes attempted to extort leaders of organized crime. Unlike law-abiding citizens, who allowed themselves to be terrorized, these criminals simply turned to the police. Although this seems an apparent violation of the underworld's law against informing, it only shows that Black Handers were considered to be beyond underworld rules. Brotherhood members despised the Black Handers, and not only because of occasional extortions against themselves. The very existence of the Black Hand was damaging to the societies' reputations. Most contemptible of all, from the crime families' point of view, was the Black Handers' tendency to sign their extortion notes "the Mafia." No true Mafioso would ever sign such a note, for it would amount to signing his own death warrant.

THE BIRTH OF
THE AMERICAN MAFIA

The American Mafia was created by a man born in New Orleans who never left the American South. His name was Joseph P. Macheca. His father, whose name is unknown, was a Sicilian immigrant who went to prison sometime around 1845 and urged Joseph's mother, Mary, to consider him dead. He said she should remarry as a means of support. She followed his advice, and made a good choice. Her second husband, a respectable and hard-working fruit-stand vendor named Joseph Macheca, adopted the boy and later had two sons of his own by Mary. In 1855, when young Joseph reached his majority, he and his stepfather opened their own shop on the New Orleans waterfront.

Joseph was tall for the era, standing above six feet. He was dark haired and handsome and known for a quick humor and charm. He had an especially open and friendly nature. By 1859 he and his stepfather had acquired sufficient means to buy a building in the French Quarter and become food wholesalers. During the Civil War Joseph Jr. moved his operations to Houston, where he acquired a boat, and by war's end had put together a fortune of more than $100,000. Returning to New Orleans in 1865, he used his Texas wealth to take advantage of depressed prices and bought several properties. Most of them were in the French Quarter, but his new residence was uptown, in a section favored by the American nouveaux riches. He expanded his business, founding the steamship company that inaugurated the fast banana trade between Central America and United States ports. Always loyal to his adopted family, he called his profitable new enterprise the House of Macheca.*

Until this point Macheca had behaved as an exemplary young man. He had overcome deprived origins, worked hard, built a sizable fortune by the age of thirty, and was a property owner and a faithful son. But there was a hint of elusiveness about him. He had managed to avoid service in either army during the Civil War, and, despite his youth, wealth, appearance, and charm, he remained unmarried.

In 1868 Joseph gave the first hint that he was a man capable of organizing and manipulating a group like the Mafia. The occasion was that year's presidential campaign. The Republicans had nominated Ulysses S. Grant who, unlike the incumbent, Andrew Johnson, was not committed to continuing Lincoln's policy of healing the breach between North and South. The Democratic candidate was Horatio Seymour, a man who had declared the Emancipation Proclamation unconstitutional when he was governor of New York. The Republicans were offering a harsh policy toward the South and special privileges for Southern blacks. The Democrats, at least in Confederate eyes, lined up as the pro-South, pro-white party.

Joseph Macheca had sat out the Civil War, but he suddenly

---

*The House of Macheca was not included in the stepfather's will when he died in 1878, so it seems likely that Joseph was in fact the owner of the business. The House of Macheca was eventually acquired by Joseph's half-brothers and became the foundation of a respected New Orleans fortune.

took an interest in politics and launched an extraordinary campaign for Seymour, which was described by the New Orleans *Daily Picayune.* "This popular and pleasant-mannered gentleman organized and commanded a company of Sicilians, 150 strong, known as the Innocents. Their uniform was a white cape bearing a Maltese cross on the left shoulder. They wore side arms and when they marched the streets they shot at every Negro that came in sight. They left a trail of a dozen dead Negroes behind them. General James B. Steedman, managing the [Seymour] campaign, forbade them making further parades and they were disbanded."

This matter-of-fact account is the first report of a formal Sicilian organization in New Orleans, and it is likely that from the ranks of these armed Innocents came the nucleus of Macheca's Mafia. That remarkable newspaper, *The True Delta,* which eight years earlier had discovered the existence of the American Black Hand, caught the American Mafia in the very act of organization. The events reported in the *Delta* on March 19, 1869, took place less than nine years after the creation of the Sicilian Mafia in Palermo. The newspaper account shows Macheca struggling with Palermo refugees for control of the new American outpost of the Mafia:

> There is now in the second district of this city a band of about twelve well-known and notorious Sicilian murderers, counterfeiters, and burglars who, in the last month, have formed a sort of general co-partnership or stock company for the plunder and disturbance of the city. Three or four of these men have been residing here for years and have always formed part of an extremely dangerous class. The others are but recently in the country. These men have been driven out of Sicily by laws which appear more strict and severe than any we have in this. Much as we imagine ourselves the superiors of anything that is old, these men in Palermo, the city whence they come, are held to a strict and careful account. Once a man is there suspected of being a dangerous character, he is either incarcerated altogether, or he is required by the police to report every night at the stationhouse and be locked up. There are no American theories of liberty there about thieves.

Finding that the license and bail bond system of this city afford much more liberty and personal security than Sicily, these men have come here and deliberately organized for mischief, and when it is stated that several of the best known murders ever committed in this city have been committed by them, it will be understood how dangerous the class is. . . .

One of the murders committed by these men is alleged to have been that of Lethario Barber, whose death was at one time attributed to another party. Barber, it now appears, was met at a late hour of the night, and advantage having been taken of the political excitement of October, he was shot down by two balls, one through his left hip, one through his abdomen. Four weeks ago, on Sunday night, these men were all together at their place of rendezvous on Royal Street,* drinking and carousing together. Suddenly, while all were dancing and playing together, they commenced stabbing and shooting. About ten shots were fired and several blows of the dagger were dealt. Two parties were seriously wounded, and another of the party shot through the mouth. This difficulty was between the members themselves, among whom, as is always the case in every organization, there was an opposition party.

A week after, a similar affray occurred on Chartres Street between Dumaine and St. Philip. On that occasion about a dozen more shots were fired and some of the balls penetrated Leyadore's Drug Store.

The party consists of nine 'soldiers' and three 'captains.' The soldiers follow no regular occupation; or if any at all, it is that of fruit sellers; and this occupation is only followed for a blind. Their more serious occupation consists in the manufacturing of spurious nickels and such occupation or employment as the captains may find for them.

The editors asked in conclusion that the attorney general give police powers to an "Italian society of Citizens" and allow them full powers to deal with the new organization. Excep-

---

*The "political excitement of October" is a reference to the affair of the Innocents; Barber was shot during that political fracas. The "rendezvous on Royal Street" was a bar located in a building owned by Macheca and operated by the immigrant Matranga family, who would play a significant role in the American Mafia some twenty years later.

tional measures were needed, the *Delta* explained, because experience had shown that "honest Sicilians and Italians are stabbed in the back when they give true evidence on the witness stand."

In the next two weeks *The True Delta* reported three more murders and several woundings resulting from the ongoing conflict. Two men, "part of the same gang to which reference has been made," came under police suspicion. One, Pietro Attuchi, fled to Galveston. The other, Francisco Valloti, was captured by police and confessed, probably under torture, that he had been paid five hundred dollars to assassinate a society captain named Gregorio Guglielmo, one of the Palermo refugees. Valloti refused to say who hired him, but at the end of the two-week shooting spree the windows of Joseph Macheca's business on Old Levee Street were fired into. It was an indication that Macheca was making war on the new immigrants.

His opponent was one Ralph Ajnello, a newly arrived Sicilian who established himself promptly as a man of wealth and substance. Ajnello won the early skirmishes in March of 1869, and following the shooting-out of Macheca's windows he spent two days, flanked by bodyguards, strutting down every block of the French Quarter to show that no one dared challenge him. On the second day he concluded his parade on the sidewalk in front of Macheca's store. But he had misjudged his man. Ajnello and his three bodyguards were cut down by a single gunman, one Frank Saccaro, who used a *lupara** and two revolvers. One guard survived. He wept to police that "our godfather" had been killed. Years later, the assassin, Saccaro, turned up as an important member of Macheca's Mafia.

Behind all these events was a power play between Macheca and members of the Sicilian Mafia. In late 1868 or early 1869, members of the Sicilian brotherhood arrived in New Orleans and began to organize a new society of criminals. Macheca, a

---

*A sawed-off shotgun with a twelve-inch double barrel. The stock was also sawed off, near the trigger, and hollowed out for lightness. The stock and barrel were then rejoined by a hinge, so that the barrel and butt could be folded up like a jackknife. The gun was also fitted with a hook so it could be concealed inside a coat.

violent man, found his position threatened. For three years he had been *the* leader of young Sicilians in the city, taking charge by force of his personality, reputation, wealth, and his ability to provide young men with jobs on the waterfront. Suddenly he was challenged by Ajnello, a new arrival from Palermo who was called "godfather" and had organized a gang into "soldiers" and "captains."

Macheca pondered this Mafia, whose mystique among young Sicilians was such that a newcomer could usurp an established leader's position almost overnight. He reacted by killing Ajnello. He then incorporated the new Mafia phenomenon, bringing his own young men and the Palermo refugees together under its institutions. Dating from this war of 1869, Joseph Macheca's Mafia became a profitably functioning organization under American leadership.

Macheca's citizenship was important to the early growth of the society, for as an American, he had certain political advantages which, in 1869, would not have been available to an immigrant. Macheca also enjoyed some political stature because of his wealth, his property, and his leadership of Sicilian voters. Five years later, in 1874, he added to that influence. In that year the city of New Orleans experienced a civil war, and Macheca managed to become a major participant. The struggle was between the city government and a Democratic party faction called the White League which was determined to overthrow the Republican carpetbaggers who had been in power for years. The war was no petty street brawl. Into the French Quarter both sides poured several thousand armed men and dozens of cannons. Macheca, as he had in 1868, lined up with the pro-South Democrats.

"At the head of the White League attack "reported *The Daily Picayune,*" was Joe Macheca who had organized a company of 200 Sicilians and armed them with bayoneted rifles." The Democrats launched an attack from Canal Street into the French Quarter and "as the rest of the White Leaguers pursued the retreating Republicans, Macheca led his company to attack the wounded and just as they were about to bayonet the fallen General Badger [leader of the Republican party's force], a

White Leaguer named Douglas Kirkpatrick leaped forward with a pistol aimed at Macheca's head. He stopped Macheca in his tracks and, with the pistol still pointed at his head, forced him to obtain a stretcher and carry General Badger to Charity Hospital."

At the hospital Macheca took credit for rescuing Badger, and when the general regained consciousness, he was informed that he owed his life to Macheca. Kirkpatrick's account became lost in the confusion, and Macheca accomplished a feat rare in civil wars: he emerged a hero to both sides, to the White League for his bravery and to the Republican administration for his chivalry. After the civil war, Macheca's political star continued to rise. His influence was such that foreign nations sought him out. In 1875 Bolivia appointed him its consul general in New Orleans. The following year three other Latin nations did the same.

His Mafia leadership was eclipsed only briefly, from 1879 to 1881, when he temporarily deferred to Giuseppe Esposito (See page 43). But within six weeks of Esposito's capture, he was back in power and had sufficient political clout to remove from the police force the detectives who had arrested Esposito. He replaced them with his own man. In 1888, however, David Hennessey became chief of police. From then on, Macheca was doomed.

Hennessey's appointment resulted from one of New Orleans's rare reform elections. The appointment was popular in New Orleans and elsewhere. Congratulations came from across the nation, including a letter from William Pinkerton, head of the celebrated detective agency.

Hennessey had not forgotten Joe Macheca and the Esposito episode, which had brought about his dismissal seven years earlier. In his first year of office he compiled dossiers on ninety-four murders, which, he claimed, had been committed by the Mafia since 1868. Hennessey's Mafia investigation also revealed that after Esposito's arrest in 1881 the New Orleans Mafia had split into two factions, with both groups recognizing the overall leadership of Macheca. The more powerful of the factions was headed by a young Sicilian named Charles Matranga, the other by an old-line Mafioso named Joe Provenzano, a man who had been close to Esposito and one of the witnesses who had perjured himself for the Sicilian leader in the extradition hearing.

Matranga, born in 1857, was one year old when his family emigrated to New Orleans. His father ran a saloon, and he and his brothers grew up in an underworld environment, toiling dutifully in the ranks of Joe Macheca until the Esposito episode. Following that arrest, Esposito's friends, led by Provenzano, challenged Macheca's leadership on the grounds that the American had failed in his responsibility to protect the Sicilian leader.

To bolster his defense, Macheca decided upon a solution that would be used by American brotherhood groups repeatedly in the next century and unto the present day—he would import reinforcements directly from Sicily. However, he had a problem: American-born, his parents unconnected with crime, Joe Macheca had no connections in Sicily. But his young lieutenant Charles Matranga had excellent Sicilian contacts, and it was he who was given the responsibility of recruiting.

Matranga's roots were not in the Mafia country in Sicily but in Monreale, the home of a rival brotherhood society called the Stoppaglieri. The Stoppaglieri had been organized in 1870 by a suppressed political faction which overthrew the local Mafia government. The group was structurally more complex than either the nineteenth-century Mafia or Camorra, both of which lacked a boss of bosses and a consigliere, or advisor. The society survived for twenty years in the neighborhood of Monreale, only two hours from the Mafia's center in Palermo. But by the time Matranga began looking for recruits, many Stoppaglieri members were only too glad to make the crossing. Economic opportunity had become severely limited in Sicily, and their rivalry with the Mafia and another minor brotherhood, the Fratuzzi, was turning into open warfare. By 1889 the Italian consul estimated there were at least 320 members of the Stoppaglieri in New Orleans. With these 320 Stoppaglieri imports and a dozen old-time Macheca soldiers, Matranga and Macheca would confront the Provenzano faction of some forty to sixty Mafia members.

THE BIRTH OF THE AMERICAN MAFIA

Shortly after he began his inquiries, Hennessey received an anonymous letter informing him that the Mafia had sworn an oath to kill him. The letter named Macheca, Matranga, and Rocco Geraci as principals in the plot. As a protective measure, Hennessey began to keep his confidential secretary, George Vanderwoort, intimately informed about the investigation. One of the chief strengths of the society, the chief told Vanderwoort, was its ability to provide services for new immigrants. This function was supervised by Mafioso Frank Romero. He saw that all Italian immigrants were interviewed concerning their skills, family, personal history, and resources. He helped them obtain peddling permits and get jobs, and in general established the image that the Mafia was their protector and their government.

This question of who would be able to supply jobs was at the root of the Matranga-Provenzano war. Macheca and Matranga were struggling with Provenzano for dominance, and the battleground, the territory to be gained or lost, was the New Orleans docks. Under Esposito, the Mafia's Provenzano had been given a monopoly on the hiring of all dock workers. In the late 1880s Matranga set up a rival association composed of Stoppaglieri members and through beatings, murders, and other intimidations gained substantial power over Provenzano's clients, the steamship lines that needed dock workers to load and unload their vessels.

In 1889 Provenzano made several peace offers. His association and Matranga's could split up the work. His delegate, Vincenzo Ottumvo, was to get together at a friendly card game with Rocco Geraci, Matranga's chief enforcer, to negotiate. But while Ottumvo sat at the playing table, his head was split open with an axe. It was a treacherous act, but Mafia tradition has it that if a body is not found, revenge cannot be sworn. To keep Provenzano from declaring all-out war, the murderers dismembered Ottumvo's body and buried it secretly.*

---

*The Ottumvo murder in 1889 has been cited by numerous authorities as the first Mafia murder in the United States. It is, however, rather far down the list, following some ninety such murders in New Orleans in the period 1869–1889 and the 1888 New York murder, which was identified on the spot by Chief Inspector Byrnes as "a Mafia killing."

Provenzano responded by murdering a capo of the Stoppaglieri faction. At that point Hennessey sent for the principals, Macheca, Matranga, and Provenzano, and according to his secretary, "told them he meant business, that there must be no Mafia trouble and that they must live in peace. He threatened, in case of trouble, to send them all to the penitentiary, and that they knew him well enough to know he would keep his word. The factions shook hands, took a drink, and seemingly parted friends. Hennessey stated afterwards that Macheca went to Matranga and told them he had made a mistake [in letting Hennessey make peace], as the Provenzanos would not keep their word and were backed by the chief of police [Hennessey]. Between the two factions, the chief did lean towards the Provenzanos, considering them more Americanized."

Whatever his motivation, Macheca reneged on his word and the war began in earnest. Before dawn on April 6, 1890, the Provenzanos set up an ambush outside the French Quarter at Claiborne and Esplanade streets. This was a route traveled by the Matrangas on their way to the docks. When a wagon carrying Tony Matranga, Rocco Geraci, a capo named Jim Caruso, and four others came by, the Provenzanos opened fire with shotguns. Two were wounded; the others escaped.

Within two hours, still before dawn, Hennessey rounded up the Provenzanos and jailed them, both for their own protection and to prevent a gang war. To his surprise, the Matrangas came in and swore out complaints, identifying the Provenzanos as would-be assassins. It stunned the chief, for in all previous cases Italians refused to bear witness against one another. He did not realize that in cases where rival brotherhood societies were involved, the rules went out the window.

Once formal charges were made against the Provenzanos, Hennessey took himself off the case to give an appearance of impartiality. At the trial, held in July 1890, some two dozen policemen of every rank, from captain to patrolman, gave perjured testimony in an effort to prove that the Provenzanos were carousing elsewhere in the city at the time of the shootings. The Matrangas, however, told a consistent and well-rehearsed story of the attack. Despite police perjury, the Provenzanos were convicted. The next day, the fix was put in again. The presiding judge overturned the jury verdict and, ignoring the Matranga testimony, ruled that no positive identification had been made of the defendants. He ordered a new trial to be held October 17. Meanwhile, the Provenzanos were to remain in prison for safekeeping.

At this point there existed a bizarre situation: The police chief and the town's Mafia leader, Provenzano, had sided against Macheca, Matranga, and the "less Americanized" Stoppaglieri. Hennessey publicly declared that he would "show up Macheca and the Matrangas, giving their records and showing that they are not worthy of credence."

For his role in this affair, any other police chief but Hennessey would be suspected of being in Provenzano's pay. There is no evidence, however, that Hennessey took bribes, from the Mafia or anyone else. On the contrary, he tended to beat up people who offered them to him. And in 1881, when the Mafia had wanted to give him $50,000 to help Esposito, he had refused, and been dismissed from the force. So why did Hennessey favor the Provenzanos, defending them, as we shall see, to the very end? Part of the answer may lie in his statement above that they were more Americanized than Macheca's imported troops. But more importantly, Macheca had engineered Hennessey's dismissal, while Provenzano had done Hennessey no such disservice. Provenzano seems to have been a fairly reasonable, cautious Mafioso, who cooperated with the police when it was advantageous, and kept the peace. He and Hennessey, indeed, were friends. The police chief sponsored Provenzano for an exclusive club membership, and the two were frequently seen together socially.

After Hennessey made his allegiance public, Macheca replied with an ever more astounding interview. He told reporters, "Hennessey is investigating the Provenzano case the wrong way and he will answer for it." The cold threat, made against a man who was both police chief and town hero, was a testament to Macheca's confidence.

On August 12, 1890, Hennessey wrote to the chief of police of Rome, L. Bertin, asking for the names, records, and photographs of known Mafiosi wanted in Italy. He said he believed many of them to be in New Orleans. On September 1 Chief Bertin replied that he would be pleased to comply and would send the information as soon as he had gathered it. But shortly after receipt of the letter, Hennessey learned that his correspondence with Bertin was known in New Orleans, although he had tried to preserve the utmost secrecy. He suspected that agents in Rome had tipped off the New Orleans Mafia. The records were never sent. A week after he wrote Hennessey, Chief Bertin was murdered in Rome.*

More determined than ever, Hennessey contacted the Italian consul in New Orleans, Pasquale Corte, who said he could provide a list of about one hundred criminals in the city who had escaped from Italian prisons. Shortly afterward an attempt was made to murder the consul. He was asked to supper at Macheca's house and, although he felt he couldn't refuse the invitation of such a prominent man, he ate sparingly of everything. Hours later he became desperately ill and later told Hennessey, "My symptoms bore all the evidence of poisoning and I am satisfied that my life had been attempted."

Corte was intimidated. He refused to produce the list of fugitives he had promised Hennessey, saying he needed authorization from the ambassador in Washington. Later, when a New Orleans grand jury called for it, Corte admitted he had the power to release the list, but he refused to do so on the grounds that it would only serve to harm Italian citizens. Thus, wherever Hennessey turned for outside information he was stymied.

Unknown to him, his fate had been decided by his letter to Chief Bertin in Rome. Macheca knew of the letter on August 13, the day Hennessey mailed it from New Orleans. On that date Macheca made a house call which set in motion the machinery to put an end to Hennessey. Using the alias "Mr. Paul Johnson," he went to the house of Mr. and Mrs. John Petersen

---

*In this era, the Mafia had an exceptionally strong influence in the Italian government. Parliamentary hearings in 1885 disclosed that at least ten members of that body were also members of the Mafia. It was further revealed that the commandant of the Royal Army had repeatedly acted on behalf of the Mafia and may have been a member.

THE BIRTH OF THE AMERICAN MAFIA   ○ 85

and inquired about a property of theirs he wished to rent. The property, on Girod Street near the corner of Basin, was an old wooden shanty of three rooms, with a shed projecting over the sidewalk. The two back rooms, Mrs. Petersen told Macheca, were already occupied by two Negro families. Macheca replied he was only interested in the front room, which he wanted to rent for a friend for a period of three months. Mrs. Petersen accepted a month's rent in advance and handed over a receipt to "P. Johnson" in the amount of three dollars.

The value of this shack was its location. It was half a block from Hennessey's cottage and lay directly on his regular route home from police headquarters. Macheca installed an immigrant shoe cobbler named Pietro Monasterio. The cobbler, an illiterate, was instructed to keep a log of Hennessey's habits, especially the times he left and returned to his house; who, if anyone, accompanied him; how he was armed; and when, if ever, he seemed to be intoxicated. For six weeks Monasterio watched and scratched his records on the wall with matchsticks.

In early October, Charles Matranga, Rocco Geraci, the enforcer, and two soldiers moved into the one-room shack, sharing it with the cobbler and his fourteen-year-old nephew, Aspari Marchesi. A few days later, on October 15, two nights before Provenzano went on trial a second time for assaulting Matranga, thirteen more gang members joined them, making a total of nineteen in the shack. That night a meeting was held, presided over by Macheca. Straws were drawn to determine who would be on the assassination team. Eight men were chosen. The remainder, including Macheca and Matranga, departed.

At eleven o'clock that night, the electric streetlights, which normally were dimmed at 10:00 P.M., came up bright, bathing the street with light. It was later established that the city electric department had been bribed. At 11:25 neighbors heard a long, trilling whistle. It was the fourteen-year-old nephew signaling that Hennessey was in sight. The chief, returning from a police board meeting, approached from the corner of Basin and turned onto Girod. Two men stepped out and dropped him with blasts from sawed-off shotguns. Others fired from the shack. Hennessey tried to crawl away. More men ran out and, standing over him, pumped shots into the body. Then they ran away. Neighbors came out into the street. Some saw the fleeing killers. Others heard Hennessey say, "The Dagoes done it." He was lifted into a wagon and taken to Charity Hospital.

Long before dawn, the news was out. Great crowds assembled at the scene to watch while police searched the sidewalks, gutters, and houses for discarded weapons. A ramrod was found on the sidewalk in front of the shanty, and several witnesses had seen fire coming from a doorway next to the shop. Bullet holes in the houses opposite Monasterio's shop proved that Hennessey had been killed by persons waiting in ambush there. Those findings, supported by Hennessey's own words, led to the arrest of many Italians. By noon the prison held one hundred of them. In the evening, Hennessey died.

The help he had sought came only after his death. In Chicago, William Pinkerton assigned his top investigator, Frank Dimaio, to New Orleans. There Dimaio would have sensational results in obtaining one of the few confessions ever extracted from an active Mafioso. Pinkerton himself spent weeks of his own time working without fee to solve the case. It was Pinkerton who first named the Mafia as the killer of Hennessey. "It all began twelve years ago when Hennessey arrested Esposito. He was head of the Mafia here in the United States. This brought down the hatred and wrath."

In the excitement, the Mafia leaders were nearly forgotten. Joe Provenzano, his brother Pete, and Mafiosi Nick Giulio, Nick Pellegrini,* Tony Gianfoccaro, and Gaspardo Lombardo were in Parish Prison, where they had been since the previous April. They were not uncomfortable. The section where they lodged was known by prisoners as "the Orleans Hotel," separate from the regular cells. The Provenzanos had clean linen three times a week, and good meals and wine were brought in. They wore fashionable clothing and had the run of their tiers. The only

---

*Pellegrini was among the men who perjured himself in the New York extradition hearings of Esposito in 1881. Rocco Geraci was a second member of the five-man alibi team from New Orleans; Joe Provenzano a third.

time they were locked up was on October 18, three days after the murder, when a reporter from the *Daily Picayune* came to visit them. Through a grated window in the cell door, the reporter interviewed Joe Provenzano. The Mafia leader talked freely about his enemies and gave himself the role of helpless, persecuted victim.

"Who do you think shot him?" he was asked.
"I don't know."
"Nobody knows; but who do you think?"
"Matranga, sure."
"Why do you think so?"
"Because he [Hennessey] was going to be a witness for us and was going to expose them. He knew all about Matranga and Geraci. He got some things from Italy about them and he was going to tell what he knew and that would break them up." Then Provenzano unexpectedly said, "Matranga was head of the Stoppaglieri society."
"The what society?"
"The Stoppaglieri. They are the people who work for the Matrangas; there are about twenty leaders of them. They are the committee, and there are about 300 greenhorns who have got to do anything the leaders say. I'll tell you about that. When Jim Caruso came to me about four years ago with a letter asking $1,000 for the Mafia or they would kill us, Caruso told me Matranga was the president of it and Rocco Geraci was a leader. Caruso said he had been in it, too, but got out of it as soon as he could." Provenzano described how Caruso was initiated into the Stoppaglieri. "They brought him into the room, and he saw Matranga dressed in a black domino [a loose robe with wide sleeves, a hood, and a mask] and others were in dominoes, and they made him swear on a skull with a dirk in it."

The reporter asked, "Are there any Italians in the Mafia besides the people who work on the ships?"

And, in the year 1890, the Mafia boss of New Orleans replied, "I don't know. They've got the Mafia society everywhere. They've got it in San Francisco, St. Louis, Chicago, New York and here."

"Did you ever belong to it?"

"Me? No, indeed."

"Where does this Mafia or Stoppaglieri society meet?"

"They meet anywhere out near the levee, back of town and in Carrolton. Their headquarters is in Carrolton, I think." This must have jolted readers, for the Carrolton section was the city's wealthiest residential area.

The reporter moved in with a hard question: "Weren't you at the head of the [Mafia] association?"

Provenzano sidestepped it. "We had a laborers' association when we had the stevedore business," he said, "and never let any greenhorns in it. All our men were Italians who were raised here. They were Americans." Provenzano shifted the subject back to the Matranga brothers. "Their own men hate them, but have to do what they say or get killed. They make the greenhorns do the killing. They pay them ten, twenty or one hundred dollars to get a man out of the way, and if the man they order to kill someone doesn't do it, they have him killed so he can't tell anything to the police."

It was remarkable for a ranking Mafioso to confide society secrets to a newspaper. But Provenzano was undoubtedly scared now that his protector, Hennessey, was gone, and he was anxious to line up with the "Americans." A lynch wind was blowing. In the days following Hennessey's death, anti-Italian demonstrations and riots occurred in New York, Chicago, Cleveland, St. Louis, New Orleans, and San Francisco.

As the weeks passed, the many innocent Italians who had been arrested were released, and by the end of October the true assassination squad had been charged and placed in prison. It was at this time that the Pinkerton detective Frank Dimaio infiltrated the gang. New Orleans authorities were not informed of the plan. Instead, from Chicago, Pinkerton sent phony wanted notices which led to the arrest of Dimaio as a notorious counterfeiter. The detective, who spoke Sicilian, was placed in the Parish Prison hospital where eight suspects in Hennessey's murder were being held. Dimaio played the role of a big-time operator, treating the Mafiosi with scorn, which he later softened to condescension. He called them small-time dagoes too stupid to live by their wits. Weeks passed, and the more arrogant Dimaio became, the more he was admired. Some members of the gang began to boast about jobs they had done and to tell certain aspects of the Hennessey killing.

Conditions in the prison, even in the hospital, were so bad that by December Dimaio's weight had fallen from 185 to 140 pounds. This was noticed by his "lawyer," another Pinkerton agent who was the only person outside the prison with access to Dimaio. Pinkerton sent word that Dimaio was to leave the prison immediately. The detective refused, arguing that he was on too good a footing to leave now. Instead, Dimaio concentrated his efforts on a minor recruit named Joe Polizi. He told Polizi his cellmates were trying to poison him, because they were afraid Polizi would talk. When food was brought, Dimaio warned Polizi not to eat it because it might contain arsenic. The two of them shared Dimaio's food and both men starved and weakened.

Finally, the strain caused Polizi to tell Dimaio all the murder details. The detective made notes on a small piece of paper, had Polizi make his mark, and passed the confession to his lawyer that evening. The next day Pinkerton effected the detective's release and in mid-December Dimaio went before the New Orleans grand jury. His testimony was instrumental in the indictment of ten men for murder and of nine, including Macheca and Charles Matranga, for conspiracy. The confession gave dates, names, and places. Polizi identified Charles Matranga and Joe Macheca as the engineers of the assassination and described the drawing of straws in the shack. Polizi also gave his version of the society's history. He said Mafia was the name of a legendary bandit who formed the society centuries ago, at which time it was composed only of gentlemen. Polizi joined, he said, because La Mafia was under the patronage of Saint Joseph, for whom he was named.

During the period Dimaio had been in jail, mob passions had swept across the city in several waves. American gangs beat up Italians, usually being careful enough to pick on old men, women, and adolescent children. Italians responded, in one incident, by tearing down the U.S. flag at city hall and raising that of Italy. On October 18 the city council met in special session and Mayor Shakespeare appointed a committee of fifty citizens and charged them to "investigate the existence of murder societies and to devise means to stamp out the same if they exist."

On October 21, 1890, there began a series of diplomatic exchanges between Italy and various officials in the U.S. government. First Italy complained to James Blaine, United States secretary of state, that Italians were being oppressed in New Orleans because of the Hennessey killing. Blaine, in turn, passed on the communiqué to Louisiana Governor Francis Nichols. The latter referred the Italian government and the U.S. government to the New Orleans government. Unable to comprehend the separation of city, state, and federal powers in America, the Italian government continued to bombard Washington with cables. In the Italian Parliament several deputies introduced resolutions for the navy to begin bombardment of the Atlantic and Gulf ports of the United States. These threats in turn alarmed the American Congress, which immediately allocated funds to expand the White Squadron, a small but highly modern collection of warships, into the world's second-most-powerful navy, the Great White Fleet.*

On February 16, 1891, the murder trial was opened in St. Patrick's Court on Lafayette Square across from city hall. Great crowds—anxious, muttering, and menacing—filled the grounds each day. Police used rear exits to bring prisoners and witnesses in and out. The state was represented by a curiously apathetic district attorney, Charles Luzenberg, and three assistants. The defense was glittering. Chief of the counsel was Thomas J. Semmes, former state attorney general, and a former Confederate senator. His grandniece, Mrs. Myra Menville of New Orleans, states that he accepted the Mafia leaders as his clients

---

*In 1898 the existence of this powerful fleet played a major role in the U.S. decision to begin the Spanish-American war. Its victories added Cuba, Puerto Rico, the Philippines, Guam, the Caribbean Sea, and the Pacific Ocean to the American sphere of influence.

"with great reluctance. He tried, in fact, to discourage them from retaining him by setting a very high fee. But the next night they brought the money, a pillow-case full, and he was stuck." Semmes was assisted by a former district attorney named Adams, three lawyers, and an incumbent judge who had taken a leave of absence for the occasion. They were paid by a defense fund of $75,000, most of which was raised by extortions which ranged as far afield as Texas and New York.

Ten men were charged with murder—Polizi, Pietro Natali, Antonio Scaffidi, Charles Traina, Antonio Bagnetto, Antonio Marchesi, Pietro Monasterio, Bastian Incardona, Sal Sunseri, and Lorretto Comitz. Nine were charged with conspiracy—Macheca, Matranga, the fourteen-year-old boy Aspari Marchesi, Jim Caruso, Rocco Geraci, Charles Patorno, Frank Romero, John Caruso, and Charles Pietza (or Piazza).* The evidence, physical and testimonial, was extensively incriminating. Among the more significant items introduced were five shotguns, four of them Sicilian luparas, the traditional Mafia assassination weapon. According to testimony from experts, the lupara's charge was large enough to down an elephant, and, when loaded with buckshot or ball, the gun had a range of about thirty yards. But the prosecution's major piece of evidence was the confession of Joe Polizi, and a great uproar resulted when District Attorney Luzenberg announced in court that he would not use it. Polizi leaped to his feet and demanded to repeat his testimony. He asked the court to let him take the stand and tell the events that led to Hennessey's death; to tell where the firearms were procured; to tell where the conspirators met. He would reveal the names of everyone involved, including a mysterious capo named S. Oteri, who had fled to Sicily. Polizi recited all this in Sicilian while, according to courtroom reporters, the defendants, especially Macheca and Matranga, turned "absolutely pale, blood drained from their face." Prosecutor

---

*All these names, with the exceptions of Monasterio, Macheca, and Comitz, can be found in lists of men who were members of the Louisiana Cosa Nostra family in 1972. In three cases—Matranga, Incardona, and Geraci—the present-day members are known to be direct descendants of members of the 1890 group.

Luzenberg, who had an interpreter, objected that Polizi was obviously deranged and shouldn't testify. The defense counsels, surprised first by Polizi's offer, were further surprised by Luzenberg's refusal of it. They joined him in the motion to keep Polizi silent. The presiding judge agreed. He ordered Polizi bound and gagged and ordered him kept that way during recesses so that he couldn't talk to reporters. The bonds and gag were removed only during long recesses, when Polizi was kept confined in the sheriff's office. During one of these breaks he began screaming that Matranga and the lawyers wanted to kill him, and tried to jump out the window to his death.*

After testimony ended, two whole days were given to argument. The judge delivered his charge at midnight and gave his final instructions to the jurors. He ordered them to acquit the defendants Matranga and Incardona, who could be linked to the conspiracy only by Polizi's inadmissible evidence. The jury went out at 6:22 P.M. on March 12. Twenty-one hours later it returned with the verdict. Three men—Polizi, Scaffidi, and Monasterio—were granted a mistrial. The other defendants were declared innocent.

First in the courtroom, then swelling out the windows, down the corridors, and into the park of Lafayette Square, there arose a howl of rage that didn't subside until midnight. Crowds roamed the streets. Angry meetings were held. At the prison, eighteen of the defendants (Polizi was not present) held a victory supper of wine and Italian dishes. For their own protection they had not yet been released.

Of all the gatherings that night, the most important was held at the socially exclusive Boston Club, the second-oldest private club in the United States. About forty men attended.

---

*Three months after the trial, when a majority of the defendants were dead and there was no legal pretext for secrecy, District Attorney Luzenberg continued to withhold the confession given to Dimaio and repeated in the judge's chambers to Luzenberg, the defense counsel, and the judge. A newspaper, however, obtained a copy of the court reporter's notes, and these were eventually published, at least in part. There is no direct evidence that either Luzenberg or the judge was bribed. Nevertheless, their actions were highly irregular and served to protect Macheca and Matranga.

Here it was soberly decided that the trial proved that the city's political and judicial structure was controlled by criminals. The group determined to regain control of the city's institutions. W. S. Parkerson, a man of impressive moral and civic credentials, was named to head a "movement to correct the failure of justice." Newspaper publishers who had been invited agreed to hold the presses so that a last-minute notice could be inserted on front pages. Appearing the next morning, it read: "A Call. All good citizens are invited to attend a mass meeting on Saturday, March 14 [the day of publication], at 10 o'clock A.M. at Clay statue to take steps to remedy the failure of justice in the Hennessey case. Come prepared for action." The notice was signed by sixty-one of the best-known citizens of New Orleans, and long before the appointed hour an immense crowd had gathered at the Clay statue in front of city hall.

Parkerson, thirty-four-year-old attorney, campaign manager for Mayor Shakespeare, and leader of the reform movement, made the key address. "When courts fail, the people must act. What protection is there left us when the very head of our police department, our chief of police, is assassinated in our very midst by the Mafia society and his assassins turned again loose on the community?"

There was an hour of such speeches. Then Parkerson led the crowd to the Parish Prison on Treme Street. Inside were the nineteen Sicilians, Polizi among them. What followed was the largest lynching in American history. It was graphically described by reporters.

> At each corner the great assemblage of people gathered new strength and hundreds fell in who had entertained no faintest notion of taking part in the affair and were swallowed up in the seething tide, and went shouting to the very gates of the jail. Men, women and children from doorways and galleries raised their voices and applauded as if at some favorite carnival parade but in notable contrast was the bearing of the armed men and leaders who marched like a regiment of mutes. In a moment's space the streets which fronted upon the grim old prison streamed with people. Every avenue was jammed from curb to curb—telegraph

poles, lamp posts, and trees—these held a burden of human forms.

Windows and house tops were filled in every direction. The army of vigilantes drew up before the main gate of the prison and a man smote upon it with the butt of his shotgun, demanding entrance. The crowd anticipated a volley and surged back, while a dozen policemen struggled to clear the sidewalks. In answer to a command the armed men scattered, surrounding the building with a cordon of steel and the main body renewed the assault. The strong oaken door stood fast so they made their way to a small side door which was both locked and barred. Some one noticed a wagon loaded with timber, hopelessly wedged in the press, and a rush was made toward it.

A giant Negro picked up a huge paving stone and smashed it through the side door. The crowd was momentarily awed and stilled by the feat. Then beams of ashwood were snatched from the timber wagon and used as battering rams to further breach the door. Every crash provoked shouts from the people, and after repeated blows the door fell. Thirty armed men entered the building and disappeared one by one. Four others stood guard with their backs to the door, facing the crowd. The vigilantes were within.

The crowd listened, hushed and still. Moment after moment that hush continued, then from within came a renewed hammering; hollow, measured, and the faint cries of terrified persons. A little later a dull, unmistakable reverberation rolled forth like a smothered explosion, followed by another and another. Gunshots fired within brick walls . . . the crowd gave tongue in a howl of hoarse delight. Then followed a peculiar shrilling chorus. It was that signal known as the "dago whistle" which was like the piercing cry of lost souls.

"Who killa da chief?" screamed the people, then puckered up their lips and piped again that mocking signal. The booming of the guns continued and the maddened populace sought to enter the prison but were forced back by the guards. The streets heaved and tossed and men and women shrieked aloud.

Terrible as was the sight on the streets, it was worse within. Once they gained entry, the posse quickly obtained the keys from a terrified deputy. An iron-ribbed door barred them from the main body of the prison. They battered it down. Inside, the prisoners begged to be allowed to hide and save themselves if they could, and the jailers released them. There were all the confusions of hell. The Sicilians cried out to God, and were joined in the appeal by other inmates, black and white, who feared their crimes had overtaken them too. Men and women, felons and minor offenders alike, rushed along the galleries, fighting with one another, tearing each other from places of refuge. They huddled in dark corners, crept under beds, beneath stairways, and into barrels. Some kneeled to pray and were trampled. The vigilantes were inside.

They found Macheca and two of his men on the third floor crouching in the farthest cell. All three were shot in the cell, and died with their bloody hands clinging to the iron bars.

Polizi and another assassin had squeezed themselves into a dog kennel beneath the stairs. They were found, dragged out, and rushed into the street, where they were beaten with clubs and hanged from lampposts. The bodies were then shot to pieces.

The other prisoners, finally realizing which way the game was flowing, now began to point out where the Italians were hiding. One vigilante group was led to the women's department, where six Sicilians tried a desperate breakout but were caught between crossfire in the open courtyard. Wounded, they fell to their knees and shrieked for mercy. "Then followed a nightmare scene," reports *The Illustrated American*, "a horrid bellowing uproar of voices and detonations, of groans and prayers and curses. The armed men emptied their weapons blindly into these writhing forms, and as one finished, he stepped back while another took his place. The prison rocked with the din. The wretches were shot to pieces, riddled, by that hail which mowed and mangled all alike."

Now and again, a man struggled to his feet only to be so devastated with gunfire that his clothes were torn from his body. By the time the firing stopped, the prison pavement was wet and slippery. Out of the sodden heap of bodies, Monasterio the cobbler rose up, his gray hair matted with blood. The vigilantes, merciless, struck their rifles against his chest and killed him.

It was over. Eleven were dead. Five were critically wounded and soon would die. Three had been spared, including the boy Marchesi, who had been discovered hiding between two mattresses and was put into another cell unharmed. Matranga and Bastian Incardona had escaped by burying themselves in a pile of rubbish in a far corner of the prison yard. That evening, when the mob had departed, they came out.

In the aftermath, all charges against the surviving Sicilians were dismissed. The lynchings, an instant international sensation, were condemned by most of the Continental European press and cautiously endorsed by papers in England and the United States. The *Times* of London and *The New York Times* justified the lynchings on grounds that the Mafia had corrupted the judicial process to such an extent that there was no other remedy.

Meanwhile, in New Orleans the various committees—Parkerson and his vigilantes, the city council, the grand jury—set their jaws, damned their critics, and plowed ahead with the work. Testimony and evidence against the Mafia continued to be heard. In May 1891 an American grand jury officially reported for the first time on the presence and influence of the Mafia:

> The extended range of our researches has developed the existence of the secret organization styled 'Mafia.' The evidence comes from sources fully competent in themselves to attest to its truth, while the fact is supported by the long record of bloodcurdling crimes. . . .
> The officers of the Mafia and many of its members are known. Among them are *men born in this city of Italian parentage,* using their power for the basest purposes, be it said to their eternal disgrace. The large number of the society is composed of Italians or Sicilians who have left their native land in most instances under assumed names to avoid conviction of crimes there committed.

The jury went on to list ninety-four murders, dating from 1869, which had been committed by the society, and filed with the court clerk the names of 360 "Italian fugitives under Mafia protection in New Orleans." It reported further that several of the murder trial jurors had been bribed and others intimidated. This, said the grand jury, was the reason for the mistrial and acquittals. It also criticized the prosecutor, Luzenberg, and the judge, Baker. Most significant was the grand jury's identification of American natives as an integral part of the Mafia.

Five days after the report, an unfazed Charles Matranga, now Mafia boss of New Orleans, resumed personal control of the stevedores on the docks. Non-Italian workers, who had broken the Sicilian labor monopoly in recent years, complained anew that restrictions by nationality were back in force. The shipping companies replied that they did not intend to jeopardize their investments by defying their contract with the Matrangas.

The Provenzanos, retried in January 1891 on the old charge of shooting the Matrangas, were acquitted. They moved across the Mississippi River, where their descendants operate today.

Joe Macheca had been lynched intestate. In the absence of direct heirs, his property and shipping interests passed into the hands of his half-brothers. In 1900 Joe Macheca's shipping line merged with four others to form the giant United Fruit Company, which remains one of the largest of all U.S. firms.

The amazing thing about the 1891 lynchings is that they had so little effect on the Mafia in New Orleans. They did not diminish the society's power in the least—it operated as brazenly after 1891 as before, perhaps more so. The society's power was not checked until the Prohibition era, when Irish gangs temporarily dominated the city's organized crime.

The power of Charles Matranga grew steadily from 1891 onward. He was never again linked to any public scandal, though he continued as boss until about 1922, when he allowed a protégé, Sam Carolla, to succeed him. Some of Matranga's descendants went into Cosa Nostra rackets, but most entered legitimate businesses and professions. Like the Machecas, the main line of the Matranga family eventually became part of the New Orleans social establishment.

Matranga died on October 28, 1943, at the age of eighty-six.

He left four children, ten grandchildren, and seven great-grandchildren. Until he died he continued to receive income from steamship lines and longshoremen's associations. His funeral was large and attended by executives of United Fruit, Lykes, Standard Fruit, and other large steamship companies which had benefited from his good will.

Other than the victims themselves, the only party to suffer from the lynchings was the U.S. Treasury. In 1892, for reasons of diplomacy, Congress agreed to pay the Mafiosi survivors an indemnity of 125,000 lire.

The Stoppaglieri society absorbed the remnants of the Provenzano Mafia, and, having achieved a territorial monopoly, settled down to make peaceful profits. Its days of intersociety combat were over. It became part of the American Mafia.

SAN FRANCISCO, 1878

During the 1870s and 1880s, while the Mafia was establishing itself in New Orleans and New York, it was also spreading to other cities. After the arrest of Giuseppe Esposito, his men resettled in St. Louis. Another of the cities penetrated by the Mafia was San Francisco.

In the late nineteenth century, San Francisco had several things in common with New Orleans and New York, including a relatively large Italian population, political corruption on a grand scale, and a general tolerance of lawlessness. In one important respect, however, San Francisco was different. It had not ostracized its Italian community, and when Italians complained of hoodlums the police paid as much attention to their complaints as they would to any member of a comparable economic class. Because of early police opposition, the San Francisco Mafia lasted only a few years before it was exiled to the young city of Los Angeles, where while never a major influence in the government or the police, it has managed to survive into the present time.

The leader of the short-lived San Francisco Mafia was Rosario Meli. He was the first man to be identified as a Sicilian society member in America, and his capture in 1879 sent shivers through the national press. He was described as a "prominent member, if not the chief of the Mafia" in the western reaches of the United States. In addition to the exoticism of this Old World society, the Mafia excited the press with its ruthless methods of operation—suborning witnesses, bribing officers, killing informants.

The center of this storm of publicity, Rosario Meli, was indeed a prominent member of the Old World brotherhood. He was not, however, so prominent in the American Mafia. From the beginning, the American Mafia and its lineal offspring, the Cosa Nostra, were autonomous societies. A Sicilian Mafioso was not automatically given membership just because he had arrived in the United States.* Respect had to be earned and a sponsor had to nominate him for American membership.

Meli, a member of the original Palermo society, was among the most notorious brigands of Sicily by the time he was nineteen years old. In 1867, at age twenty-two, he was captured, convicted of several murders, and sentenced to life imprisonment. En route to the mainland he escaped and, according to the San Francisco *Examiner,* arrived in New Orleans in 1868, where "he was one of the founders of the order in this country."

This report gave more prestige to Meli than he deserved. He had started out as a lieutenant to the "godfather" Ralph Ajnello, who tried to take over New Orleans. When Ajnello was defeated, Meli became an ordinary soldier in the ranks of Joe Macheca and remained there until 1875. Then he set out with a few followers for San Francisco, where he hoped to reestablish himself as a leader.

---

*In only two instances have ranking Sicilian Mafiosi immediately stepped into comparable roles in America. One of these chiefs was Giuseppe Esposito, who arrived in 1879, and the other was Salvatore Maranzano, who arrived in 1927.

SAN FRANCISCO, 1878   ○   101

His traveling Mafia launched itself energetically in San Francisco. "Many mysterious crimes are committed in this city and surrounding towns," the *Examiner* reported. "Nearly every day the police receive information of burglaries having been committed the night before while robberies are perpetrated in broad daylight on the street." Many murders were committed, mostly in the Italian quarter. "The crimes are credited to the members of La Mafia. Several times members of the gang [have been] arrested but they invariably escaped conviction owing to the lack of witnesses for the prosecution."

Meli himself was "a walking arsenal. He carried a serpentine dagger, a loaded cane and a revolver fully two feet in length which carried a very large-sized bullet.... The serpentine dagger was of Turkish manufacture and had large scallops on the edges. The object of a man who uses such a weapon is to wound his victim in the abdomen, if possible, and turn the blade while it is in the body. The raised edge in the center, which acts as a fulcrum in turning the blade, makes this possible with a very slight twist of the wrist. The fact that such wounds were found in the bodies of several persons caused detectives to suspect that Meli was responsible for the crimes, but they could secure no other evidence against him."

In 1878 the body of a Sicilian named Catalani was found on a hill back of Sausalito "and in his abdomen was a gash judged to be inflicted by a serpentine dagger." Police arrested Meli and his confederates, Ignacio Trapani, Salvatore Messino, and Giuseppe Bianchi. Trapani confessed the murder, but said it resulted from a duel. The district attorney refused to prosecute the murder, claiming that a jury wouldn't convict, despite the confession. But police pressure forced him to prosecute a robbery charge against the foursome, and each was sentenced to a long term in San Quentin. Meli, however, wasn't beaten yet.

"On his way from the court, Meli threw a handful of flea powder into the eyes of the deputy who accompanied him and sought to make his escape, but was caught at the corner of Washington Street and Brenham Place. Detective [Appelton] Stone succeeded in fastening upon Vincent Trapani, a brother of Ignacio, the crime of having supplied Meli with the powder and he, too, served a term in San Quentin. Like the others, he was a member of La Mafia."

In a subsequent interview, Detective-Captain Stone described Meli's background. "Rosario Meli was held in abject terror by his countrymen who knew his bloody record in Italy. It was he who murdered the mayor of Syracuse, Italy, for which crime the power of La Mafia was bootless to save him from capture and a sentence of imprisonment for life. Through the intervention of his friends, however, he was pardoned and had not long been at liberty before he murdered the brother of the mayor. For this crime, he was sentenced to death, but again the Mafia saved him. He was assisted to escape from prison by the very men whose duty it was to carry out the sentence. Upon regaining his liberty, Meli ranged through the mountains of Sicily as a bandit for awhile until he came to this country. Detectives from Sicily traced him to New Orleans but then lost all trace of him there. It is said that they sent word of their approach so that he might escape."

Soon after Meli entered San Quentin, the warden received extradition papers from Italy, where Meli was wanted as a fugitive. Captain Stone took him by train to New York, where he was handed over to Italian detectives and placed in the Ludlow Street jail to await completion of the extradition process. In New York Meli became the object of a public uproar. Italian community leaders in New York and New Jersey, possibly beguiled by resident Mafiosi, created the argument that Meli was the wrong man, an innocent who was being persecuted. It was an ironic preview of the Esposito extradition when, two years later, the Sicilian chief would be placed in the same jail and given the same defense.

On September 2, 1880, *The New York Times* presented the argument of the Free Meli movement. "The prisoner denies he is the wanted man. He says he is a native of Palermo, born 34 years ago, and came to the United States 16 years ago and went to live in Philadelphia for 12 years." In 1876 he moved to San Francisco and opened a rifle gallery on Kearney Street, where "his prosperity made his Sicilian friends jealous and they determined upon his ruin" and framed him on the robbery charge.

He said "he knows nothing about La Maffia Society and that he was never connected with it in any way whatever."

At the extradition hearing, however, Italian officials used photographs and personal identification to prove that Meli was the man convicted of murder in Sicily. Even so, the Free Meli faction refused to give up. On September 8, 1880, when Meli was scheduled to depart for Europe, a huge crowd of Italians, many of whom were armed, gathered at the pier. Officials averted an incident by sneaking Meli aboard in a cargo net, and from there history loses him. The Italian consul in San Francisco later said, "I have newspapers and correspondence from Sicily and they never heard of Meli's arrival." Twelve years later, Captain Stone said Meli had been allowed to escape and resume his career elsewhere in the world.

Of Meli's colleagues, Salvatore Messino died of consumption in San Quentin. Bianchi took up operations in Los Angeles, and the Trapani brothers eventually returned to New Orleans. The Trapani group and some of their descendants became sort of the wandering Jews of the Mafia. They remained in New Orleans until 1910 when they were driven out for having once again sided with Sicilian fugitives against a resident American leadership. The capo took his followers to Los Angeles where they operated modestly for fifteen years. In June 1925 the capo was murdered in Los Angeles by the New Orleans Mafia for reasons unknown. Some of the Trapanis returned to Louisiana, where they prospered until the Kefauver hearings of 1950. The publicity sent them wandering again, through several Southern states, and they eventually settled in Florida.

The penetration of the Mafia into California and the wanderings of the Trapanis both reflected the fortunes of the international Mafia. The Mafias in New Orleans, New York, and Palermo were separate societies, but they cooperated closely. A member who was properly sponsored could be transferred from one city to another, from one family to another. Every purge in Sicily, therefore, had a reaction in the United States because it sent over new Mafiosi. American families had a choice of absorbing the new arrivals or fighting them, and it was almost always wiser to absorb. Thus the pressures of growth were constant, and new fields of enterprise had to be found to employ an expanding membership. Such interaction first appeared in New Orleans in 1869 and within ten years was found in New York. By the 1880s there existed a Palermo-New Orleans-New York axis that would dominate Mafia activity in the United States for the next thirty years.

NEW YORK, 1878-1918

Organized crime in New York began not with the Mafia but with Tammany Hall, a club founded in the eighteenth century that became dominant in New York politics about 1828. Coincident with the 1828 rise of Tammany came the first of the politically protected neighborhood gangs, the Forty Thieves, composed of American natives and English immigrants. They were soon rivaled in their neighborhood by the Kerryonians, made up of natives of County Kerry, Ireland. It was the Irish who made the significant innovation of acquiring political protection. Soon after 1832 they replaced the American-English gangs as the major criminal class, and a proliferation of Irish bands arose in the Bowery and Five Points neighborhoods. Their patron was Captain Isaiah Rynders, a former Mississippi River gambler and knife fighter who came to New York in the mid-

1830s, organized the Five Points gangs, and became Tammany's boss of the Sixth Ward. He endured as a significant power in Tammany for the next twenty-five years, and men like him—bosses of criminal gangs—were the foundation of Tammany's vote-gathering power. By 1855 there were at least thirty thousand men in the city who owed allegiance to gang leaders and through them to Tammany Hall.*

During this period the Italian criminal population was insignificant. The earliest report of the Italian professional criminal in New York comes about 1864–1865, when the Spanish-Italian Black Hand gang of Brooklyn became notorious. But after the Black Hand uproar the newspapers said nothing more about the Italian professional until 1872, when a small outbreak of murders caused *The New York Times* to editorialize on the subject, "Murder: Palermo and New York." The editorial observed that the same law of silence prevailed on either side of the Atlantic in connection with Italian murders. This spate of killings, along with the *Times*'s editorial, may indicate the arrival of the Mafia in New York. In 1873, however, the public discovered a practice which, by its very opposition to Mafia ethics, argues that the society had not yet entered New York in any significant strength. The crime was a form of kidnapping known as Italian slavery, a phenomenon which later served as a model for the famous children's story "Pinocchio." The victims of this slave trade were boys, usually between the ages of four and twelve. They were kidnapped from their homes in Italy and transported to America, where they worked for *padroni* in the city streets. One could see them any hour of the day or night, playing musical instruments and begging. Finally, in 1873, one such boy, twelve-year-old Joseph Rocco, escaped from his *padron* and came to the attention of the police. Joseph

---

*This represented an important voter nucleus in an era when only American male citizens could vote. Manhattan Island's total population in 1860 was 813,669, of which slightly more than half were foreign born. Of these the Irish numbered 203,740, and were mostly settled in the Five Points and Mulberry Bend districts. The next-largest foreign group was the Germans, numbering 119,974, massed on the Eastside. The Germans caused no crime problems and, to the contrary, organized patrols to assist the police.

was placed in jail and charges were filed against the padron, Joseph Macino, and Vincenzo Motto, who had kidnapped the child three years earlier from his father's home in Italy. Also tried were several other padroni who lived with their boys at Macino's house on Crosby Street. As the star witness, Joseph did a magnificent job of keeping to his story despite two days of vigorous and aggressive cross-examination by the defense. The defense lawyers accused him of lying. They accused him of being ungrateful to his "Uncle" Motto. They told him his father had sold him, a lie which nearly broke Joseph because he feared it might be true. (The next day, however, the prosecution produced a complaint of kidnapping filed in Italy by Joseph's father in 1870.) These defense tactics seemed even more appalling when it was revealed that the lawyers' fees were being paid by the earnings of Joseph and the other slaves. In spite of everything, the boy's nerve held. When asked to name all the padroni at Forty-five Crosby Street, he surprised everyone by going into the audience and laying his hand on the shoulder of a well-dressed spectator, who fled before he could be stopped by bailiffs. Other boys' testimony showed that Motto made regular trips to Naples to procure slaves for the Macino house. The prosecution rested its case, only to hear the court order the defendants freed, on the grounds that no one had testified against them except children.

Back on the street, the padroni promptly put in claims for their escaped slaves. Their claims would have been honored, but sympathetic policemen had already hidden the children away in foster homes and then conveniently forgotten where they were placed. Later that same year, a U.S. marshal estimated that there were still eight thousand boy slaves on New York streets. The practice wasn't defeated until 1878, when the immigrant community, backed by actions of Congress and the Italian Parliament (but without any aid from the New York City government) put the padroni out of business—men who, except for the actions of an occasional outraged Irish policeman, never had been molested by the New York structure of justice.

During the 1870s, Italian slavery flourished in many other cities besides New York. But it never took hold in Sicily, New

Orleans, or any other area of Mafia dominance, because the brotherhood would never allow such practices. One of the Mafia's strengths was its respect for blood-family bonds, and kidnapping children would only arouse its own people against the society. But the scandal did draw Americans' attention to the presence of the Mafia elsewhere, and in 1874 reports of brotherhood activity in Sicily and Naples began to appear in New York newspapers.

Mafia stories were back-page items, however. The front pages concentrated on New York's own forms of organized crime. In the centennial year of the republic, 1876, a New York state legislative committee reported that the police—especially the New York City detective force—were crooked, and charged that they "habitually protected gamblers, thieves and prostitutes from whom they received regular payments of large sums. The committee are of the opinion that while all kinds of crime have been winked at by the police force at sundry times, from the detective force [the criminals] have received constant and systematic support."

In the same year, William Marcy Tweed, the former boss of Tammany, was extradited from Spain. He and his subordinates, Mayor A. Oakley Hall and City Comptroller Richard Connolly, had stolen a minimum of $30 million by padding vouchers, and had made inestimable amounts of money by means of graft and kickbacks. Tweed was convicted and died in 1878. Into the power vacuum he left behind stepped Giuseppe Esposito, newly arrived from Sicily, and the New York Mafia began to organize.

There was no *True Delta* newspaper to catch the New York Mafia in the act of forming, but a report made by New York's chief of detectives, Thomas Byrnes, indicates that the society was in existence by 1881 and was probably organized by Esposito three years earlier than that. Byrnes was the first official to make public mention of a New York Mafia. He was also the indirect cause of a Mafia-Camorra gang war in New York which lasted twenty-eight years and involved, at minimum, fourteen hundred murders and twenty-three hundred bombings.

Byrnes, whose family immigrated from Ireland when he was a child, became a policeman in 1863. He had a distinguished career and was named head of the detective bureau after he solved a $3 million bank robbery in 1880. As chief of detectives, Byrnes fascinated some of the great journalists of the era, including Lincoln Steffens and Jacob Riis, who thought him "quite without moral purpose or the comprehension of it, yet with a streak of kindness in him that sometimes put preaching to shame.... Byrnes was for Byrnes ... but he made the detective service great."

He was a master at controlling street crime. From his headquarters at Three Hundred Mulberry Street he directed forty-two sergeants and fourteen patrolmen who were expected to know the "style of work of every professional thief in the country and when a robbery and the circumstances attending to it are reported [to] name the operator to whom it should be credited." Like many policemen, Byrnes felt his primary function was to protect the wealthy and powerful. To do so he developed a neatly defined system of treaties with the underworld. Local thieves agreed to practice their craft outside the more exclusive neighborhoods. Thieves from out of town could not practice in New York, for that would be poaching on the locals, but they were allowed to hide out in New York and spend money there. Anyone who broke the treaties promptly felt the weight of Byrnes's detectives smashing down on him: He would be arrested on sight, beaten with fists and clubs, then either imprisoned or banished from the city.

Byrnes's first official experience with the Mafia was a routine stabbing at Third Avenue and Eighth Street on the night of October 14, 1888. The principals were all Sicilians from Palermo, including the victim, Antonio Flaccomio; the killers, Carlo and Vincenzo Quarteraro; and three witnesses who had "seen nothing." It was not the sort of murder to attract a chief of detectives, but for some reason Byrnes investigated personally. Eight days later, after using harsh interrogation techniques, he announced he had "obtained statements from the suspects, who had broke and told all."

The murder, Byrnes told *The New York Times,* had been

"decreed by a secret society . . . by order of the Mafia." It was the first mention of the Sicilian society's existence in New York. Byrnes added that breaking up the Mafia might be difficult. "There are two principal headquarters in this country—one in this city and the other in New Orleans—so that members of the society who commit serious crimes in this city can find friends in the South, and vice versa."

It was a remarkably quick piece of detective work. Although the Mafia had been in the United States for nearly twenty years, it had been so clandestine that Byrnes seemed unaware of its presence until the murder investigation. Byrnes's ignorance is attested to by a book he published two years earlier, in 1886, *Professional Criminals of America*,* in which he mentioned not a single Mafioso or Camorrist and very few Italians.

Five months after the stabbing, on the eve of the Quarteraros' trial for murder, Byrnes issued a second statement to the *Times* and was joined in it by John Goff, the assistant district attorney who was prosecuting the case. They said the murder was the result of a "Mafia feud caused by the betrayal" seven years earlier of Giuseppe Esposito. The trial was attended by "delegates from the Mafia in this city, Brooklyn,† and New Jersey who were in court to watch every witness." When it ended in acquittal, Byrnes announced in disgust that the Italian criminals could "go ahead and kill each other." His implied condition was that police would not interfere as long as they confined the killing to their own people and didn't embarrass anyone uptown. With that green light, the New York Mafia-Camorra war ensued and in its first year, 1889, it accounted for forty-seven murders.

---

*Republished in 1969 by Chelsea House, with introductions by Arthur Schlesinger, Jr. and S. J. Perelman.
†Brooklyn was a separate city until 1898 when, with a population of one million, an enormously profitable waterfront, and great cultural and economic resources, it became a borough of New York City. It was annexed over the howling objections of Brooklyn's mayor who, it is reported, wept when he had to sign over Brooklyn's $15 million treasury surplus to the Manhattan administration, in whose hands it promptly vanished.

The gang murders accelerated in 1890–92, the body count going up each year. The most significant of these early deaths, some two hundred in number by the end of the fourth year, occurred on December 4, 1892, when Antonio Morello shot Francesco Meli. Morello, a Sicilian, was a nephew of Ignazio Saietta, then in Sicily and later to be the second-most-powerful Mafioso in Manhattan. His victim, Meli, was a Neapolitan member of the city's only Camorra family, which held sway in Brooklyn.

Within six months, police and the newspapers began to refer openly to the shootings as a Neapolitan-Sicilian conflict. "The Neapolitan rascal speaks contemptuously of the Sicilian cut-throat and vice versa," the *Times* noted in 1893. At that time the war was in full swing, with both sides recruiting reinforcements from Italy. On May 15, 1893, for instance, police removed nine identified Camorrists from a ship entering New York harbor. A few months later eight Mafiosi were similarly seized, coming in from Palermo via Marseilles. Despite the death toll, then, gang power was maintained by a constant influx of old-country shooters and old-country discipline.

In 1895, in the midst of the Mafia-Camorra war, Byrnes was forced to resign. Theodore Roosevelt, serving a two-year term as head of the police board, claimed he could not reduce police corruption unless Byrnes was removed. Lincoln Steffens reported that bankers and pickpockets alike were dismayed at the ouster. Each felt that the major force for order in the city had been removed.

In the same year there commenced a series of slayings called "barrel murders." A low-ranking patrolman named Joseph Petrosino was assigned to solve them. Petrosino was a Calabrian, born near Salerno in 1860. He came to New York in 1879, an immensely strong young man, five-feet six inches and two hundred pounds. His first four years in New York he worked on the docks, then in 1883 joined the police as a uniformed patrolman. He was one of those rare persons who are both intellectual and capable of effective physical action. His usual law enforcement technique was simply to corner the hoodlum and wham him half to death, thus avoiding the frustrations of trials, lawyers, and political interference. At the same time he was a man of cultivated sensibility who adored music. He read prolifically and, like Sherlock Holmes, was a scholar in those matters that might pertain to his work. He was also like Holmes in his approach to difficult crimes, which he'd attack by playing his violin at night until he had deduced a solution. And, like Holmes, he was a firm believer in undercover work and disguises, the maintenance of dossiers, newspaper clips, and intelligence reports.

Petrosino's abilities soon earned him a national reputation. As head of the police board, Theodore Roosevelt used him frequently on special projects, and the two became friends. Petrosino also was on speaking terms with President William McKinley. In the spring of 1901 the Secret Service asked Petrosino to investigate rumors of an anarchist plot to kill the President. Petrosino reported there was no organized conspiracy, but that there was much talk of assassination among anarchists and an individual attempt was likely unless security measures were improved. For the meantime Petrosino advised that McKinley be kept away from large crowds. Three months later, McKinley was fatally shot in Buffalo, New York, by Leon Czolgosz, an anarchist acting independently and shooting from a crowd.

Petrosino did not begin to specialize in Italian crime until 1895, when he was assigned to the "barrel murders." Killings of this type were taking place in several cities, and the modus operandi was always the same.

An Italian would be either shot or stabbed to death, packed in a barrel, and deposited in some obvious place, like a street corner, or shipped by railroad to a fictitious address in another city. Barrel murders had occurred occasionally in New York ever since the 1870s, but their regular appearance was coincident with the arrival in the United States of a pack of brothers, half-brothers, and brothers-in-law from Corleone, Sicily, who were known as the Morello family. It was perhaps the deadliest kinship group ever to enter the country.

The most notorious members of the clan were Antonio Morello, the eldest brother, credited with some thirty New

York murders in the 1890s; Joe Morello, another multi-murderer and later the boss of the New York Mafia; his brother Nicholas Morello, who eventually was killed by the Camorra; a half-brother, Ciro Terranova, a significant power in the Mafia and later the Cosa Nostra; and Ignazio Saietta ("Lupo the Wolf"), Ciro's brother-in-law, who owned the "Murder Stable," a property at 323 East 107th Street where the Secret Service would find remains of more than sixty murder victims. Saietta, who sneaked into the country in 1897 under the alias Ignatius Lupo, was so fearsome that Italians used to ask their priests for protection against Lupo the Wolf. The superstitious would cross themselves if they saw Lupo in the streets, and some would throw out extended fingers to ward off his evil magic.

In addition there was one more Morello brother, Vincent, and three Saietta brothers, all of whom were leaders in the New York-New Jersey Mafia and Cosa Nostra at some time or other during the period 1895–1940. This one extended family from the town of Corleone would provide a continuous link in New York's organized crime history. All the later Camorra, Mafia, and Cosa Nostra leaders, from Joe Masseria to Lucky Luciano and Vito Genovese, had to deal with the Morellos. Usually it was a simple choice of fighting them or joining them.

The family leader, Joe Morello, was born in 1863 in Corleone, a once-prosperous town which Mafia wars nearly denuded of male inhabitants.* In a parole application Morello stated, "I attended school until I was 12 years of age after which I worked on my father's farm. At 21, I was married and continued to work on the farm up to the time I emigrated to America in 1892" (when he was twenty-nine years old). Morello's statement omits, perhaps for the parole board's benefit, any mention of his reason for leaving Sicily. He had been charged on two counts of murder and one of counterfeiting.

The careers of Joe Morello and Joseph Petrosino came together as the result of a barrel murder discovered on the night

---

*Corleone, with a modern population of eighteen thousand, experienced 153 Mafia murders in the period 1944–1948 alone. Working-age males make up only 10 percent of the population.

of July 23, 1902. The victim had been sewn up in a sack, jammed into a barrel, and dumped in Brooklyn where Seventy-third Street meets the bay. This site, south of the Gowanus docks, was a popular swimming spot. The water was relatively clean and there was a nice bank of tall grass and reeds shaded by big trees. Two fourteen-year-old boys went there to swim, and, while hiding their clothes in the grass, found the barrel. They went to the police. The man inside the barrel was described by the *Times* as "unusually handsome, extremely well built and powerful looking." The throat had been slit from ear to ear and the neck trussed to the knees in such a fashion that movement would have strangled any life that might remain. In addition, the body had been beaten so savagely that all major bones had been broken. The gratuitous brutality was the trademark of a Mafia execution. Going far beyond what was necessary to kill, the excess was not generated by passion, but was intended as a horrifying warning to potential offenders. A second trademark was the neck-to-knees trussing, a form used to identify the death as a Mafia-sanctioned execution.

The man in the barrel was identified as Joe Catania, forty, "a Brooklyn grocer."* Catania was a Mafia capo in charge of the southern Brooklyn docks area, which was being used by the Morello family for a new smuggling operation. The contraband was counterfeit U. S. bank notes, which, by arrangement with Don Vito Cascio Ferro, were printed in Palermo and entered the United States across Catania's docks concealed in olive oil shipments. The Morellos then passed the bills to Mafia organizations in Buffalo, Pittsburgh, New Orleans, and Chicago for distribution. The bogus, mostly two-dollar, bills were entering the country by the tens of thousands every shipment. Coincident with this new responsibility, Catania, always a quick man with the bottle, settled into systematic drunkenness. His remarks in saloons became increasingly indiscreet. A trial was held and his execution was ordered.

Petrosino spent a month working neighborhoods in Brook-

---

*Father of Joe ("the Baker") Catania, a Masseria lieutenant murdered by Joe Valachi and "Buster from Chicago" in 1931.

lyn and Manhattan but was unable to produce any witnesses willing to testify on the killing or on Catania's associates. At that time he was unaware of the details of the counterfeiting scheme, although he had learned that Catania, in his drunken ramblings, had been preoccupied with the Secret Service. He informed that agency and the Morello-Lupo gang was placed under long-term surveillance.

The break came eight months later, on April 14, 1903, at five-thirty in the morning when a scrub woman on her way home from work inspected a barrel standing on the sidewalk at Eleventh Street near Avenue D. Inside, packed in sawdust, was the body of Benedetto Madonia. His throat had been cut, his bones broken, and he was trussed neck to knees. Thanks to the surveillance, Madonia was known to be an associate of Morello. Petrosino promptly obtained a warrant to raid a café owned by Morello at Two Twenty Elizabeth Street. There he and the Secret Service found nine men, all armed with revolvers and daggers. These men, including Morello, Lupo, and a man named Genova, were arrested.* On the premises Petrosino also found bogus notes, and barrels and sawdust that matched the murder barrel and its contents. The Secret Service was puzzled not to find any counterfeit plates. It would be another six years before they learned that the currency was actually printed in Sicily. Also discovered was a cache of letters, memoranda, and bookkeeping entries, all justifying the Secret Service's conclusion: "Morello is the head of the Palermo society of the Mafia in this country and directs the affairs of the various branches in many cities. . . . These cities include New Orleans, Buffalo, Chicago and Pittsburgh. . . . Lupo is believed to be the treasurer of the Palermo society of the Mafia. . . . In Italy there is a general society and in each province a branch. When residents of a certain province come to America they preserve their affiliation with the branch organization." To this statement Petrosino added the charge that the New York Mafia was engaged in the principal crimes of levying tribute on the Italian community

---

*The others were Tomasso Petto, Joseph Fenaro, Lorenzo Lobiodo, Vito Lobiodo, Dominico Pecoraro, and Pietro Inzarillo.

and of counterfeiting. Murders, he said, were committed "to create an image of terror and enforce discipline."

At the Madonia inquest, Petrosino handed over the following letter as evidence of the close cooperation between the New York, New Orleans, and Palermo organizations. Dated March 4, 1902, postmarked New Orleans, and addressed to Morello, it read:

> You are a man born without influence from anybody. Do not take it in bad part if I tell you, as I am older than you, that you have to be afraid of false friends who are the ruin of good ones. Do me the favor to remember me as I remember you. In the house of Lupo there is a young man just come from Italy by name Francesco Paolo Marchese, condemned from the tribunal of Palermo to thirty years in prison. This for your intelligence, he has been sent by persons in New Orleans to Lupo. I can tell you he is a good young man, and for his small age is in need of help, and salute him for my part. With every regard I kiss you and believe me am your friend ready to your orders. [signed] F. Genova

It was a remarkable communication, written with perfect Mafia courtesy. Paolo Marchese, the fugitive mentioned in the letter, had originally fled from Palermo to New Orleans. There he went to work for Genova, who was himself wanted for murder in Sicily. One of Genova's projects was a defunct macaroni factory in the nearby Louisiana town of Donaldsonville. His men put it back into operation, then made the rounds of Italian grocers, informing them that the Donaldsonville factory was to be their source of macaroni. The only complication was that the grocers already had a supplier, a law-abiding family named Luciano. When the Lucianos objected to the Mafia takeover, Marchese replied by killing the elder Luciano, then fled to New York to take sanctuary with Lupo. His arrival in New York was the occasion for Genova's letter of sponsorship to Morello. To Petrosino the letter was conclusive proof of the Palermo-New Orleans-New York axis.

The Madonia killing led to the creation of the New York police's Italian Squad. Petrosino was put in charge and from then on he devoted his energies exclusively to the Mafia and the

Camorra. He swept through them like a scythe. In 1905 he arrested and deported, on a murder charge, a New Jersey boss named Tony Strolle. On April 17, 1907, he interrupted all plans of the Camorra. On that date he entered a Harlem apartment house, walked upstairs, and stood outside a certain door. Behind it he heard muffled sounds. Petrosino reared back and kicked in the door with such force that it came off its hinges and flattened three men, all armed. He then collared the Camorra boss of bosses, Enrico Alfano, and dragged him down the stairs and along the sidewalks to jail, refusing to let him stand up. Alfano, the international Grand Master of the society, was returned to Italy where he was the star defendant in the Viterbo trial of 1911.

Petrosino's successes were so scary that up-and-coming gangsters like Johnny Torrio abandoned their rackets in New York and looked elsewhere for work. In Torrio's case it was Chicago.

In 1908 Petrosino outdid himself. The first to fall was Enrico Costabili, identified by *McClure's* magazine as "leader of the Camorra in New York [who] held undisputed sway of the territory south of Hudson Street as far as Canal Street and from Broadway to the East River." Costabili was given three years in prison and then deported. In the same year, another Camorra leader, Giovanni Campanillo, was shot by Petrosino and deported. Petrosino piled humiliation upon humiliation. On January 27, 1908, the steamship *San Giovanni* arrived in New York openly carrying the second-most-prestigious Mafioso in the world, Raffaele Palizzolo. Palizzolo, an ex-member of the Italian Parliament, was the predecessor of Don Vito Cascio Ferro as leader of the Sicilian Mafia confederation. He had resigned from both positions following his conviction and sentence of exile, in the murder of a Palermo banker. He had immense prestige among Mafiosi and among New York Sicilians in general. His boat was met by hundreds of cheering supporters, and for the next month his schedule was filled with a series of banquets and street parades. At that point, Petrosino stepped forward and began deportation proceedings. Palizzolo chose to leave America voluntarily.

Other Mafia notables he deported that year were Paolo

Navarra, brother of Dr. Michele Navarra, who later became Mafia boss of Corleone; and Genco Russo, a young man who became the Sicilian boss of bosses in the late 1950s.*

In 1908 Petrosino also brought about the conviction of Vincenzo Cantone and two brothers named Pelletieri on charges of committing twenty murders, and the deportation of sixty other Camorrists and Mafiosi. Petrosino's one-man campaign in 1907 and 1908 is one of the principal reasons why the Camorra was never truly powerful in America. Its leaders were systematically knocked over by the New York detective. His success with the Mafia, though considerable, was never as complete, probably because his Calabrian background gave him a common ground with Neapolitan informers that he lacked with Sicilians.

Petrosino's performance in 1908 was stunning. His one-man record surpassed the accomplishments of any Italian army, parliament, U.S. law enforcement officer, or Senate subcommittee, before or since. But his success was also his downfall, for in that same year the leader of all the Sicilian Mafias, Don Vito Cascio Ferro, secretly entered New York.

Don Vito did his business and departed without being detected by Petrosino. His visit to America is mentioned briefly by a few Sicilian writers, but they do not give details and the purpose of the visit must be deduced. Very likely it had to do with Petrosino's accomplishments. Sicilian writers have always maintained that Don Vito had a direct interest in the United States and exported Mafiosi to establish a foothold for him. Petrosino held a somewhat similar view, believing that the influx was a deliberate Mafia plot masterminded in Palermo with the cooperation of Morello and Lupo in New York. Petrosino never

---

*Other deportees whose family names will show up in an account of later Cosa Nostra activities are Ludovico Liuzzo, Filippo Melodia, Salvatore Messina, Francesco Russo, Salvatore Schifanni, Girolamo Asauro, Giuseppe Bonura, Pasquale Carbone, Carlo Cioppa, Giuseppe Conoscenti, Francesco Consoli, Gustave Di Martino, Giuseppe De Primo, Paolo Genovese, and Filippo Giannone, all of whom were named in later years as important Mafia or Cosa Nostra figures, according to investigators of the Italian Parliament and the U.S. Senate.

named the man at the top of the scheme, and it is possible he didn't know of Don Vito's existence.

Following Don Vito's visit, Saietta spread word that he, Lupo the Wolf, would kill Petrosino. News of this threat reached the detective in October 1908. He walked into Lupo's warehouse at Two Ten Mott Street, closed the office door, knocked Lupo down, and stomped him. The following week, Lupo abruptly left the city and went to Palermo.

The week Lupo departed for Sicily, reform police commissioner Theodore Bingham received a report on how the Italian criminal societies might be eradicated. The report had been commissioned by Bingham and written by an Italian professor of law whose name has never been disclosed. He recommended that an agent of the police be sent to Rome, Naples, and Palermo to gather the photographs and police records of all fugitives. The dossiers would then be used to identify those criminals that were in New York and provide cause for immediate deportation. It was further recommended that the attack could be made nationwide by circulating the dossiers to other American cities.

In the first week of February 1909, Bingham called in Petrosino, handed him a copy of the report, and asked if he would undertake the mission to Italy. Petrosino agreed to gather the dossiers and was also empowered to set up a permanent liaison with his counterparts in Italy "so that the Camorra and Mafia may be watched on both sides of the ocean." His first stop was Rome, where he was welcomed by the head of the Italian police. Petrosino spent a week in Rome and gathered a suitcase full of documents. As he left, he was warned by U.S. Ambassador Lloyd Griscom to be cautious in Sicily for there "are perhaps a thousand criminals who know you there."

The remark was an understatement. Throughout Italy, Petrosino's name and face were known by perhaps hundreds of thousands of people. During the previous five years, his exploits in New York had become the subject of an Italian dime-novel boom. Forty-four different adventures of *Giuseppe Petrosino II Sherlock Holmes d'Italia* had been published there in paperback book form. In rare instances these unauthorized books described his true adventures, but more often the stories were highly romantic fictions.

In Rome, Petrosino wrote his wife* that he had visited St. Peter's, the Sistine Chapel, and the "Michelangelo galleries which are the wonders of the universe . . . above the human imagination." He complained that "Rome is as expensive as New York" and that he was already lonesome and anxious to be home. He went next to Naples, where he was again received with warmth and cooperation by the authorities. But his letters home began to worry his wife. He was being "followed everywhere." On the boat to Palermo he saw that one of his fellow passengers was a Mafioso he deported in 1908.

He arrived in Palermo on February 28, 1909, and checked into the Hotel de France under the name Guglielmo De Simone. He then notified the prefect of police of his presence and embarked on a rather curious and as yet unexplained tour of towns—Trapani, Noto, Caltannisetta, Partinico, Monreale, Bisacquino—all in the Mafia-infested districts of Trapani and Palermo. He could not have expected much cooperation from citizens or police in those communities. Perhaps he wished to see firsthand the roots of the society. It was not a reassuring trip. In Noto he sent a telegram, not a letter, to his wife: "It is very uncomfortable to be here alone."

The last town he inspected was Bisacquino, the birthplace and residence of Don Vito Cascio Ferro. He returned to the Sicilian capital on March 12 in time for a meeting scheduled for the next day with the chief of police. That night, Petrosino, unarmed, went for a walk before dinner in the Piazza Marina. Located in the heart of Palermo, this lively square was usually crowded, and patrolled by at least six policemen. On the night of March 12, however, the crowds had disappeared and there were no policemen in sight. A few blocks from Petrosino's hotel, Don Vito Cascio Ferro had already sat down to dinner in the house of a deputy to the Italian Parliament. Midway through the cheese he excused himself and, borrowing his host's carriage, drove to the Piazza Marina. There he waited.

---

*Adelina Saulina. They were married in 1907 and resided at Two Thirty-three Lafayette Street, Manhattan.

Petrosino walked into the plaza. Two men stepped from behind a tree and fired three times, wounding him in the back and head. Blood streaming from his face, Petrosino turned and grabbed the iron grating of a window to hold himself up. A third man stepped out and fired a pistol into his face. The third man was Don Vito Cascio Ferro, administering the coup de grace. Petrosino fell dead on the spot. Don Vito returned to the deputy's villa for his pousse-café. The deputy would later testify that his "guest had never left the house."

The prefect of police and his chief let twelve hours elapse before informing the U.S. consul in Palermo of Petrosino's death. The consul, conducting his own inquiry, later reported that the assassination had been "carried out in Palermo with military-like obedience by the Mafia. . . . There was a connivance with the police in this killing. . . . There is no doubt the public officers in Sicily are in league with the Mafia."

Subsequent research has turned up more details. In the two weeks of Petrosino's Sicilian stay, Palermo entertained what amounted to a brotherhood convention. Campanillo, a deported American Camorrist, was there, as were two deported New York Mafiosi, Francesco Palizzoti and Carlo Constantino. Lupo the Wolf, by his own statement, was there. And also on the scene were three New Orleans gunmen, who may have helped in the actual shooting. These three left New Orleans one day after Petrosino had departed New York and journeyed directly to Palermo. After the shooting they returned to New Orleans. Italian police reports, post-mortem, showed that Petrosino had been followed every hour of his journey. Known Mafiosi had been on his boat from New York. In Rome he was under constant surveillance. In Naples he himself grew alarmed and at one point grabbed a stranger in his hotel lobby. The man denied involvement in anything sinister and ran away. On the boat to Palermo, Petrosino spotted several Mafiosi, and even spoke to Palizzoti. He was also followed during his tour of small Sicilian towns.

No one was ever prosecuted for the Petrosino killing. A month after the murder, four men were arrested but were later released. The four were identified by Palermo police as "Palizzoti of New York and Palermo; Carlo Constantino of Bisacquino; Vito Cascioferro of Bisacquino; and Antonio Pascanante of Partinico." No amplification on these men or their past was given. Constantino was a new arrival in Sicily, for he had been deported from New York only a few months earlier. Antonio Pascanante was not a resident of Partinico but of New Orleans. He was one of the three gunners who left that city right after Petrosino sailed and returned immediately after the shooting.

But although they escaped prosecution, the leaders of the Sicilian Mafia, the Camorra, and the New York Mafia each claimed credit for the murder. It was the only specific crime ever admitted by Don Vito Cascio Ferro, who said, "My action was a disinterested one and in response to a challenge I could not afford to ignore." In Naples the Camorrist chief Enrico Alfano said he had "arranged" the Petrosino shooting. And in New York, Mafia boss Joe Morello said he was responsible. So did his underboss, Ignazio Saietta, "Lupo the Wolf," who claimed the shooting as the reason for his trip to Palermo. The conspiracy may have been even larger. In the three days after Petrosino's death, assassinations of Italian police specialists were also attempted, in some cases successfully, in New Orleans, Chicago, and Kansas City.

All in all, the Petrosino murder was a victory for the brotherhood societies. Their first triumph concerned the dossiers Petrosino collected, which compromised one thousand fugitives, seven hundred of them in New York. A third of these photographs, police records, and warrants were in a suitcase in his hotel room when he was murdered. Within minutes of his death these papers were impounded by the Palermo police chief, the same man who, it turned out, had personally withdrawn all patrolmen from the piazza. He then kept the records for several weeks, despite the American government's insistence that they were the victim's private property. The chief, ignoring Petrosino's credentials from Rome, took the position that in Italy the detective was a private citizen without any official standing and his possession of the records was therefore improper. In April 1909, however, he eventually surrendered three hundred dossiers, which were sent to New York. The balance of the dossiers was being compiled by police authorities in Rome at the time of Petrosino's murder. They were subsequently couriered to New York by detectives in Petrosino's Italian Squad.

Round two of the dossier battle began in New York, where Commissioner Bingham wanted to use the material immediately to deport the three hundred Italian criminals. At that point, Tammany Hall came into the picture, pointedly suggesting that Bingham drop the deportation matter since the alleged fugitives were now reformed citizens. When Bingham persisted, Tammany leaned on Mayor George McClellan, who promptly caved in and fired Bingham. There were some subsidiary reasons why Bingham became a target of Tammany, but his crucial offense was insistence on the deportations.

In those same months after Petrosino's death, the societies humiliated the detective's widow. Through their Tammany allies, the societies managed to deprive her of full police pension rights. As compensation, the New York police force organized a benefit concert. Italian hoodlums, however, intimidated would-be ticket buyers, and when the concert did begin before a meager audience they broke it up. The widow remained in impoverished circumstances, not even owning her home.

The concert incident aroused the police to an all-out effort, in which the federal Secret Service joined against the only available Mafia target, the Morello family. In 1910 Morello, Lupo, and nine other members were convicted on charges of passing more than $170,000 in fake currency. Both were sentenced to the federal prison in Atlanta, Georgia; Morello for twenty-five years, Lupo for thirty. The judge himself later admitted that the sentences were based not on the counterfeiting charge, of which they were indeed guilty, but on their roles as Mafia leaders and their connection with the Petrosino murder. He was further influenced, the judge said, by the fact that the defense fund had been buttressed by some $30,000 obtained through "Mafia extortions throughout the country as far south as New Orleans and including $3,000 extorted from Enrico Caruso."* Ironically, Caruso had been a close friend of Petrosino.

---

*Although the Caruso money was used to help pay defense fees, Salvatore Mistretto was later convicted of the extortion. The information above and the judge's quote are found in Morello's parole application.

Morello and Lupo stayed in prison until 1920, when their sentences were commuted and they were paroled on the recommendation of several U.S. congressmen, the U.S. attorney general, and those acting on behalf of the mentally disabled President Woodrow Wilson. During their imprisonment the New York Mafia had been dominated by two other Morello brothers, Nicholas and Vincent, who were assisted by their half-brother, Ciro Terranova. Then, in 1916, Nicholas Morello—who was Lupo's nephew as well as Joe Morello's brother—was killed en route to a meeting with Pellagrino Morano, chief of the New York Camorra. Operating out of the Santa Lucia Restaurant on Coney Island, Morano had always controlled large chunks of Brooklyn. But after Joe Morello and Lupo went to prison, he began steadily moving in on portions of Harlem. When the shooting began to get heavier than usual, Nick Morello asked for a meeting to negotiate a truce. Morano agreed, but Nick Morello no sooner climbed out of his car at the meeting place in Brooklyn than he and one of his bodyguards were shot and killed.

With stunning swiftness there followed the arrest of Morano; one of his most important captains, Alessandro Vollero; and one of the gunmen, Antonio Natara. Wanted circulars were put out on a second gunman, Ralph Daniello. The arrests were based on information given to the police by the crippled Morello family.

The missing gunman, Daniello, fled to Reno, Nevada, where, short of funds, he wrote his New York superior for money. It was refused. He wrote again, asking a pension for his wife and children, which was his right under Camorra law. It too was refused. Daniello surrendered in Reno and agreed to become an informer. He was brought back to New York, where an excited assistant district attorney announced the results of the prisoner's cooperation. "The arrest of Daniello and his statement to the district attorney clears up 23 murders. He is a member of a gang which established a reign of terror in Brooklyn and which through affiliations with gangs in New York and Philadelphia was even able to reach out and strike its enemies far off." The prosecutor termed the confession "one of the most remarkable in police history; unequaled on conditions in the underworld. . . . According to Daniello, the Neapolitans together with a gang in Manhattan known as the Sicilians had combined for the purpose of controlling certain forms of gambling in the two boroughs. Those who objected, the Independents, were murdered."

This statement was the first official recognition of Italian control of New York crime. In spite of its importance, it received little attention in the newspapers, and the trial that followed received even less. The key witnesses for the state were the two gunmen, Daniello and young Natara, who had also turned informer. Natara said that in 1916 he had been rather suddenly called down from Springfield for the purpose of being made a Camorrist in the family of Morano under the sponsorship of Tony Paretti. Natara told in detail how he had taken the oath, on Easter Day, at an assembly presided over by the Camorra boss.*

The hasty induction of Natara proved a major mistake for the Camorra. As a small-time hoodlum, American born, whose Neapolitan parents had no criminal connections, Natara was a bad risk. He was a half-hearted criminal without any experience in gang discipline or Camorra tradition. His testimony showed that in his short Camorrist career he had to be bullied or cajoled into every one of the thirteen executions he carried out. He was a reluctant recruit, and had the Camorra not been depleted by the twenty-eight-year gang war, he would never have been made a member.

Daniello was another matter. He was tough and unrepentant and only agreed to inform because his boss had denied him his rights. He and Natara between them revealed enough about the murder conspiracy to send Morano and his underbosses to the electric chair. Daniello revealed too much. He said that a New York detective, Michael Mealli, had been paid off after the shootings. As Daniello prepared to go into the whole system of

---

*The same blood-gun-and-knife ceremony described in the second chapter, "Mazzini."

Camorra-police payoffs, the gavel banged down. Enough. The judge leaned over from the bench, excused the witness, and called a recess. When court resumed two days later, the judge declared a mistrial. He also claimed to have come down with a case of "la grippe," and said he was too sick to continue on the case. Simultaneously, the police department issued a press release announcing that "Detective Mealli [had] been reduced in rank and assigned to patrol duty."

There would be no further disclosures of the ties among the Italian gangs, the politicians, and the police. The new trial held in May 1918 was far more circumspect. Testimony was restricted to the murders and excluded peripheral matters like the bribes. Morano and his underbosses were found guilty and sentenced to life imprisonment, which Morano told the press represented a victory since he could have gotten the electric chair. Daniello and Natara were allowed to plead guilty and received terms of six years. Their cooperation had shortened their sentences, but eventually both paid the price. After his release from prison, Natara vanished and was probably killed. Daniello was found shot dead in 1925.

After the trial, the Camorra-Mafia war ended. Following the events of 1918, the Camorra vanished and was heard from no more, although individual Neapolitan criminals did appear afterward. Johnny Torrio and Al Capone were both Neapolitan, but neither was a Camorrist. They were free-lancers who (Torrio in particular) made alliances with the Mafia. Vito Genovese was also born in Naples. As a young man, he visited some of the Camorrists convicted of the Morello killing, during their prison terms. He might have preferred to have been a Camorrist, but there was no Camorra. Instead, he aligned himself with the Sicilians during Prohibition and rose up in their ranks. Eventually he would be an important member of a new organization, a melting-pot society that combined features of the Mafia, Stoppaglieri, and Camorra. The new society was Cosa Nostra.

BOOK FOUR
COSA NOSTRA

COSA NOSTRA: RIVALRY AND CONSOLIDATION

Petrosino only temporarily blocked the ascendancy of the Italians in New York's underworld. Two years after his murder, *The New York Times* published statistics showing that the number of Mafia crimes in the city had doubled. By the end of 1912, the rate of crimes attributed to Italians had risen even further, and the first seven months of 1913 broke all previous records. By 1917 Italians dominated illegal activities in New York. They controlled gambling, narcotics, and much of the political patronage throughout Harlem and Brooklyn. They claimed portions of Manhattan's Eastside, where they competed with older organizations of Jewish criminals, and were totally shut out only on the Westside, the last vestige of the old Irish-American hegemony. The Italians seemed to have totally altered the crime setup in New York. Then came passage of the Volstead

Act, in January 1920, and the picture changed almost overnight. Prohibition had caught the Italians unprepared. The specialties they had built up over the years—gambling, burglary, protection rackets and the new narcotics market—were suddenly penny ante compared with the millions being raked in by the bootleggers, who were relative newcomers to organized crime.

Typical of these arriviste criminals was William Vincent Dwyer, known throughout the twenties as "king of the bootleggers." In 1920 Dwyer was a dock worker. When Prohibition was voted in, he saw his chance and talked a saloon keeper into financing him to a fleet of boats. He then established himself with the police and the Coast Guard by means of a well-thought-out system of bribery, and earned their trust by keeping his mouth shut about the payoffs whenever he did happen to be arrested. Within five years Dwyer was a multimillionaire whose assets included race tracks in Montreal, Cincinnati, and Miami. His rapid rise to success was not unique; it was paralleled by the career of Owney Madden, an English-born holdup man who quickly adjusted to the new market for alcohol, and several others.

Prohibition proved to be a greater stumbling block than Petrosino had ever been. Bootleggers like Dwyer and Madden used their enormous profits as capital and neutralized the Italians' influence by outbidding them for the favors of police and politicians. By the time the Italian mob recognized what was happening it was too late. More than ten years would pass before they would regain dominance in the New York underworld.

The man who led the eventual Italian resurgence was Joe Masseria, a stocky, five-foot-two gunman who, charged with murder in Sicily, fled to the United States in 1903. Four years later, when arrested in New York for burglary and extortion, he was identified as a member of the Morello gang. At that time, however, Morello and Lupo the Wolf were in prison and the leadership of the Morello gang was split. Vincent and Nick Morello ruled in Harlem, and their half-brother Ciro Terranova had been given the Bronx. Downtown had been more or less

COSA NOSTRA: RIVALRY AND CONSOLIDATION   ○ 131

surrendered to the Jewish gangs, and Brooklyn was mostly in the hands of the Neapolitans, although a Mafia group, whose leader is unknown, held certain territories there. At the time of his arrest Masseria was one of Terranova's men.

In 1913, however, Masseria split with the Morellos and announced it dramatically by gunning down their cousin, Charles Lamonti, on the doorstep of the gang's headquarters at One Hundred Sixteenth Street. Six months later he killed Lamonti's brother on the same spot. He was temporarily removed from action in 1914 when he was sent to Sing Sing for four years on a burglary conviction. Upon his release he resumed his private war and got a lucky break from the Mafia-Camorra rivalry of that year. The Camorrists in Brooklyn put Nick Morello out of the way, and were then removed from competition themselves when they went to jail for the murder. By 1920 Masseria was the most powerful Italian boss in the city.

Nineteen twenty was also the year that Joe Morello and Lupo the Wolf were released from the federal prison at Atlanta. They returned to New York to find Masseria bossing the Italians, and the bootleggers making millions. The new situation so disheartened Lupo that he disengaged himself from big-time competition. In return, Masseria gave him a form of Mafia pension—the exclusive franchise to levy protection on Italian bakers. It was a small monopoly but one which guaranteed an income. Joe Morello, however, made war against Masseria. He adopted a new first name, Peter,* and became known as Peter "The Clutching Hand" Morello. The nickname, marvelous for its sinister image of greed, was in fact only a reference to Morello's left hand, maimed at birth.

Masseria and Morello began by picking off each other's men. But in 1922 Masseria, known in the New York press at that time as "Joe the Boss," went after the Morello leadership. On May 7, Joe's brother Vincent was ambushed and killed by Mass-

---

*Why Morello changed his name to Peter is unknown. But it had the effect of confusing all subsequent chroniclers of New York underworld history. Peter Morello, who would become Cosa Nostra's first boss of bosses, has never before been identified as Joe Morello, who bossed the Mafia from 1895 to 1910. Federal Bureau of Prisons records, however, establish that they were the same man.

eria gunners shooting from cars. Morello's death was followed by a flurry of shootings over the next few days. Public outrage was finally aroused when six innocent civilians were wounded during a sixty-bullet fusillade that took place on Grand Street, just one block from police precinct headquarters.

Masseria, identified by police as "an auto dealer residing at 80 Second Avenue," was arrested at the scene and held without bail. An alarmed city administration convened a highly publicized "crime conference" of prosecutors, judges, and police officials. During the conference's hearings it was learned that Masseria had a permit to carry a gun, signed by Justice Seleh Strong of the Supreme Court of Suffolk County.* The crime conference was also informed that at least three hundred more New York gangsters were carrying pistols on permits issued by judges in Suffolk and Nassau counties. Written into these permits, and Masseria's, was a special clause that allowed the bearer to carry a gun anywhere in the state. Despite such revelations, the highly publicized crime conference ended in three days with nothing done. Masseria was released.

On August 9 Masseria was ambushed by Rocco Valenti, Pete Morello's ace shooter. Masseria survived, however, under circumstances that made him a legend. He was walking on Second Avenue with two bodyguards when Valenti stepped out of a doorway and emptied his revolver into the two gunmen. The bodyguards fell to the pavement, leaving Masseria—whose pistol permit had been revoked because of his arrest—completely unprotected. Valenti coolly began to reload. While he did so, Masseria ran into a millinery shop at Eighty-two Second Avenue. Valenti followed. The proprietor, Fritz Heiney, watched the men. "The man with the revolver came close to the other fellow and aimed. Just as he fired, the little fellow [Masseria] jumped to one side. The bullet smashed the window of my store. Then the man fired the gun again. Again the other man ducked his head forward. The third shot made a second hole in my window."

---

*Justice Strong survived the scandal and continued his public service. In 1931 he ruled that slot machines were not gambling devices.

COSA NOSTRA: RIVALRY AND CONSOLIDATION   ○   133

Valenti, a man who had committed at least twenty murders, was recognized as the coolest, most accurate shooter in gangland. He had emptied a revolver at Masseria in a closed room and not hit him once. For the rest of his life, Joe Masseria was known as "the man who can dodge bullets."

Demoralized by Masseria's amazing escape, Morello sued for peace. Terms were to be arranged at a sitdown meeting in a restaurant on Twelfth Street near Second Avenue. Instead of attending themselves, both bosses sent three delegates. Morello also sent Valenti to supervise. The seven men met outside the restaurant. "Valenti and his companions seemed friendly. Suddenly, however, Valenti seemed to take fright and began to run. With weapons out, [the] three [Masseria] men pursued him and the firing began." In front of hundreds of spectators, Valenti wheeled and fired back. He then tried to make his escape by jumping onto the running board of a passing taxi, but was brought down with a bullet through his body.

In the confusion two of the spectators, an eight-year-old girl and a street cleaner, were accidentally wounded by the nervous assassins. But one gunman was cooler than the rest. He planted himself in the street and fired shot after shot at the fleeing Masseria men, taking careful aim and squeezing off shots until his revolver was empty. He wounded two men and killed Valenti. The gunman was a young hoodlum named Salvatore Lucania, later known as Lucky Luciano.

With Valenti dead, Morello sought peace. Masseria dictated the terms: Morello, forty-nine years old, would go into retirement. Morello's half-brother, Ciro Terranova, could retain control of family interests in Harlem and the Bronx, but would be subject to the orders of Masseria.

The war was over and Masseria relaxed. He opened a penthouse overlooking Central Park at Fifteen West Eighty-first Street where he entertained his gang at opium-smoking parties. During this relatively quiet period of the mid-1920s, the New York Italian criminals organized themselves into six principal Mafia groups, or families, with Masseria at the top. Beneath him, the bosses were Terranova in Harlem; a man named Frank Uale (he changed it to Yale) in Brooklyn; Masseria's own family on the Eastside of Manhattan from Harlem south; and three bosses who received no publicity in that era—Gaetano Reina of Brooklyn, and Alfred Mineo and Stefano Ferrigno, whose territories are unknown.

One of Masseria's principal assistants was Salvatore Lucania, Lucky Luciano. His position is rather hard to pinpoint, but he seems to have been a consigliere, which was an unusual but not unheard of position for a young man. His rise in the Masseria family was coincident with the 1922 war and the death of Valenti. Until that shooting Luciano had been a small-time dope pusher. In *The Luciano Story*, by Feder and Joesten, one woman who hung around with twenties mobsters recalled that in 1921 Luciano was at the bottom of the ladder. "And he looked it," she said. When she saw him two years later, at a party in Masseria's penthouse, he was top assistant to the boss. "I could hardly tell it was the same fellow. He was going up fast, the closest man to Masseria. The first time, I didn't give him a tumble. The next time I was more friendly."

Lucky Luciano was born in 1897 in Lercarda Friddi, a sulphur-mining town in the province of Palermo.* His parents brought him to America in 1907, when he was nine. At age eighteen he was convicted of peddling heroin and morphine and was committed to a reformatory for six months. Upon his release he resumed narcotics peddling and, around the start of Prohibition, worked for a while as a pusher for Legs Diamond. Luciano's acquaintance was never limited to Italian gangsters. His closest friend, from his late teens until his death, was the Jewish gunman Meyer Lansky. Through Lansky, Luciano met and became friendly with other Jewish gunmen from the Eastside, among them Lansky's partner, Buggsy Siegel. Others in this entourage of young, ambitious Jewish gangsters were Dutch Schultz, Lepke Buchalter, and Jacob ("Gurrah") Shapiro.

Luciano joined Masseria's operation no earlier than January 1921, when he was twenty-four years old. Part of his value was his friendship with the Jewish gangsters. Another asset was the diplomatic ability he demonstrated. After he put Luciano

---

*The same small town where Leone and Esposito kidnapped the Englishman John Forester Rose in 1876.

COSA NOSTRA: RIVALRY AND CONSOLIDATION   ○   135

on the payroll, Masseria's troubles with non-Italian gangs ended.

The year 1922 should have marked the beginning of peace and prosperity for Masseria. He had commenced his shooting war, in which he often found himself one man against many, in 1913. It had finally ended. But 1922 was also the year in which Mussolini took over the government of Italy and began his purge of the Sicilian Mafia. Those events would directly affect the United States, New York City, and the life of Joe Masseria.

When the Mafia leaders of Sicily replied to Mussolini's invasion of their territory by assassinating his Fascist appointees, they selected their best young men to do the killings. No mistakes could be risked. As a consequence, those gunmen who were forced to flee the island after the killings were the youngest and brightest of the Sicilian Mafiosi. They were polite, intelligent, adventurous, energetic, and disciplined. Collectively, they constituted the Twenties Group.

The first to arrive was Carlo Gambino. He passed through New York immigration on December 23, 1921. Within the next five years he was followed by Joe Bonanno, Stefano Maggadino, and Antonio Maggadino (1924); Joe Profaci, Joe Magliocco, and Mike Coppola (1926); and Salvatore Maranzano (1927). All eight men would become bosses or underbosses of Cosa Nostra families. The last arrival, Maranzano, would create Cosa Nostra.

When the Mafiosi first arrived, they took shelter in an existing organization called Unione Siciliana, which found them housing, jobs when they wanted them, and identities to cover up their illegal entries. Originally the Unione was a legitimate fraternal organization, founded in Chicago in 1895. In the early 1900s it actively fought Italian criminal organizations and Black Hand terrorism. With the advent of Prohibition, however, Mafia members (such as the Genna family in Chicago and the Brooklyn boss Frankie Yale) took over the Unione. They organized thousands of Unione members into making alcohol in tenement distilleries. Thereafter the Unione became so closely identified with the Italian crime organization that it was believed to be the organization itself.

The Unione provided a convenient hiding place for the

refugees while they adjusted themselves to America. Then the Twenties Group moved out into power positions, and they did it with amazing quickness. Gambino, Bonanno, Profaci, and Magliocco suddenly surfaced in high-ranking positions with families in New York City. Maggadino turned up as an underboss in the Buffalo family. Mike Coppola did the same in Detroit.

In 1927 Salvatore Maranzano arrived in the United States. He came not as a fugitive but as a direct representative of Don Vito Cascio Ferro. The Sicilian boss of bosses had sent him to organize the American crime families, including non-Italian groups, under one leadership. This goal was a long-time ambition of Don Vito, who probably envisioned himself as the leader. Once on American soil Maranzano was the undisputed boss of the Twenties Group. His authority also was recognized by certain resident American Mafiosi such as the boss Gaetano Reina of Brooklyn and his capos Thomas Lucchese and Gaetano Gagliano, by Joey Aiello, the Mafia boss of Chicago, and by Joe Zerilli, underboss of the Detroit family. Each of these men had entered the United States following Petrosino's death and were identified by the Italian police records as members of the Sicilian Mafia.

Arrayed against the Maranzano group were the bosses Masseria, Terranova, Ferrigno, and Mineo; the capos Frank Costello and Lucky Luciano, and three Neapolitans who were rising members of Masseria's organization—Mike Miranda, Joe Doto (known as Joe Adonis), and Vito Genovese. For a variety of reasons they owed no allegiance to the Sicilian Mafia. All of them had positions to protect. And all but two of them, Masseria and Terranova, had been in America since childhood. They regarded the Sicilian Mafia as a foreign intrusion. The conflict between the two groups, one Sicilian and the other essentially American, came to be known as the Castellammarese War.*

*A misnomer that arose from Maranzano's propaganda that his gangland enemies were waging a race war against all Castellammarese, a reference to a coastal locale near Palermo where Maranzano and many of his men had been born.

COSA NOSTRA: RIVALRY AND CONSOLIDATION 137

In the beginning the war was undeclared. Maranzano would kill a Masseria member; not openly, but in such a way that his own involvement would be concealed. Such mysterious killings, it was hoped, would create fear, uncertainty, and schisms in the Masseria organization. "The idea," said Joe Valachi, "was to try and get a couple of their bosses before they catch up with them, and they would be that much ahead... but when they [Masseria] find out where it comes from, naturally, they are in war with wherever it comes from."

The first sneak killing of a boss was the July 1, 1928, murder of Brooklyn's Frankie Yale. This murder has always been attributed to Al Capone, usually on the theory that Yale was the first gangster murdered in New York by a Thompson submachine gun, a weapon identified almost exclusively with Al Capone and Chicago. The Thompson weapon being rather difficult to aim and control, most researchers have felt that only Capone's men had the necessary expertise. But Yale and Capone were known to be allies, and no satisfactory explanation for the betrayal has ever been advanced. Moreover, Yale was not murdered with a submachine gun. He was killed with typical Mafia weapons, pistols and shotguns. A Thompson was found at the scene, but it had not been fired. The death of Frankie Yale weakened Masseria's hold on Brooklyn. To replace him, Masseria brought his old enemy Joe Morello out of retirement and announced that henceforth Morello was to be boss of bosses. Morello's new territory was Brooklyn, or as much of it as he could hold. The move was calculated, in part, to offset the appeal of Maranzano and Don Vito, who was rumored to be arriving soon.* Morello was a perfect choice for, like the two Sicilians, he represented old-time discipline and prestige. At the same time, he had no gang of his own, no real power, and was not a threat to Masseria. He was a puppet ruler.

Other mysterious murders followed the Yale death, and Maranzano continued to profit from his secret war. Evidence of the advances Maranzano was making may be found in a meeting held December 1928 in Cleveland, Ohio. Acting on a tip

---

*In 1928 Don Vito had not yet been arrested by the Fascists.

from a suspicious hotel clerk, police arrested twenty-seven gangsters from New York, Chicago, Philadelphia, Tampa, Cleveland, Hot Springs, New Orleans, Buffalo, Kansas City, and Detroit. Among those arrested at the meeting—which newspapers referred to as a gathering of "the Mafia Grand Council"—were Joe Profaci, Joe Magliocco, and Vincent Mangano, all close allies of Maranzano. The purpose of the convention—from which, according to police, non-Sicilian gangsters such as Al Capone had been excluded—was to work out a solid Mafia front in preparation for an upcoming national bootleggers' meeting in Atlantic City. At the Cleveland session it was decided that New York Italian interests would be represented by a delegation led by Lucky Luciano and including Joe Adonis and Joe Magliocco. This makeup reflected the New York leadership race: Masseria in front and Maranzano moving up fast.

Five months later, on May 13–15, 1929, the Atlantic City bootlegging convention was held. The seven bootlegging syndicates represented at the meeting were the New York Italian delegation, Al Capone, Longy Zwillman of New Jersey, Charles ("King") Solomon of Boston, Siegel and Lansky representing Philadelphia, and Waxey Gordon and Owney Madden, who had separate enterprises in New York. By the end of the convention they had agreed to pool resources and share profits. Once formed, this alliance was almost immediately in control of 40 percent of all illegal alcohol sales in the United States.

Five months after the Atlantic City meeting, Masseria's main man, Luciano, was kidnapped and beaten. It was reported thus in newspapers the following day:

> Charles (Lucky) Luciania [sic], associate of the late Arnold Rothstein, the notorious Diamond brothers and the late Thomas (Paddy) Walsh, awoke at 2 A.M. yesterday [October 17, 1929] on Huguenot Beach, Staten Island, and thought he was dreaming. He had been "taken on a ride" the night before and was alive to tell about it.
>
> His lips were sealed with adhesive tape, his head was aching from fist and gun butt blows and there was a knife wound on his chin. Luciania tore off the tape and staggered almost a mile before

he reached the police booth at Prince's Bay avenue where he was intercepted by Patrolman Blanke of the Tottenville Precinct.

"Get me a taxi," Luciania pleaded. "I'll give you fifty bucks if you do and let me go my way." Blanke ignored the offer; instead he took Luciania to the Richmond Memorial Hospital and telephoned to Detective Charles Schley. To Schley, the battered man told the story of his ride.

Luciania said he was standing on 50th street at Sixth Avenue at 6 P.M. when a limousine, with curtains drawn, rolled up beside him. Three men leaped from the tonneau, prodded Luciania in the back with gun muzzles, forced him into the machine, and the ride began.

The adhesive tape was applied, then came the kicks and punches and knife wound. Luciania became unconscious and hours later woke up on the beach, staring unbelieving at the waves rolling in from lower New York Bay.

When the detective began to ask questions, Luciania suddenly became mute.

"Don't you cops lose any sleep over it," he finally burst out, impatiently. "I'll attend to this thing myself later." He refused to say any more and denied that he had recognized the men who had taken him for the ride and wearily insisted that he had no enemies. . . . The detectives were inclined to the theory that Broadway racketeers had thrown Luciania on the beach in a belief that he was dead. He has been arrested many times, but he has been convicted only once, according to his fingerprint record. In that he was sentenced to the penitentiary for possessing drugs.*

Several months later, after recovering from the beating, Luciano met secretly with Maranzano and agreed to betray Masseria.

In the meantime, two months after the Luciano kidnapping, a second Masseria boss was disgraced. The victim was Ciro Terranova, one of the original Morello clan, and he was subjected to a curiously Sicilian punishment—loss of face, loss of respect.

---

*Many writers have attributed Luciano's nickname "Lucky" to this event, claiming it was bestowed on him because he was lucky to be alive. The first line of the newspaper story, however, shows that he was known as Lucky prior to the beating.

The occasion of Terranova's disgrace came to be known as "Magistrate Vitale's Supper." Besides embarrassing Terranova, the dinner had political effects which went far beyond the immediate concerns of the Mafia. The Vitale Supper tripped off a chain of investigations that changed the entire political picture in New York.

The date of the supper was December 7, 1929. That night the Tepecano Democratic Club had taken over the Roman Gardens Restaurant in the Bronx for a private supper in honor of Magistrate Albert Vitale. The room was festooned with red, white, and green decorations, and every table setting included a bottle of red wine. Applause greeted the guest of honor, Magistrate Vitale, as he entered with his friend Ciro Terranova, who was the organizer and host of the testimonial. Of the forty some guests, approximately one-third were gangsters, one-third politicians, and the remainder in-between types. Among the last was Detective Lieutenant Art Johnson.

After a brief welcoming speech by Terranova, supper was served. While the guests ate a comedian told jokes. "Did you hear about the two guys who jumped out of the tenth floor of the Ritz? They went down holding hands. They had held a joint account. If you check into a hotel now, the clerk asks why you're taking the room. For sleeping? Or jumping?"

Midway through the supper, the comedian suddenly stopped his patter. Gradually the guests fell silent too. With no announcements or crashing of doors, seven men had materialized, as if from nowhere, at the front of the room. All were waving pistols. One of them, the leader, was masked. He ordered everyone to line up against the wall. Ignoring Terranova's objections—"We're all paisans here"—the gang methodically passed down the line of men taking money and jewelry. Magistrate Vitale was relieved of all he had in his pocket, forty dollars. Detective Johnson lost more—his credentials, police badge, and service revolver. When they reached the end of the line, the bandits had collected about two thousand dollars in cash and another twenty-five hundred dollars in jewelry. They cleared out, leaving their victims stunned. Represented at the dinner was the combined power of orga-

COSA NOSTRA: RIVALRY AND CONSOLIDATION   ○   141

nized crime, the police, and Tammany Hall, and they had all been bagged like tourists. Outraged, the participants dispersed to begin their various inquiries.

The most nervous of the lot was Detective Johnson. He was charged out at the department with his badge and gun, and there seemed no way to avoid reporting the theft and linking himself with the gangster dinner. He asked Magistrate Vitale what could be done. Vitale told him to come to his office in five hours and meanwhile to wait at home and file no report.

Terranova, accompanied by three of his gunmen, was already out searching for Johnson's gun and badge, for it was just possible that if they could be recovered the whole incident could be kept secret. His men knew precisely where to go.*

Less than three hours after the robbery, Detective Johnson was summoned to Vitale's office, where the magistrate handed over the credentials, badge, and revolver. He also turned over to him a substantial amount of the stolen jewelry, and told Johnson he could report it "recovered" in whatever kind of report he chose to submit. At that point it looked as if the humiliation might be kept secret. Neither the victims nor Johnson had any desire to carry it further.

But someone did—the robbers themselves. They tipped the newspapers off to the whole story, including Vitale's role in returning the gun and badge. The next morning the incident was the city's sensation. The police administration was outraged because one of its own had lost his gun and gangsters had to get it back for him. Editorialists wanted to know why magistrates (Vitale was the guest of honor but six other magistrates were present) were in such close association with known hoodlums like Terranova and his gunmen. And the underworld was both thrilled and puzzled as to the identity of men who would deliberately humiliate a boss, for the dinner had been under Terranova's protection.

---

*All three of these men would be killed within the next eighteen months. They were Danny Iamascia, Terranova's driver who moonlighted as a bodyguard for Dutch Schultz; Joe Catania, Terranova's nephew and son of the Joe Catania murdered by Morello and Lupo in 1902; and John Savino, who had a long police record but no other distinction.

Investigations and hearings began immediately. The first to take place was the administrative trial of Detective Johnson, held before Police Commissioner Grover Whalen on December 26. At this hearing a police spokesman offered a bizarre, but officially accepted, theory as to why the robbery had happened. According to the *Literary Digest*, this spokesman claimed Ciro had engineered it himself, "to recover a murder contract against Frankie Yale which bore Terranova's signature and which bluntly set forth the agreement to assassinate Yale, leader of a Brooklyn gang. Terranova invited the slayer to the magistrate's dinner. He asked the gunman to bring along the contract. After satisfying himself that the man had the document, Terranova gave the word for the seven men to raid the dinner. They got the contract and within four hours were sending back most of the $5,000 in jewels and money they had taken from the diners in order to make the robbery look genuine." No such written murder contract ever existed and Terranova did not rob his own guests. A clue to the true perpetrator was actually turned up at the police hearing, although its significance was never made public. It was a letter, mailed to Terranova's bodyguard, John Savino, eleven days after the robbery and intercepted by police. It read:

> It is all fixed. You and Danny [Iamascia] get rid of the rods at your place. We will get rid of that other one. Be ready to leave any time if necessary. Get in touch at once with Vitale. Tell him we will take care of that other matter at once, so he has nothing to worry about. Don't do any talking over telephones. Tell you why when I see you. We got another guy to take the rap if necessary. Tell Ciro to give Joe [Catania] the grand for me because they—the bulls—are watching him. Come down about three in the morning.
> [signed] M. C.

"M. C." was Mike Coppola, an important member of Maranzano's Twenties Group.

What happened was this: A soldier in the Maranzano-allied Reina family had been ordered to break up the Vitale supper and humiliate Terranova. Once the damage was done, Maran-

COSA NOSTRA: RIVALRY AND CONSOLIDATION   O   143

zano—who had ordered the Reinas to commit the robbery in the first place—graciously offered to serve as an intermediary. By means of one robbery, then, Maranzano was both damaging Terranova's prestige and enhancing his own, by assuming the role of supreme arbiter of Italian affairs. Terranova accepted and Coppola was assigned to make repairs, restore the loot, and save Vitale. Because they were all businessmen, Coppola charged a token fee of one thousand dollars for his services.

Although the letter clearly implicates Coppola and therefore Maranzano, they were never brought into the investigation and the robbery was never officially solved. But the furor built. On December 30, 1929, while the police hearings about the Vitale supper were going on, detectives raided one of Masseria's key narcotics outlets and arrested two of his men, Louis and Frank Saccarona, brothers who operated the Performers and Entertainers Club at Twenty-two Twenty-one Seventh Avenue in Harlem. Arrested with them were eighteen white and Negro confederates accused of running a "national distribution of narcotics, mostly heroin and opium." Seized in the raid were financial records tying the Saccaronas with Tammany leader Jimmy Hines and a variety of lesser politicians—the late Arnold Rothstein, Masseria, Luciano, and the star-crossed magistrate, Vitale.

Following on the heels of the Vitale scandal, this revelation was explosive. Once again Tammany luminaries were linked with the gangsters, and it burst the city wide open. The events led to the Seabury investigations, the eventual ouster of Vitale and other magistrates, the resignation of Mayor Walker in 1932, the election of La Guardia, and the rise of Roosevelt.

Masseria spent the next several months rebuilding the dikes. He lost some politicians, but he saved himself, Terranova, and the organization. He also figured out the identity of his mysterious tormentor. It was Gaetano Reina, or so Masseria mistakenly believed, for it was a Reina gunman who had held up the Magistrate's Supper.

On the night of February 26, 1930, Gaetano Reina, forty, walked out of his mistress's apartment house at Fifteen Twenty-one Sheridan Avenue, the Bronx. As he stepped onto the sidewalk, a man hidden in a parked car rose up and pulled both triggers of a double-barreled shotgun. Reina was dead.

Police publicly identified Reina as a "poultry dealer and wealthy wholesale ice dealer," and claimed that the murder grew out of some sort of poultrymen's dispute.

The Reina murder is generally recognized as the official beginning of the Castellammarese War. An eyewitness to the war was Joe Valachi, later to be a government informer.

Joe Valachi was born in Manhattan in 1904 of Neapolitan parents. He got into crime early, becoming a specialist in burglaries and an expert driver. Although a New Yorker, an Italian, and a rather successful street criminal, he spent the entire Prohibition era without being accepted as a member ("mobbed up") in any of the Italian families and in fact had only a vague knowledge of their existence. He was even warned against joining them by a former member, Alessandro Vollero, whom he met while serving a 1924 term in Sing Sing. Vollero, one of the prominent Camorrists convicted of Nick Morello's murder in 1918, told Valachi that the families were dominated by Sicilians and were therefore dangerous for Neapolitans. "He said if you hang out with a Sicilian 20 years and you have some trouble with another Sicilian, this Sicilian you hang out with 20 years will turn on you. You can't trust them," Valachi said.

According to his testimony before the McClellan committee, Valachi's introduction to the families came "in late 1929 or early 1930," that is, two or three months before Reina's death. He was approached by two long-time friends, James Santuccio, known as Bobby Doyle, and Dominick ("the Gap") Petrelli. "At first," Valachi testified, "I refused. I told the Gap 'I don't want to have nothing to do with those guys. Alessandro told me plenty. We [Neapolitans] don't have a chance.' The Gap said, 'Things aren't like they used to be. We got something in mind. We are going to fight some big shots.' He named Ciro. He named Willie Moretti, Dutch Schultz. He gave me names I would recognize."

What finally won Valachi over, however, was Bobby Doyle's argument that personal participation in burglaries carried too much risk. "If you are stealing, you are bound to get killed," he told Valachi. "Join us and you will be made. You will earn money and you are not to steal anymore."

This argument appealed to Valachi, the professional. He contemplated not only how he had been arrested fairly regularly in the past, but also how the impact of technology would affect his future activities. "The lights used to go out at three in the morning. Now they leave them on all night and that was against me in burglarizing. After all, if I am burglarizing and lights are on all night and if I am getting a chase from one car I will draw attention and I will have a hundred cars come after me for passing lights. They were talking about radio cars and naturally that is going to be more tough. With that in mind and the proposition I got, I accepted."

He now considered himself a member of the Reina family, although he had not yet been initiated, and in two months he established himself as a cool and competent hit man and driver. After Reina was killed, reported Valachi, the Reina family did not doubt that Masseria was responsible. The family, however, did not seem revengeful, and in this we see an example of the brotherhood's strong belief in abstract justice and its own law. The murder of their boss did not arouse great heat because the family members felt it was "justified." They seemed to feel that Reina had committed some aggression against Masseria (the Vitale supper holdup, perhaps) and therefore had accepted the possibility of being killed. It was between bosses. Masseria, however, overreached himself in the follow-up to Reina's murder. He pulled in an outsider, Joseph Pinzolo, to be boss of the Reina family and bypassed Reina's underboss, Tom Gagliano. Such direct interference in family affairs was considered unjustified and illegal, and this, rather than the assassination of their boss, aroused great fury in the Reina family.

Valachi said, "The Gap comes to me and says I got to meet this Joe Pinzolo, who is the new guy in charge." Valachi was turned off by the new boss and found him to be "gross, arrogant, . . . and a pig. He didn't know how to behave." The Gap told him not to worry about Pinzolo. "This guy ain't going to be around long. We got plans." The plans centered around the dissatisfied underboss, Gagliano, who was organizing a secret revolt against Masseria. Like many successful leaders, Gagliano did not structure his appeal on the injustice that had been done to him. Instead, he invented a disinterested cause, the revenge of Reina. The murder, he now told members, was "unjustified."

The secret war began. He did not want an open conflict with Masseria, for he felt he was without allies. Like Masseria, Gagliano seems to have been unaware at this time that Maranzano was the man responsible for Reina's attack on Terranova.

From February to August 1930, the war between Gagliano and Masseria rolled on with Masseria getting the worst of it. Some thirty of his men were killed in that six-month period. Sometime in early August 1930, Gagliano asked for a meeting with Maranzano, and their natural alliance against a common enemy was formalized. They would work together to kill Masseria. But first, to prove good faith and absolute commitment, each family would kill a boss. Gagliano's target, of course, would be the usurper, Pinzolo. Maranzano's would be the puppet boss of bosses, Peter (Joe) Morello, the man installed by Masseria to dilute Maranzano's appeal.

Maranzano struck first, only five days after his meeting with Gagliano. On August 15, 1930, Morello was shot down in his office at Three Sixty-two East One Hundred Sixteenth Street. The hit was easy enough. Maranzano's Sicilians simply walked in as trusted acquaintances and gunned down Morello and his bodyguard, Giuseppe Piranio. The leader of the hit team was "Buster from Chicago," a Maranzano soldier who was soon to be Valachi's closest friend. Joe Morello, Buster later confided to Valachi, was "a tough old man. He kept running around the office," and Buster had to pump out several more shots to bring him down.

Three weeks after Morello's death, the Gagliano target was struck. Valachi, who was a participant in neither the Morello nor the Pinzolo hits, was given the details by Joe Profaci. "The family didn't like Masseria taking the power to go into the family and name the boss. They answered him by killing Joe Pinzolo." Pinzolo was lured to an office at Fourteen Eighty-seven Broadway leased by Thomas Lucchese. There he was shot by Bobby Doyle and unknown assistants.

COSA NOSTRA: RIVALRY AND CONSOLIDATION   ○   147

With their mutual commitment thus established, the two families now merged forces under the overall command of Maranzano. The next target was Masseria himself, and for this a team of men from both families was chosen. Representing the Gagliano family were Bobby Doyle and Valachi. Representing Maranzano were Profaci and "Buster from Chicago." The plan was for the team to set up a lookout post in an apartment at the Alhambra, Seven Fifty Pelham Parkway, from which they could observe the nearby apartment of the boss Stefano Ferrigno. Masseria's people thought Ferrigno's address was a secret, and they used his home for top-level meetings.

Valachi was told by Gagliano to "move into this apartment and at this time Buster, the Doc [name unknown], Nick Capuzzi, and Joe Profaci moved in this apartment with me. We had gotten pictures of Masseria, photographs because we didn't know who he was."

Six weeks passed without a glimpse of Masseria. When the boss was finally spotted, he was too close for Valachi's comfort.

Valachi was walking from the street into the courtyard when "to my amazement, I saw Masseria get out of a car. I recognized him fast. They gave me a description of him. He was five feet two inches, and Fennuci* and Masseria got out of the car together." Valachi's stake-out apartment had an entrance on the opposite side of the courtyard from Ferrigno's so he hoped to get inside and avoid the bosses.

"To my amazement they followed me in my entrance. So I got in the elevator. They got in there with me. So I asked them where they wanted to go. They said, 'Punch yours.' I think I was on the second floor, so I punched six. When I got up to six—they were looking me over, see—we were facing one another. I had my back to the wall. They had their backs to the wall on the other side. I come out of the elevator, slowly, walking like. As soon as I reached [the stairwell] I flew down to the second floor to tell them in the apartment what I saw."

---

*Valachi knew the boss Ferrigno as "Fennuci." It is evidence of the secrecy of that era that even experienced criminals like Valachi knew virtually nothing of the makeup of the organization. Until he joined, Valachi had never even heard the names Reina, Gagliano, or Maranzano.

Buster, Profaci, and the others didn't believe him until "one who was looking out the window sees Masseria" crossing the courtyard to Ferrigno's apartment. He had taken a ride in the elevator to check out Valachi and had judged him harmless.

From this point, as would happen in all but one murder he described in his Senate testimony,* Valachi was careful to excuse himself from direct action. He said that while he was away somewhere the next day, about twenty to twenty-four men entered Ferrigno's apartment for a meeting. "As they were coming out, two by two, the ones in the apartment [that is, Buster and associates] were waiting for Masseria, letting the others pass." Finally, when they saw Ferrigno and another boss, Alfred Mineo, Buster said, 'Let's grab what we have. Maybe Joe got out during the night,' and they shot those two, which were two bosses. They were just as important as Masseria.

"After the killing, Buster ran out of the apartment right into a policeman and the policeman asked him, 'What is going on?' Buster said, 'I don't know. There is shooting down the block.' The policeman ran toward the apartment. All that Buster did was walk off."

Unaware of the importance of Ferrigno and Mineo, the police attributed the deaths to a feud in the policy business. They did find out about the ambush however, and told *The New York Times* that the "killers were in an apartment that had been rented by a man named Frank Rubin." In the apartment they found three shotguns and a violin case "which had been used to smuggle the weapons into the building."

Masseria's organization did a much better job than the police of investigating the hits. The members examined the furniture at the "Frank Rubin" apartment and found it had been purchased at One Hundred Sixth Street and Third Ave-

---

*The murder he admitted was that of John Saupp, whom Valachi killed in a case of mistaken identity in 1962 in an Atlanta prison (see p. 169). Federal sources who knew Valachi personally claim that his main value to the society was his expertise as a hit man. He is judged to have killed thirty-three men. Nevertheless, Valachi always absented himself from the scene during a murder. It is a curious lie, for he made no effort to disguise his role as an accomplice, and therefore under the law was equally guilty of the murders.

COSA NOSTRA: RIVALRY AND CONSOLIDATION   ○   149

nue. The purchaser was Joe Valachi's sister. From these two clues they deduced the whole Gagliano-Maranzano alliance. The two sides commenced open hostilities, and the war became national. "It was made in all cities," said Valachi. "Wherever the members were, in Chicago and Cleveland and California."

The brotherhood switched over to its wartime structure of government, much as a commercial nation like the United States alters its laws in wartime to make itself a more efficient fighting machine. The main change was that autonomous families deferred their independence to a commander in chief. On the one side it was Masseria, who coordinated the efforts and financial donations of his allies. His forces included the Terranova, Ferrigno, and Mineo families and the outsiders Al Capone, Dutch Schultz, and the Siegel-Lansky mob. Maranzano was the opposition warlord. "He was boss of the Gagliano family," said Valachi, "and he was going to continue to be boss throughout the trouble." Lined up with him were the Twenties Group (Bonanno, Profaci, Maggadino, Magliocco, and Coppola) and the Chicago Mafia boss Joey Aiello. A second change was elimination of the rank of *caporegime*. During war there are no capos or lieutenants. "During the trouble, there is nothing like lieutenant or anything like that. That comes after, when you make peace."

At the time war was declared, Valachi was sworn in to the society. With three other initiates, he drove to a private house ninety miles upstate where there were gathered some forty members. "The purpose of the meeting was to make us, to make new members and to meet all the family." One by one the initiates were called into a main room. It was Valachi's first meeting with Maranzano.

"When I came in I sat down at a long table and there was a gun and a knife on the table." About forty men were seated around it. "They sat me down and Maranzano made me repeat in Italian . . . I repeated some words they told me, but I couldn't understand what he meant. They were in Sicilian. Maranzano explained [presumably in Italian] that they lived by the gun and by the knife and you die by the gun and by the knife. Then he gave me a piece of paper, and I was to burn it. The paper is burning, and it is lighted and then in your hand. You say, 'This is the way I burn if I expose this organization.'

"After that they got around the table and they drew numbers, from one to five. Then they add up the numbers everybody picked and, say, they end up in a total of 38. Then they count around the table until they come to the 38th man and he is my godfather." Joe Bonanno—who according to his biographer Gay Talese and to Valachi was the youngest boss in Cosa Nostra at this time, having arrived in the United States only six years earlier—was Valachi's godfather. Bonanno stepped forward and pricked Valachi's finger. The letting of blood "is supposed to be like brothers. You are willing to give your blood or your life. Then they all shake hands and say a few more words together in Sicilian."*

The war continued. It has never been calculated how many men were involved nationally, but in New York alone more than one thousand members had taken to mattresses. The majority of these were married men with families and all had financial obligations which depended on a more or less regular income from whatever rackets they were in—bootlegging, gambling, narcotics, or loansharking. But any soldier who made his usual appearances was sure to be gunned down by the opposition, so the rackets—and the soldiers' incomes—were greatly curtailed during the year-long war. In addition to the loss of income, there were exceptional expenses peculiar to wartime. These included the cost of guns, ammunition, automobiles and other transportation, apartment rentals, and a minimum subsistence allowance for the men who were living more or less barracks-style, five and ten to an apartment.

War costs were financed by a special fund. Maranzano put in an estimated $250,000 and Gagliano another $140,000 "out of his own pocket." Taxes or contributions were also levied on allies elsewhere in the country. For instance, Buffalo boss Steve Maggadino contributed $5,000 a week, which in a year's time added up to $260,000. Another $5,000 a week was received

---

*Valachi told the 1963 Senate hearing: "This is the same meeting today, what I described in 1930."

COSA NOSTRA: RIVALRY AND CONSOLIDATION   ○   151

from the Aiello family in Chicago until October 23, 1930, when Aiello was killed by Al Capone. The money was allocated to the men on the basis of need, not rank. "It was on the basis of who needs financing," said Valachi. "If you need guns, if you need machine guns, you get it. Maranzano was in charge of all that." For subsistence, Valachi's group of four got twenty-five dollars a week. It wasn't enough, even in Depression times, so Valachi went moonlighting "on a couple of burglaries, doing this so we could have some money in our pocket. You are hiding out, you can't make money."

After about a month of the declared war, Masseria sent out peace feelers. These were rejected by Maranzano, who told his men there would be no peace until they had killed Joe ("the Baker") Catania, the nephew of Ciro Terranova. Why Maranzano focused on Catania is not clear. He claimed that Catania had once hijacked some of his alcohol trucks. What Maranzano probably had in mind, however, was an excuse to ignore the peace proposals and continue the war. Unknown to his soldiers, Maranzano had been secretly negotiating with Lucky Luciano to have Masseria killed by his own men. By creating an issue of personal honor, he silenced those in his camp who wanted peace.

Valachi, "Buster from Chicago," and two others were given the assignment to kill Catania. Such contracts were regarded as an honor. They were not done for payment or out of fear of family discipline. "It was natural as breathing," said Valachi. "We were young, we thought we were doing a duty for these people."

At the beginning of January 1931, the team set themselves up in an apartment on One Hundred Eighty-third Street in the Bronx. From there they could watch a bail bondsman's office used regularly by Catania. They manned the apartment from four in the morning until ten o'clock at night. After a month Valachi got nervous, feeling they had been there too long. "I know this neighborhood. They'll tell and Masseria will come and bomb us out of here. They'll crash in with guns."

He took his fears to Maranzano at the boss's house in Yonkers. Valachi suggested the hit team leave its stake-out location and move into an apparently vacant apartment next door to the bail bondsman's office. Catania passed there every morning and it offered a much better shooting blind than their current hideout. Maranzano agreed.

Early the next morning (February 3, 1931), Valachi and Buster used the spring leaf of a car, one of Valachi's favorite burglary tools, to crash open the door of the new apartment. It was not empty, however. Three frightened house painters were standing there, brushes in hand. "The painters wanted to give us money. They thought we were sticking them up." Valachi lined them against the wall and told them to stay there. They would be present during the ambush and shooting.

Half an hour later Buster saw Catania pass by. Valachi (in his version) said that Buster and the hit team opened the windows and waited for Catania to reappear. Meanwhile Valachi went out to the getaway car to get the motor running. A few minutes later, Buster and the other two soldiers jumped into the car and Valachi sped off. "How did it go?" he asked.

Buster said, "He came out of the office with his wife. He kissed her in front of the office, and I was worried I wouldn't get a shot. But he turned and went for the corner. She was just standing there watching when I got him. I don't think I missed once. You could see the dust coming off his coat when the bullets hit." Catania died the next day in Fordham Hospital. The police reported that "in spite of mortal wounds, he could not or would not identify the perpetrators of the crime."

Newspapers identified Catania as a bail bondsman and noted, "At first, the police supposed the bullets had come from a passing automobile. But one reluctant eye-witness pointed to a vacant first-floor apartment in a tenement house across the street. There the police found the shotguns. Later two painters who had been working in the apartment said two men had entered in the day and, displaying revolvers, had intimated they had better leave." The painters, like Valachi, had conveniently removed themselves from the scene of the shooting.

Catania's death demoralized Masseria, who was already suffering a terrible attrition. More than sixty of his key men had been killed in New York alone, balanced against Maranzano's loss of a single ally—Chicago boss Joey Aiello, for whom Capone, not Masseria, got the credit. Winners are loved in the underworld as elsewhere, and Masseria now experienced mass desertions. He was left with only a few key regimes in his family, headed by Luciano, Genovese, Adonis, Anastasia, and Pete Livorsi. Maybe half of the Terranova family remained loyal. That was all. The Capone and Schultz organizations had been among the first to abandon him. His only outside allies were Lansky and Siegel, who were loyal to Luciano rather than Masseria. "They were not members," said Valachi. "They were close with Charley and Vito, that is an allegiance group. They worked together."

Masseria, always a realist, offered surrender.

His terms were astoundingly abject. "He offered himself to be a plain soldier," reported Valachi. "He will give up anything he had if they leave him alone. Maranzano refused." For this second refusal he didn't bother concocting an excuse. The war was won and Luciano and Pete Livorsi had sent word that they themselves would kill Masseria. Their official rationale was that the Masseria family could not tolerate further demoralization. It would be better, they said, to kill the boss and preserve organizational integrity. The truth beneath the propaganda seems to be that Luciano was culminating eighteen months of intrigue aimed at making himself boss of the Masseria family. Some such high-level betrayal is the only explanation for the off-balance murder statistics. Maranzano had sixty successful ambushes; Masseria had none. Furthermore, we know from other portions of the Valachi testimony that Luciano's negotiations with Maranzano were in fact going on as early as August 1930, which was one month before the killing of the boss Joseph Pinzolo and two months before the war was brought into the open by the deaths of Ferrigno and Mineo.

The plot proceeded. Throughout March 1931, Masseria's key lieutenants, Livorsi and Luciano, worked to convince him they were setting up a peace meeting with Maranzano. On April 15 they took him to the Nuovo Villa Tammaro Restaurant at Twenty-seven Fifteen West Fifteenth Street, Coney Island. The car was driven by Ciro Terranova, who had joined the conspiracy but almost tipped off Masseria by his nervousness.

"Ciro was so shaky in putting the key in the ignition that

they threw him off the wheel. Ciro Terranova was getting what we call buckwheats, you know, like he was being stripped a little at a time of his power." Immediately after the murder, Terranova was relieved of all power. His family was dispersed to other units, and his rackets were given to Maranzano's man Mike Coppola. "After a while," said Valachi, "he took it so hard that he died from a broken heart."

At the restaurant, Masseria was seated with Terranova, Livorsi, Luciano, and Genovese. On various excuses, they all left the table. Luciano told police he had gone to the restroom and while there had heard shots. When he returned Masseria was dead. Carefully placed in his right hand was an ace of diamonds, a bit of show business the meaning of which is still unknown.

The boss was buried in a solid silver coffin. The funeral procession numbered sixty-nine cars, including sixteen filled with flowers. In the few days between Masseria's death and burial there was a flurry of other killings in New York and New Jersey, but the war was over. Maranzano had won.

On or about April 30, 1931, the new boss held a five-day celebration at a big hall on Washington Avenue in the Bronx. The get-together began with the first organizational meeting of Cosa Nostra.

Valachi was there. "There was about 400 to 500 people in this hall. After I was there awhile, Maranzano was standing on the platform when he got up to speak. Members were coming. He started to explain about Masseria and his groups, that they were killing people without justice. He mentioned some names, names that I didn't know or never even heard of. He mentioned they had killed Don Antonio without justice. They killed another name he mentioned which is Reina. I didn't know any of these men. 'Now it is going to be different,' he said. 'We are going to have, first we have the boss of all bosses, which is myself. Then we have the boss [of the families] and we have an underboss under the boss. Then we have the caporegima. Now if a soldier wants to talk to a boss, he should not take the privilege for him to try to go direct to the boss. He must speak first to the caporegima and the caporegima, if it is required and

COSA NOSTRA: RIVALRY AND CONSOLIDATION ○ 155

important enough, the caporegima will make an appointment for the soldier.' "

"This is what I call Second Government," said Valachi.

At this meeting Maranzano announced the principles by which this "Cosa Nostra" would operate. Most of these ideas had already evolved in the society by 1931; even the name "Cosa Nostra" was used by some members as early as 1927. But Maranzano was the first to enunciate them as an organized code, and demand that all members—Sicilian, Italian, or American—be aware of and observe them.

According to Valachi's testimony to the McClellan committee, Maranzano emphasized five main points. First was insulation for the leadership, which seldom involved itself directly in crimes. The boss, says the philosophy of all brotherhood societies, must be protected.

The second feature, after insulation, was respect. There is not only the boss to protect, there are the law and the family, which can be preserved only by respect.

The third feature was a chain of command. All important matters must go through channels. Meetings are formal. The matter is discussed, the justice of it is weighed, and a decision is given to the petitioner.

A fourth feature was family integrity. All disciplining, including murder, is done within the same family by the members. This greatly reduces the chances of individual or interfamily vendettas.

A fifth feature was permission. New members are always surprised to learn that they must obtain permission to enter an illegal enterprise, commit a stickup or burglary, dispose of stolen property, even borrow from a shylock. Permission is given only for those undertakings which will help the family. In return the family provides lawyers, bail bondsmen, bribes and influence, if anything goes wrong.

Further features of Cosa Nostra that had already appeared in the society by the time of Maranzano's meeting were (1) killing for fees was forbidden, (2) membership was open only to those of Italian descent, (3) dues were collected from all members, (4) pensions were available to wives of imprisoned members and to widows, (5) one would not commit a private murder; that is, a murder without permission, and (6) members could transfer from family to family only with permission of the respective bosses and after a six-month trial period.

At the meeting Maranzano also divided Cosa Nostra into new families. Valachi, for instance, was given a choice of either staying with Gagliano or joining the Maranzano family. He chose the latter.

There were five families in the New York structure. The leaders were Maranzano and his underboss Angelo Caruso, Gagliano and his underboss Thomas Lucchese, Luciano and his underboss Genovese, Vincent Mangano and his underboss Frank Scalise, and a small organization headed by Joe Bonanno which apparently was recognized as a family.*

The Terranova-Morello family, the original New York Mafia group, ceased to exist. Masseria's family was taken over by Luciano, and the Ferrigno-Mineo families combined under Vincent Mangano. Except for the Maranzano family, these are the same families that exist today. After Maranzano's death his family was divided up. Some of the members went into an expanded Bonanno family and others went into a new Brooklyn organization headed by Joe Profaci.

Families outside New York, in Chicago, Buffalo, and New Orleans, were not affected by the Maranzano realignment. It was left to Lucky Luciano, after Maranzano's death, to make Cosa Nostra a nationwide syndicate, mainly through business partnerships.

Immediately after Maranzano's speech, the five-day banquet began. It was a fund-raising affair, and donations were piled right on the table in front of Maranzano. Approximately

---

*The precise status of Bonanno in this 1930–31 period is unknown. Valachi never says explicitly that Bonanno was a boss, but he says at one point that Bonanno was his initiation godfather and at another point that only bosses can be initiation godfathers. Biographer Gay Talese also says that Bonanno bossed a family at this time, but fails to state his evidence. A sixth member of the 1931 Cosa Nostra was the New Jersey family. At one point, Valachi said the boss of it was Joe Bonanno, but not the modern Bonanno, "a different one." At another point he says the 1931 New Jersey Cosa Nostra boss was one Steve Padami.

$115,000 was raised, including $6,000 sent by Capone, $6,000 from Maggadino, $6,000 from Luciano—an apparently agreed-upon symbol of good wishes or tribute. "I saw piles of money on the table every night," said Valachi. "There were members there I never saw before. There were so many people, so many faces. I didn't know where they came from."

For Valachi, it was perhaps the golden moment of his life. For Maranzano, however, it was a rest stop. He had further plans and was already importing hundreds of new Sicilian gunners. Several weeks after the banquet he invited Valachi to his house. In a comfortable atmosphere, over some drinks, he told him they were going back to war. Maranzano's confidence was proof of Valachi's exceptional value as a killer. No ordinary soldier would have been so honored.

"He told me a list of the people we would kill. Al Capone, Frank Costello, Charley Lucky, Vito Genovese, Joe Adonis, Dutch Schultz. These were the names I remembered."

Salvatore Maranzano had been in the United States only four years. His mission had been to form a truly national crime syndicate, which his leader, Don Vito Cascio Ferro, would control. But by 1931 the don had been imprisoned by Mussolini, and Maranzano decided to take his place. Three men had stood in his way. Now Masseria was dead. Al Capone was in prison and faced serious income tax charges whenever he was released. Only Lucky Luciano remained on the field of battle.

THE MAKING
OF THE SYNDICATE

Joe Valachi was sixty years old when he testified before McClellan's Senate Subcommittee on Organized Crime, and he described his life from childhood onward. In all those years his only sources of real happiness seem to have been his relationships with his leader, Salvatore Maranzano, and his best friend, the killer "Buster from Chicago." Buster was undoubtedly the number one killer in the Maranzano organization, and he drew all the important hits: Morello, Ferrigno, Mineo, Catania, and the assignment to kill Masseria, although eventually Luciano himself did the job. After Maranzano's victory banquet in 1931, Buster and Valachi became members of the boss's personal bodyguard.

One day at Maranzano's office on Park Avenue the boss took Valachi aside. "He told me I should be at his house that night about 9 o'clock. When I got to his house, he was bandaging his son's foot. I walked in. He greeted me. I waited until he got through with his son."

In the conversation that followed, Valachi learned that Maranzano planned to kill Luciano the next day. He was scheduled to appear at Maranzano's office for a meeting, and Maranzano had arranged for him to be killed immediately afterward, as he left the office building.

The plan bothered Valachi. "There was a rumor being passed around the office not to come up with any guns, nobody to come up there with any guns because they expect the police up there. I got to talking with some of the members and I said I didn't like that order. I said I'm afraid they are trying to prepare us to be without any guns. I just don't like it."

With all of his men unarmed, Maranzano himself would be an easy target for a hit. Fearing just such a setup, Valachi tried to persuade Maranzano to cancel the meeting. "After all, if I lose you I am out in the street. I got all reasons to worry. Must you go on this appointment? Can't you let Angelo Caruso [the underboss] go?" Maranzano explained that this was to be their last meeting, and that there was nothing to fear, since Luciano would be killed right after he left the office.

"If this is your last meeting," Valachi asked, "why should you go when the other ones, they usually send the underboss?"

Maranzano replied that if Valachi were worried, he should phone the office fifteen minutes before the rendezvous with Luciano and his underboss, Vito Genovese.

The next day, Valachi called at the proper time and "Charley Buffalo said everything was all right. He said I need not go down." Reassured, Valachi and a friend took the day off and spent the next twelve hours with girl friends. In those twelve hours, the leadership struggle within Cosa Nostra was resolved.

The meeting was set for 2:00 P.M., September 10, 1931. But Luciano and Genovese never showed up. Instead, four strangers arrived at Maranzano's headquarters and identified themselves as police detectives. With pistols in their hands they marched into the waiting room and ordered seven Maranzano men, all unarmed, to line up against the wall. Three of the detectives then stalked into Maranzano's private office.

At that point, *The New York Times* reported, "there was a

sound of voices in angry dispute; blows, struggling, and finally pistol shots. Then the four men dashed out of the suite. The seven clients who had been waiting to see Maranzano lost no time in following them, the detectives. But Miss [Frances] Samuels [a secretary] hurried into her employer's office. She found him slumped in a chair, his body riddled with bullets and punctured with knife wounds. The sound of shots attracted scores of occupants of other offices. Some of them dashed out in time to see men fleeing from the office suite. But nobody interfered with them." On the floor beside Maranzano's body, the *Times* continued, police found "two hats which had been knocked from the gunmen's heads in the struggle. Both hats were of exceptionally fine make and bore the labels of Chicago hat stores."

The four killers, never apprehended, were members of the Siegel-Lansky gang. Valachi later learned the circumstances of the hit from Red Levine, one of the gunmen who had lost his hat. The murder had been done, Levine told Valachi, as a favor to Luciano. "Siegel and Lansky were an allegiance group," Valachi said. "Vito and Charley Lucky were close to them. They seem to work together at times." The Jewish gunmen had been chosen because they were unknown to Maranzano and could pass as detectives.

Ironically, as the killers left the building, they ran into the gunman whom Maranzano had sent to ambush Luciano and Genovese. His name was Vincent ("Mad Dog") Coll, and he had been chosen because, although he knew Luciano and Genovese, he too was non-Italian and could approach them without arousing suspicion. According to Valachi, the Lansky men "waved [Coll] away and told him to beat it. They met Coll coming in and whoever was with Coll and they waved them away. 'Beat it, the cops are coming.'"

The successful execution of Maranzano was the signal for the planned execution of some sixty Maranzano allies, called "Mustaches," a reference to their traditional Sicilian ways. The occasion has since become famous as Cosa Nostra's Purge Day and although no comprehensive death list has ever been compiled, there were at least eleven hits in the New York area alone.

Details of the purge are not known, even after forty years. Implemented on a national scale, it must have required extraordinary preparation and communication. Each of the sixty victims must have been kept under surveillance to establish his daily pattern. For each of the sixty, a hit team had to be organized and gunmen chosen who wouldn't betray the plan. When Purge Day arrived, the hit teams had to be delivered to their target's area. A communications liaison must have been worked out to relay the go-ahead message from New York—that Maranzano had been killed—to each of the teams. Once their jobs were done, sixty teams had to escape.

At least three hundred men must have been in on the plot. Yet it went off without a hitch, so smoothly that it took more than a year before the first hint of a brotherhood purge filtered out to police. One reason the shake-up went off so quietly was that in many cases it took days, even months, before the bodies were discovered. Some of the bodies have never been found.

Typical Purge Day victims were Sam Monia and Luigi Russo, who were, respectively, the underboss and consigliere of the Steve Padami family in Newark. Their bodies, tied to concrete blocks, washed up on New Jersey beaches a week after their deaths. They had been beaten to death with billiard cues within four hours of Maranzano's death.

Maranzano's murder touched off one of the biggest scandals ever to hit the U.S. Immigration Service. Notebooks found in his office gave evidence that he had thoroughly corrupted the Immigration Service. In response to this revelation, eleven top officials in New York and Washington immediately resigned, including the commissioner of immigration who was in charge of Ellis Island. The incriminating notebooks soon disappeared, thanks to police connivance, but it has been estimated that beginning with his own illegal entry in 1927, Maranzano had arranged the illegal entry of some three thousand Italians. Within two weeks of Maranzano's death, the Immigration Service rounded up and summarily deported 861 of the illegal immigrants.

Following Purge Day, Luciano asked for a national peace, sending word to all families that there would be no more boss of bosses. Cosa Nostra, a federation of the former American

Mafia families of New York, New Jersey, Buffalo, and Philadelphia, now became the nucleus around which a national crime confederation gathered. Its nonmember alliance groups included the Lansky-Siegel gang; Zwillman in New Jersey; Moe Dalitz in Cleveland; Dutch Schultz, who ran the New York numbers syndicate, and Lepke Buchalter, who operated Murder Incorporated, along with a variety of scattered extortion rackets, mostly in the garment district. In 1932 Luciano and Johnny Torrio visited Chicago. With Torrio, the former gang boss of Chicago and Al Capone's patron, acting as intermediary, Luciano succeeded in bringing the Italian members of the Capone syndicate into Cosa Nostra. Other families, such as the Detroit, Kansas City and New Orleans Mafias, joined in later years.

During the next five years, Cosa Nostra set about absorbing the business and territory of its allies. Schultz was killed. Lansky, Siegel,* Buchalter, and Zwillman were given the status of high-level employees but deprived of real power. Only Dalitz in Cleveland managed to remain independent. The absorption of the Jewish organizations, which during Prohibition were probably as powerful nationally as the Italian syndicates, was so thorough that by 1972 Jewish syndicates controlled organized crime in only one U.S. city, Las Vegas.

Maranzano's death, then, resulted in a nationwide syndicate and greatly strengthened the Italians' leadership role. For Valachi, however, his leader's death marked the end of Cosa Nostra's golden days. Thereafter he became a malcontent, a carping, complaining corporal in the ranks, and was tolerated only because of his expertise in killing. The Maranzano bosses who survived Purge Day—Steve Maggadino of Buffalo, Joe Profaci and Gaetano (Tom) Gagliano of Brooklyn—did not share his bitterness. The king was dead, long live the king. They made peace with Luciano, and their first duty under the new regime was to quell resentment among the lower ranks. They

---

*Luciano's old friend Siegel was killed June 20, 1947, following a death sentence adjudged at a Cosa Nostra meeting presided over by Luciano in Cuba. His crime: wasting funds in building the Flamingo casino in Las Vegas.

did so by inventing justifications for the murder of Maranzano.

Valachi was informed that "Tom Gagliano wanted to talk to me and there was an appointment made for me up around 225th street. When I got there I found Tommy Brown [Lucchese] there and quite a few members. There were about 15 members there, the old type, not Americanized, and Tommy Brown sat me down. He wanted to ask me some questions. He said they are interested in me. He asked if I ever knew about Maranzano hijacking alcohol trucks on Charley Luciano. So I put up my right hand and I said, 'Tommy, I don't know nothing, so help me God.' "

Lucchese said he believed him and that Gagliano wanted Valachi to come back into the family. Valachi asked for time and conferred with other members, who advised him he would be safer going into the Luciano family. An appointment was made for him to see the underboss, Genovese.

"Vito said, 'I want to take you along with me because I want to see the respect due you come to you.' In other words, we [that is, Valachi and Maranzano's other soldiers] had worked so hard, and now all of a sudden we lost our boss, and there would be no more respect. He went on to say the things Maranzano had done, about the trucking and about the alcohol."

Valachi asked what he could do for Genovese and was told he could go to Chicago as a known Maranzano loyalist and explain the killing to the Chicago Mafia family. Valachi, who had no desire to be so prominent, talked his way out of it, and another emissary was sent. After his meeting with Genovese, Valachi and some other recruits were taken downtown "and they introduced us to Tony Bender [Strollo] and they told us Tony Bender is the new lieutenant we have." Thus, within a few months Valachi had been with three families—Gagliano, Maranzano, and Luciano.

In the fall of 1931 Luciano imposed some modifications on the Cosa Nostra structure; since then, it has remained unchanged to the present day. As he promised, Luciano abolished the boss-of-bosses position. A commission of bosses would rule Cosa Nostra and decisions would be reached by vote. In addition, an appeals court of six consiglieri, one from each of the six families, was established for the New York area only. The purpose of this added council of consiglieri was to protect the soldiers. "For instance," said Valachi, "if a lieutenant wants to have a soldier killed or something like that, he cannot do it no more. If he has anything he wants to do, anything like that, he must come up and talk to these six and state what he has got, what is his reasons before he is able to carry out. They never had that before." In case of a tie vote, a boss would be invited to sit in and break the tie.

The commission of bosses, varying in number from seven to twelve, acts as legislature and supreme court for the entire society. It rules on all matters concerning more than one family and negotiates with all non-Cosa Nostra syndicates. No outsider ever attends commission meetings.

Beneath the commission is the council of six. This body is purely judicial in function, ruling only on matters of direct concern to the New York area families.

Beneath the council of six is the individual family, headed by a boss, who is assisted by an underboss, and a consigliere. The family is divided into regimes headed by capos.

Within each family there is a body called the administration, consisting of the consigliere and the capos, which acts as a judicial court for minor disputes and advises the boss on important decisions. Unlike the commission or the council of six, however, its rulings are not final, and a boss can refuse its advice. The existence of this body was not publicly known until June 10, 1969, when the FBI released transcripts taken during four years of electronic surveillance of the office of Sam DeCalvacante, boss of the New Jersey family.

Since 1931 there have been no structural changes in Cosa Nostra with the exception of an experiment, begun that same year under Luciano, known to outsiders as Murder Incorporated.* Its function was to commit certain murders which Cosa Nostra did not want to handle directly. It was composed of professional killers, some Italians, some Irish, mostly Jewish, who were kept on a regular payroll and paid from $100 to $250 a week. Murder Incorporated did not begin as a specialized

---

*The name was invented in 1940 by the New York journalist Harry Feeney.

THE MAKING OF THE SYNDICATE   ○   165

unit. Originally the group was a run-of-the-mill Brooklyn gang put together in 1927 by Lepke Buchalter. During the closing years of the twenties, however, it was repeatedly pressed into service by Luciano, acting on the recommendation of a Brooklyn Cosa Nostra soldier named Albert Anastasia. The arrangement was formalized in 1931, and Luciano used Murder Incorporated for many of his Purge Day executions. From 1931 to 1940, when it was broken up by the arrest of its leaders, the group committed an estimated one thousand murders on contract to Cosa Nostra.

In the year of its breakup, a well-informed article was written by Meyer Berger for *Life* magazine on the subject of Murder Incorporated and "The Combination." (The name Cosa Nostra was unknown to Berger.) Berger pointed out that the members of Murder Incorporated could work for no organization other than The Combination and could do no free-lance operations for fear of jeopardizing their value as hit men. This was the reason they were kept on regular payroll. Murder Incorporated, Berger went on, had six national branches. "Six men dominated the branch in New York's metropolitan area. Six more men run a Chicago branch. In Los Angeles, the management is mostly made up of expatriate New Yorkers. It has personnel on call in Newark, Jersey City, Chicago, St. Louis and Florida."

Berger identified the employer of Murder Incorporated as "the Combination, formed about nine years ago [that is, 1931] when the head men from different cities met and agreed to adopt new rules for the conduct of murder under a loosely formed national syndicate. Murder is not the Combination's business. It does no murder for outsiders and no killing for a fee. Indeed, its revised rules sharply restrict the uses of homicide to business needs and have probably reduced rather than increased the total number of U.S. murders committed annually.

"The new handbook sternly forbids murder for personal or romantic reasons, or even for revenge. Executive heads of the Combination debate each murder before causing it to occur, much as a Wall Street syndicate might discuss a maneuver in the stock market."

Berger's analysis was correct. Murder Incorporated was an

execution squad used to insulate Cosa Nostra members from the risks of killing. The modus operandi was that the killers were given the name of the victim and usually a briefing on his habits and a place where he was most likely to be found. Once the murder was done, the killers vanished and the police were left without clues. The usual avenue to solution—motive—was absent, and the Murder Incorporated client always had an ironclad alibi. The only connection between the clients and the killers was the liaison between Cosa Nostra and Murder Incorporated, Albert Anastasia.

This arrangement broke down with the arrest of a Murder Incorporated killer, Abe Reles, in 1940. Faced with an absolutely certain murder conviction, he talked enough to implicate six other Murder Incorporated shooters, and each of them told what he knew to escape the electric chair. Their confessions resulted in a number of convictions by the Brooklyn prosecutor, Assistant District Attorney Burton Turkus. Several electrocutions eventually took place, including that of gang leader Lepke Buchalter.

When the investigation turned toward Anastasia, Turkus's boss, District Attorney Bill O'Dwyer, suddenly seemed to lose interest in pursuing the case further. Prosecutor Turkus, however, would not be deterred. With an ace witness like Abe Reles, he was confident of convicting Anastasia. He scheduled Reles to testify before the Brooklyn grand jury on how Anastasia arranged for the payroll, expenses, and political protection of Murder Incorporated.

Two days before Reles was to testify, he plunged to his death from a window of the hotel where he was being held for safekeeping. Whether he was pushed or fell has never been resolved. At the moment of his death, seven policemen were standing guard or sleeping in Reles's three-room hotel suite. The underworld, including Valachi, has long maintained that one or more of the police guards threw Reles out the window in return for a large Cosa Nostra bounty. Whatever the explanation, Reles's death ended Turkus's hopes of prosecuting Anastasia.

Luciano had set up the contract between Cosa Nostra and

Murder Incorporated, but he was not around to witness its dissolution. In 1936, Prosecutor Thomas Dewey tried him for running a prostitution syndicate. Luciano was convicted and sentenced to thirty to fifty years. Although he was paroled only ten years later for his wartime "services" (see p. 62), Luciano never again held direct control of Cosa Nostra.

Between 1948 and 1952, Luciano established short-term residences in Mexico, Cuba, and Venezuela, in repeated attempts to regain control by use of couriers. Each time, however, extraordinary American diplomatic pressure forced him back to the Mediterranean region—Italy, France, and Monte Carlo—where he spent the last ten years of his life. There he bought night clubs and established the narcotics syndicate now operating between Sicily and the United States. He died of a heart attack in Italy in 1962.

From 1937 to 1948 the acting boss of the Luciano family was the consigliere, Frank Costello. Luciano's underboss, Vito Genovese, was himself absent from the country, having fled to Naples in 1937 to avoid a murder indictment. Genovese returned to the United States under arrest in 1946. The main witness against him in the murder case was killed shortly after Genovese's return, on Genovese's orders. Charges were dropped and Genovese became boss of the Luciano family, Valachi's family, in 1949.

Following the dissolution of Murder Incorporated, Cosa Nostra relied on its own personnel to carry out executions. One of the most efficient of the death specialists was Joe Valachi. From 1930 until his final arrest in 1959, he was directly involved in at least thirty-three killings, averaging more than one per year. In that time, however, he was never picked up as a suspect in any of the murders.

It was this expertise that kept Valachi alive, because the bosses were not pleased with his general attitude. From the moment he joined the Luciano family, Valachi complained. He and his lieutenant, Tony Bender Strollo, got along like a knee in the groin. Valachi protested that only the higher-ups made money in Cosa Nostra. "Lieutenants automatically make money, through different soldiers who give them different propositions. They have a hundred percent edge over the soldier. The soldier has to do it himself, whereas the lieutenant, they bring it to him."

Valachi carried his resentment so far that he spurned normal services of Cosa Nostra, including lawyers, bondsmen, and similar aid. "I got my own bondsmen, my own lawyers for 35 years." Nevertheless, every month from 1931 to 1959 he paid his monthly family dues of twenty-five dollars.

Valachi's favorite racket was usury. At any given time, he had an average of forty thousand dollars out on loan. Over a year, the profit on this forty thousand dollars capital amounted to thirty-two thousand dollars, which he would plow into new enterprises or into more usury. He threatened deadbeats but never beat them up. It didn't make good business. "You put a guy in the hospital and how's he going to work to pay you back?" His customers were mostly bookies, but included "all occupations—even lawyers," he told the Senate subcommittee counsel with a grin. Occasionally Bender and other lieutenants would try to cut in on Valachi's profits, but he was always quick to carry such disputes to a Cosa Nostra court. Usually the mere threat of such action made the lieutenant back off.

Valachi also ventured into legitimate businesses, and there he did benefit from Cosa Nostra membership. "I had a dress shop, a negligee and dress contract, on Prospect Avenue. I never belonged to any union. If I got in trouble, any union organizer came around, all I had to do was call up Johnny Dio [Dioguardi] or Tommy Dio and all my troubles were straightened out." Valachi was in the dress business twelve years. He got in by interceding in a strike. "I ran them [the union] out and got things fixed up with the Dios. My partner was a legitimate guy. I made him do everything. [In return], I got him business and kept the union straight."

After the war, Valachi bought the Lido Restaurant and began selling narcotics. In 1948 his family's acting boss, Frank Costello, passed a law against narcotics activity, a law that was enforced by Vito Genovese when he became boss a year later. Nevertheless, the Lido Restaurant continued to be known as a place of sale. Federal narcotics agents became interested in the restaurant, and, in 1952, convinced Valachi to turn informer. He gave them information from time to time, and informed his boss Genovese that he was doing so. Genovese allowed him to continue on the theory that Valachi would get more information from the narcotics bureau than he would give.

In 1955 Valachi was convicted of selling narcotics but served only a short term, thanks to his friends in the bureau. In 1959, however, he was convicted again and given fifteen years. In the same year, Genovese, who had always supported Costello's antinarcotics trade position, was himself convicted on a narcotics charge. His conviction was based on fraudulent testimony which was apparently manufactured by the federal government in a deliberate frame-up. Both Valachi and Genovese were sent to the federal prison in Atlanta, where Genovese used his influence to become Valachi's cellmate. While sharing the cell, Genovese decided that Valachi, a known narcotics informer, had been involved in the frame-up. In the cell one afternoon, Genovese gave Valachi the "kiss of death," a traditional marking of the victim which was first publicly reported in the Viterbo, Italy, trial of Camorra leaders in 1911. From then on, Valachi knew he was marked. He refused to eat, for fear of poison, and kept to himself in the exercise yard.

On June 22, 1962, a group of prisoners surrounded Valachi. Fearing he had been ambushed by Genovese's men, Valachi picked up a pipe and killed a man he believed to be Joe Di Palermo, a Cosa Nostra soldier. Guards intervened and Valachi was rushed to solitary confinement. While in that cell he learned he had killed the wrong man. The dead prisoner was one John Joseph Saupp, who bore a remarkable physical and facial resemblance to Di Palermo.

Shamed by his mistake (Valachi was after all a professional) he was now even more fearful for his life. If Genovese somehow failed to get him, then he most certainly would be tried, possibly executed, for killing Saupp. At this point federal agents decided to approach Valachi again. After a series of conferences, he agreed to answer any and all questions about Cosa Nostra. He would open up the Genovese family like a diary, and tell what he knew about other operations of the society. But Valachi's value as a witness went beyond his willingness to talk. He had an absolutely amazing memory for detail and could recall with precision events that had happened thirty-five years earlier. A corollary to that was a quality even rarer in informers —whenever he didn't know an answer, Valachi said so. He didn't hedge, theorize, or fabricate. He either knew or didn't know, and what he knew he remembered. Attorney General Robert Kennedy called him "the biggest intelligence breakthrough in organized crime yet in the United States."

During September and October 1963, Valachi appeared for six days before a national television audience as he answered questions put to him by the McClellan subcommittee. Following that appearance, he testified secretly before New York grand juries. He even signed a book contract with writer Peter Maas.

In the meantime, the Kennedy Justice Department made arrangements to transfer Valachi to a Pacific island where he could live out the rest of his life in peace. Department lawyers made several exploratory trips and picked out an atoll, one of the Caroline Islands, which as a United Nations mandate group was under United States supervision. The atoll consisted of one main island and several smaller ones, averaging five acres per island. On the main island was a jail and a small American colony. The plan was to transfer Valachi from his American prison to the jail and then from the jail to parole him to one of the smaller islets, where he would have a cottage and the run of the place.

The promise was canceled upon orders from the Lyndon Johnson White House. President Johnson's reasons seem to have been entirely political. Valachi's testimony had aroused the hostility of Italian-American defamation groups and, in turn, a variety of senators and congressmen, particularly those from the New York area. The most outspoken was Brooklyn congressman John Rooney, head of the appropriations committee, who spent a couple of years screaming on the House floor, and privately to the Justice Department, about "all the cost in maintaining this bum."

Valachi spent the last seven years of his life being transfered from prison to prison. His final move was to La Tuna, near El Paso, Texas. La Tuna is a traditional place for hiding informants, because its convict population is almost entirely Mexican, men unconnected with U.S. organized crime groups. There, in 1973, he died.

LOUISIANA IN THE TWENTIETH CENTURY

During Joe Valachi's career, Cosa Nostra became one of the world's most profitable corporations. Techniques developed by U.S. government agencies in the 1960s made it possible to estimate Cosa Nostra's revenues and assets.* In 1969, in the first reasonably accurate estimate made, the Department of Justice announced Cosa Nostra netted a minimum gross of $22 billion from gambling, loansharking, narcotics, stock swindles, and contrived bankruptcies.

An Internal Revenue Service study stated that "in one midwestern city, racketeers had control of or large interests in

---

*The estimates are made from extrapolations of captured financial records, income tax forms, surveillance of gambling operations, and electronic interception of conversations.

eighty-nine businesses having total assets of more than $800 million and annual receipts of more than $900 million. Among those businesses were savings and loan associations, auto dealerships, breweries, construction companies, insurance agencies, and food and liquor distributorships."

The Pennsylvania Crime Commission in the same period compiled a list of more than 375 Pennsylvania businesses controlled partially or wholly by members of crime families. The late J. Edgar Hoover testified before a congressional subcommittee that "ultimate control" of the Port of New York was in the hands of Cosa Nostra. President Richard Nixon, in a speech to the Congress on April 23, 1969, reported that Cosa Nostra had estimated annual revenues of $20 billion at minimum and $50 billion at maximum. America's largest corporation, General Motors, reported gross revenues that year of $24.3 billion, followed by Standard Oil of New Jersey, $14.9 billion; Ford, $14.75 billion, and Sears, $8.86 billion.

In 1972 the Internal Revenue Service released statistics compiled from the tax returns filed by approximately two thousand Cosa Nostra members. The report stated that 85 percent of the members were engaged in one or more legitimate businesses and that collectively they controlled 1,188 separate, distinct, and ostensibly legitimate corporations. The most popular categories were restaurants, bars, hotels, and motels; followed by real estate and insurance corporations, casinos and race tracks, banks and stock brokerages, construction firms, manufacturing firms, and trucking and transportation companies. Control of most of these businesses was gained by extortion. A typical scenario would show a businessman applying to Cosa Nostra for a loan. If he defaulted or was late on a payment, he would be informed that henceforward he would have a silent and controlling partner—Cosa Nostra.

The success of Cosa Nostra as a profit-making corporation was noted at a 1972 California state university seminar on business. The speaker observed that Cosa Nostra, which emphasizes individual initiative, and is divided into only four levels of hierarchy, was not as crippled by bureaucratic inertia as other types of corporations. He recommended that its management techniques, but not, one assumes, its acquisition methods, be studied by businessmen.

Cosa Nostra's profits are distributed among an estimated five thousand members* and are shared with an unknown number of associates, such as financial technician Meyer Lansky, who is a highly paid partner but not a sworn member. Nevertheless, many members whose status is well below the boss level have made fortunes. Joe Valachi was a millionaire, and he testified that he personally knew forty to fifty millionaire members in the Genovese family alone.

One of the richest members is Carlos Marcello, boss of the Louisiana family, whose personal assets are estimated at $60 million. The Louisiana family, dating back to 1869, is the oldest and least harassed in the nation. It has been protected by both geographical isolation and Cosa Nostra tradition. Joe Valachi, for instance, was asked about Louisiana in 1964 interrogations.

"Louisiana?" he replied. "I don't know a thing except that they don't want visitors. Once I was going to go see Mardi Gras and I checked it out with Vito, which I was supposed to do if I took a trip. He said, 'Don't go.' No explanation, just 'Don't go.' They didn't want anybody there. And I was told if I ever had to go to Louisiana, Genovese would call ahead and get permission. Genovese himself had to get permission. It was an absolute rule."

At the turn of the century, the Louisiana family adopted a structure unique among American brotherhood families. It created rural based satellite organizations, country Mafias such as existed in Sicily. Charles Matranga's 1890s Mafiosi invested their profits in fishing boats, farms, and other agricultural enterprises. When possible they themselves moved away from the city and opened up small monopolies in the areas around New Orleans that were heavily populated by immigrant Italian farmers. Although only a fraction of the Italian population had any sinister connection with the society, almost every community

---

*The membership figure is a Justice Department estimate. A full list of Cosa Nostra's members has never been compiled. The closest to a comprehensive listing is a 1971 FBI memo that lists 1,086 known members and 401 suspected members. The IRS tax survey cited "2,000 organized crime figures" but the figure included nonmember associates.

within a two-hundred-mile radius of New Orleans had its resident Mafioso. As in Sicily, there was a strawberry Mafia, an orange Mafia, a vegetable Mafia, each of which levied tariffs on Italians growing and selling these products. At the same time, the country Mafias kept their hands in with an occasional bank robbery or truck hijacking. At all times they were under the control of the New Orleans family, which had guns and prestige to back its authority. These country Mafias were eventually destroyed by a prosecutor in Amite, Louisiana.

Amite is in the parish of Tangipahoa, a land of cool hills, pine forests, and strawberry farms north of New Orleans. It had a fundamental, frontier morality and was not the type of place one expected to find a Mafia. Or so the town thought. In 1923 the Amite bank was robbed and a guard killed.

A posse was formed and almost immediately rounded up six young Sicilian immigrants. Italians of the community came forward and identified them as members of a local Mafia that, it was revealed, had been secretly extorting strawberry farmers for twenty years. All six were charged with murder by the district attorney, Matt Allen. Immediately after the arrest, Allen was beleaguered with bribe offers from local Mafiosi, first from the Amite farms, then from New Orleans. When they failed, the government of Italy introduced itself and demanded custody of the "Italian citizens over whom the parish government" and the United States "has no jurisdiction." District Attorney Allen, described by a descendant as a "tough, craggy-faced old Anglo-Saxon bastard," stood his ground. The bribes and diplomacy then changed to threats against Allen and his family. He bowed his neck, obtained convictions, and ordered six scaffolds to be set up in a row. All six men were hung at once, panoramically.

The hangings were followed by two to three years of vigilante action. By 1927 the country Mafias had vanished as organizations and most of the members had retreated to New Orleans, where Charles Matranga was boss. Matranga, who had survived the New Orleans lynchings of 1891, continued as boss until 1922. In that year he voluntarily retired and named as successor his young protégé, Sylvestro ("Sam") Carolla.

Sam Carolla and his Sicilian parents had arrived in New

Orleans in 1904, when Sam was eight years old. By 1918, at age twenty-two, Sam had earned the nickname "Silver," and was the French Market supervisor for Charles Matranga. The French Market was the symbol of the New Orleans Mafia's power and wealth, and Matranga's office was just across the street. Carolla's duties were to make collections and convey orders from the boss. With the advent of Prohibition, however, the old boss, Matranga, decided not to compete in the new game. He named Carolla his successor; one of Carolla's first acts for the family was to buy a fleet of sea-going trawlers for rum running. In 1923 Carolla was convicted of stealing eighty-six drums of alcohol and was sentenced to two years in the federal prison at Atlanta. Sam told the newspapers that the charge was obviously a frame. He didn't need to steal any piddling eighty-six drums, he was too big for that. When the newspapers asked how big he was, he revealed that he averaged a $12,000-a-week profit from the fleet—$600,000 a year.

The conviction seems to have been engineered by the bootleg king of New Orleans, William Bailey, as the easiest method of removing a young rival. But Sam was back on the street again in 1925 and began to put together a regional operation. By early 1929 he controlled the majority of liquor smuggling in the South and sold legitimate, imported booze to syndicates in Kansas City, St. Louis, Detroit, and (in rare instances when their regular sources dried up) to Washington and Baltimore. One man he refused to sell to was Al Capone, who at the time was competing with the Chicago Mafia boss Joey Aiello. In 1929, just prior to the meeting in Atlantic City that established national bootlegging territories, Capone came to New Orleans. What happened on that visit testifies to the independence of the Louisiana family and its truculence toward uninvited visitors.

Capone had notified Carolla that he was coming down for a talk, and when the Chicago train pulled in at Union Station Sam was on hand. Capone and his bodyguards stepped off and walked toward Sam with big smiles. Then, from behind posts, out stepped three uniformed policemen. Carolla waited until Capone reached him, hand outstretched. Then Sam, his hands behind his back, spoke only one sentence. "You're not welcome." At that point, the policemen stepped forward, grabbed the bodyguards, and broke their fingers. Capone wheeled without a word and returned to the train.

For the remainder of 1929 and all of 1930, Carolla concentrated on eliminating his only competitor in organized crime, the gang of William Bailey. The war between them made New Orleans look like movies of Chicago. There were ambushes from doorways, machine guns from speeding black sedans, and classy funerals. Bailey's men were mowed down like wheat in the field.

A few days before Christmas 1930, Sam trapped Bailey. As the bootleg boss was leaving his house, two cars roared up and braked to a tire-squealing halt. Bailey scrambled back to his front door but found it locked. As he frantically dug for his keys, Silver Sam and his men stepped out of their cars. Sam himself carried the ritual weapon, a sawed-off shotgun, and walked almost leisurely over to Bailey, still fumbling for his keys. Carolla turned Bailey around and blew his chest half apart.

Bailey didn't die until four days later. When asked who had shot him, he gave the same answer as had many of his men earlier that year: "Sam Carolla and his gang." Carolla, a soldier named Joe Madonia, and a Kansas City import, Sam Rubde, were arrested but never prosecuted. Confronted with Bailey's accusations, Carolla simply claimed he had been home in bed.

Shortly before that killing, Carolla himself had been caught in an ambush. A Ford coupe had rammed his chocolate-colored Buick roadster on Esplanade Avenue and forced it to the curb. Sam and one of his capos, Frank Tedaro, jumped out and shot the man, who they figured was a Bailey gunman. He wasn't. He was a federal narcotics agent named Cecil Moore who was trying to serve an arrest warrant on Carolla. Moore survived the shooting, and Carolla and Tedaro were indicted.

The trial was held early in 1931. Carolla was thoroughly protected by the New Orleans police force.

Although agent Moore was not sufficiently recovered to testify at the trial, he made an affidavit from his hospital bed identifying Carolla and Tedaro as the shooters. The statement was corroborated by eyewitnesses who saw the ramming and saw the defendants do the shooting. The prosecution's case seemed to be a strong one. But when the defense got its turn, it surprised everyone with a parade of policemen who testified that Carolla and Tedaro could not have shot agent Moore because they were elsewhere at the time—in New York.

Typical testimony was given by officers Charles Poretto and J. T. Ford. Asked if they knew why agent Moore would falsely identify the defendants as his attackers, both policemen had an answer. They said Moore hated Carolla and was determined to frame him. Poretto's testimony was especially energetic, for he was the city policeman who had interviewed Moore at the hospital.

The prosecution: "Did he identify his assailants?"

Officer Poretto: "Yes, sir. He identified two other men, not the defendants. He's changed his story."

"Do you have your notes of that interview?"

"No, sir."

The police effort went on. Another officer testified he had been sent to New York to check out the defendants' alibis. He then produced records of a New York hotel showing that the defendants had been registered in that city on the day of the shooting.

The jury didn't believe any of it and convicted Carolla and Tedaro. The judge, however, imposed extremely light sentences for the shooting of a federal agent: two years in Atlanta. Carolla entered prison in 1932 and left late in 1934, but in that relatively short period of time two power hungry competitors joined forces to make a move on the New Orleans family.

The competitors were Senator Huey Long and Frank Costello, consigliere and later acting boss of the Luciano family. Beginning in 1933 and continuing into early 1934, Costello and Long met perhaps a dozen times in the New Yorker Hotel. In the early thirties Huey Long was one of the hottest political properties in the nation. He planned to run against President Roosevelt in the 1936 election, and was even writing a book in his spare moments, titled *My First Days in the White*

House.* To finance his ambition, Long needed money. Costello, in turn, had money and needed a place for his thousands of slot machines that had been ordered out of town by mayor-elect Fiorello La Guardia. Eventually they made a deal. In return for 10 percent of the take, Long would allow Costello to have a slot machine monopoly in Louisiana. Details were to be left to Costello.

Costello immediately began moving down his machines and men. Simultaneously he opened negotiations with Carolla, first by messages and visitors to the Atlanta prison and, when Carolla was released, face to face. Neither man was in a dominant position. Silver Sam's political power rested with the New Orleans city administration, the only anti-Long enclave in the state. It had no power beyond the boundaries of New Orleans. On his side, Costello had Long's alliance, but he needed New Orleans, Carolla's stronghold, to make big profits on his slot machines. Furthermore, Costello didn't want to use guns, for fear of touching off a national war that would disrupt the fledgling Cosa Nostra organization. Both sides seemed aware that the Detroit and Kansas City families, allied to New Orleans by tradition and marriage, would side with Carolla in the dispute. Other families might join them, for New Orleans had territorial "justice" on its side.

A compromise was reached. Carolla would become boss of all Louisiana activities, a greater territory than he had had before, and would join in the Huey Long alliance, a political protection he hadn't had before. Frank Costello would operate the slot machines as a franchise in Louisiana. New York and Louisiana men would share key positions where they could watch each other. It also appears that Costello arranged to give part of the action to Meyer Lansky and some out-of-work members of the Chicago syndicate. Some of their men moved into the state at this time and became members of the slot machine syndicate.

For four years Silver Sam enjoyed the fruits of this compromise. Then, in 1938, he was again convicted by the federal

---

*Published in 1935.

government, this time for narcotics trafficking, and spent two more years in Atlanta. In 1940 he was officially informed that he would be deported. The war interrupted this plan, but the proceedings were resumed in 1945. At that point, Louisiana's most powerful congressman, Jimmy Morrison, interceded on Sam's behalf with a series of private bills to give Carolla American citizenship and thereby prevent deportation. Such special-privilege bills almost always pass, but Morrison's bills were defeated by Drew Pearson, who repeatedly used his column to expose Morrison's scheme. Morrison then tried to intercede with the Immigration Service but was again intercepted by Pearson.

Finally, in April 1947, the deportation proceedings began. Congressman Morrison vouched for Carolla's good character and wrote a letter saying Sam was an innocent and wronged man. Numerous politicians and policemen came forth to testify to Silver's "excellent character and reputation." In spite of the testimonials, Sam was deported to Sicily on April 30, 1947.

He stayed less than a year. In 1948 he was openly operating out of Acapulco, Mexico, as liaison between the United States crime families and Lucky Luciano. In 1949 he sneaked back into the United States, but was found and redeported a year later. Finally he settled in Sicily. He bought a villa on the outskirts of Palermo and took his place as ranking member of the Cosa Nostra in exile headed by Luciano. In 1970, an old man, he returned to New Orleans illegally and died there two years later.

His legacy was the Costello slot machine arrangement, which brought Louisiana into the mainstream of national organized crime. It also indirectly provided the boss who would take Carolla's place.

In 1934 Frank Tedaro, a Carolla capo, assigned a new soldier to an administrative job in the slot machine operation. The new man was Carlos Marcello, just released from Angola State Prison, where he served four years for talking two teen-agers into robbing a grocery store for him. When he joined Tedaro at the age of twenty-four, he had never before been involved with the Mafia or any other organized gang. Thirty years later he would be the Cosa Nostra boss of Louisiana.

Marcello's real name was Calogero Minacore. He arrived in New Orleans in 1910 as an infant in the arms of his parents. The Minacores were Italian citizens who had emigrated from Sicily to Tunisia, then under French government. There Carlos was born, and the circumstances of his birth—the son of Italian citizens, born on French-Tunisian soil—would later complicate his deportation status and impel the federal government to the extreme of kidnapping him.

His father opened a wine and dry goods store in New Orleans, and the family was doing moderately well. Then, when Carlos was about three, his father shot and killed a burglar who had broken into the store. Afraid that he would be unfairly tried, Carlos's father packed up their belongings and moved his family across the river in the middle of the night. They started over in another part of the city and took the name "Marcella," later masculinized to "Marcello."

The first entry on Carlos's police record was made in 1929, when he recruited three young men to execute a bank holdup he had planned. His father's influence obtained his release, but only six weeks later he arranged the grocery store heist, and his family's influence could not save him from four years in state prison. From there he joined up with Tedaro and married the capo's daughter in 1935. Then came the war, and Marcello engaged mostly in black-market activities. During the war years, however, he was also the principal suspect in several murders.

The most interesting case was the murder of Constantine Masotto, a New York Mafioso who had been sentenced to death by the New York family for robbing his own sister. He fled to New Orleans and hid out under an assumed name, but in 1944, after a year-long national search, he was located. According to a later FBI report Masotto died in the kitchen of a country restaurant, lashed to a chair and beaten with rubber hoses by Marcello and another man. Masotto's lime-encrusted skeleton was found several months later in a swamp adjacent to the restaurant. Although brought in for questioning in that killing and several others, Marcello was never charged.

Marcello's step up from talented soldier to man of authority probably came in 1947. In that year Frank Costello, Meyer

Lansky, and Sam Carolla met several times in New Orleans to discuss expansion of the Louisiana operations. One project they agreed on was to create a national communications center in New Orleans to transmit financial information. Such a clearing-house would, for instance, make it possible for the bookmaking syndicate in New York to know instantly if a horse, ball team, or what have you was being heavily wagered elsewhere in the nation. Any break in the betting patterns would indicate a fix or an attempt to swindle the syndicate.

The second project was to open and operate plush Las Vegas-style casinos in the New Orleans area. Costello and Carolla* picked two men to supervise these projects. Chosen to represent New York interests was Frank Coppola, a capo in the Luciano-Costello family. Representing the Louisiana family was Carlos Marcello. Shortly after these meetings, Coppola was deported and Marcello became the supervisor for New York's interests as well.

The more ticklish of the two jobs was setting up the casinos. New Orleans had just elected a reform mayor, Chep Morrison, so the city proper was ruled out. Likelier sites were the neighboring parishes of Saint Bernard to the north and Jefferson to the south. When approached by Marcello, the sheriff, political figures, and business community of Saint Bernard welcomed the prospect of a new source of jobs and tourist money. In that parish the casinos opened promptly.

Jefferson, however, was the choicer of the two sites because its population was much larger and because it was the location of the New Orleans International Airport, where the tourists arrived. But here Marcello hit an obstacle, Sheriff Frank Clancy, an old-style political boss.

Sheriff Clancy had allowed the syndicate to place more than five thousand slot machines in his parish, but he balked at the idea of casinos. The reason was competition. Whereas the slot machines brought in new jobs and new money, the Mafia

---

*Although present at at least two of the meetings, Meyer Lansky did not have decision-making powers. He functioned only as financial advisor and safeguarded the investments of other Cosa Nostra families whom he represented.

casinos would compete directly with established, and illegal, gambling halls that were run by local Jefferson Parish families. These local people constituted a strong part of Clancy's political base, and he did not want to antagonize them. Furthermore, his experience with the slot machines had taught him that the Mafia's presence in the parish tended to erode his own power. He said no.

In the kind of maneuver that would become typical of him, Marcello sought a compromise. With the outgoing governor of Louisiana, Jimmie Davis, acting as arbitrator, Marcello and Sheriff Clancy agreed that the mob would open three casinos on the New Orleans side of the river. These casinos would not compete with the locally owned gambling halls on what was then the more populous western side of the river. Clancy would be given a share of the casino profits and the right to hire all personnel below the administrative level, which amounted to about five hundred jobs.* With that compromise, the Jefferson casinos opened and the profits poured in, amounting to a minimum of $600,000 net per year per casino. The most lavish of the casinos was the Beverly Club, which became nationally famous and featured such entertainers as Jimmy Durante and Zsa Zsa Gabor.

Within three years, however, Senator Estes Kefauver opened his subcommittee hearings in Louisiana and named Marcello, incorrectly, as the boss of the Louisiana Mafia. Sheriff Clancy reluctantly explained his role in the casinos, and al-

*Governor Davis's compensation, if any, is unknown. However, in the mid-1960s, the FBI came up with a possible theory. A dredging operation in New York's East River hauled in nearly one-hundred-thousand old 78-rpm phonograph records. The bureau heard about it and came for a look. All the recordings were songs of Jimmie Davis, who had been a country music singer prior to being governor, and most of them were copies of "You Are My Sunshine." Subsequent inquiry in the New York area developed the information that back in the forties Governor Davis had done a favor for Cosa Nostra and in return the mob-owned jukebox companies of America had bought the Davis recordings and placed them in tens of thousands of jukeboxes in bars and restaurants across the country. After about six months, however, the owners of these establishments, who shared in the jukebox profits, rebelled at Davis's rendition of "You Are My Sunshine." The mob took them out and, having no other use for them, dumped the records in the East River.

though Governor Davis was not pursued in the public questioning, his involvement was detailed in confidential staff memos. Despite all the publicity, which made Marcello's name prominent for the first time, the hearings produced no lasting results. The casinos continued to operate for more than ten years, until they were finally closed in 1964 by a reform sheriff.

There was, however, a sinister epilogue to the hearings. It was the murder in April 1955 of Frank Bourg. Mr. Bourg, aged sixty-four, was a bank teller of thirty years' experience with no criminal involvement of any kind. As he lay in the bed of his hospital room recovering from a heart attack, a stranger walked in, cleaved his skull with a hatchet, and walked out. It looked like a gang hit, but there was no motive. It now appears that the intended victim was not Bourg but Sheriff Frank Clancy, who testified at the Kefauver hearings. The night of the murder he occupied the room adjoining Frank Bourg's. The police report noted that "from the time Clancy has entered the hospital, he has had a guard outside of his door but the guard was removed —on the morning of the attack—by somebody representing themselves as the sheriff's wife." Three days after the murder, a nurse's aide who had seen the killer and given police a detailed description claimed she had no idea what the man looked like. As for Sheriff Clancy, he ceased giving information to federal agents.

The Kefauver subcommittee had been premature in tagging Carlos Marcello as "the Mafia boss of Louisiana." Sam Carolla's successor in 1950 was an obscure boss named Leoluca T.* He was an old-time Mafioso dating back to the pre-Prohibition Matranga days and had served as consigliere to both Matranga and Carolla. His only arrest was a minor bootlegging incident, and his name has only once been connected with mob activity, in a highly confidential U.S. Narcotics Bureau report compiled in 1951, in which he was listed as an "important figure in the southern narcotics syndicate."

Leoluca served as boss from 1950 until he died of natural

---

*Mr. T's last name has been omitted by the author.

causes in 1963, without any publicity whatsoever, without police surveillance, and without any outsiders having knowledge of his role. During his tenure he employed Carlos Marcello as a "buffer man," an informal position in Cosa Nostra which is similar, but inferior in rank, to the job of underboss. The buffer man insulates the boss and carries messages between him and the family. In many cases it is the buffer man, rather than the underboss, who represents the family in dealings with businessmen, other organized crime figures, and politicians. Because of this exposed role, he usually attracts a lot of public and police attention and consequently is too hot to succeed to the post of boss. But in Marcello's case an exception was made, and in the summer of 1963 he succeeded Leoluca as boss. In the meantime, however, he had to fight off a number of deportation attempts.

The first deportation proceedings began in 1956, and Marcello responded by sending a New Orleans lawyer to Rome with a bag of money. The lawyer spread the money around among key members of Parliament, averaging about ten thousand dollars a bribe. The result was that the Italian foreign ministry announced to the American government (which had not as yet made any inquiries about Marcello) that he was not recognized as an Italian citizen and would not be accepted by that country for deportation. The payments and unsolicited pronouncements continued for at least another three years.

The parliamentary bribes were not the only precaution taken by the Louisiana family. Italy was closed, but Tunisia or France might decide to accept him. If he were deported, they preferred to have him closer to New Orleans, so they decided to invent a citizenship for him in Guatemala. The Central American republic had several advantages. Less than a thousand miles from New Orleans, it was linked to that city by telephone, telegraph, and commercial air service. And in addition, the Central American coasts were routinely visited by Louisiana fishing fleets, which passed in and out of those waters with absolute informality. The Guatemala adventure which ensued ranks among the more bizarre Cosa Nostra tales.

The events began with the arrival in New Orleans of a sometime electrical engineer, adventurer, and ex-convict named Mr. Franks. In 1956 Mr. Franks was looking for action. He introduced himself around the New Orleans underworld and in the course of the circuit met Joseph Marcello, younger brother of Carlos. Nothing much came of this meeting, but in the same week Mr. Franks also met a man by the name of Quervada Narcissus, who was a buyer for the Guatemalan government. He and Franks hit it off well, and Franks was invited down to Guatemala as a possible investor. In Guatemala Franks met two cabinet ministers, the secretary of the interior and the attorney general. He returned to New Orleans with a valuable conclusion: the ministers could be bought.

Franks had no idea how this fact could be used, but in his con-man, bragging, way he sought out Joe Marcello and let it come out that he was on good terms with some cabinet members. A second meeting was held a week later. In the interim, Joe Marcello had come up with a brainstorm. He and Mr. Franks would make Carlos a Guatemalan citizen.

Franks was given a small amount of expense money and told to explore further. He returned to Guatemala and conveyed the citizenship proposition to the attorney general, Antonio Valladares. The minister, according to Franks's later testimony, kept his expression blank. He said it certainly could be done. All that was needed was a birth certificate. He even suggested the means of obtaining one. If Franks could locate a church and enter Marcello's birth date in the birth recordings book, that book could then be used as the basis for issuing a certificate, and no government records would have been forged.

Two months later an official car of the Guatemalan secretary of the interior was parked in front of an eighteenth-century church in the mountain village of San Juan Punula in the highlands of the Maya. The townspeople were excited because inside the church were an American, Mr. Franks, and the attorney general of Guatemala, Antonio Valladares. The two men, traveling in a chauffeured government car, had visited ten other village churches in the preceding weeks. In each they had looked at record books for the period 1909–1914, hoping to find a blank line where they could fill in the name Carlorgas Minacore Karrugia. Their search had ended in San Juan Punula, where they had found their vacant line at the bottom of a page.

It was not enough simply to enter Carlos's name and the date. The forgery would probably be challenged by U.S. agents and therefore had to be good enough to withstand scrutiny. The penmanship of the 1910 pastor had to be matched, as did the ink he had used. Valladares and Franks decided to hold a contest. All the literate Indians in the village area were rounded up and one by one taken inside the church where they were pledged to secrecy. They were then asked to imitate the 1910 penmanship. According to Franks's later testimony, the man who succeeded was the thirty-seventh Indian to try. With the forger chosen, they held another contest to duplicate the 1910 ink. This time they found a winner quickly, for the ink came from native plants and was still a local product. The forgery was done, and the date entered. The two Indians were paid a hundred dollars each; the church custodian was given two hundred fifty dollars.

Back in Guatemala City, the attorney general executed an affidavit of authenticity based on his own forgery. Using the fraudulent affidavit, the interior minister issued a certificate of citizenship for Carlos Marcello, along with a Guatemalan passport bearing Marcello's name and photograph.

Franks took these papers back to New Orleans. There, according to his testimony, he was handed $100,000 in cash by a Marcello man, which he couriered back to Valladares as payment for the citizenship. The fake papers, which had cost a small fortune, were then put aside. As it turned out, the papers were not used by Carlos Marcello, but would be used by the U.S. government.

On December 27, 1960, the attorney general designate, Robert Kennedy, announced that he was reviewing Justice Department files on men investigated by the Senate rackets committee, for which he had been chief counsel during the 1950s. From those files he selected two priority targets. Target one was Jimmy Hoffa, president of the international teamsters union. Target two was Carlos Marcello.

A few days after the inauguration, high officials of the Immigration Service came to Kennedy and said they could deport Marcello.

"Where?" asked Kennedy.

"Where do you want?" said the official, holding up two passports. "Guatemala or Okinawa?" Kennedy was told that Marcello had been granted citizenship by both countries. He did not ask the details of the citizenships, and did not know they were based on forgeries.*

Three months later, on April 4, 1961, Carlos Marcello, accompanied by his attorney, walked out of his $200,000 house in Jefferson Parish. They entered Marcello's limousine and drove into New Orleans. Following them, more or less in a line, were agents of three separate federal agencies—the FBI, the Internal Revenue Service, and the Alcohol and Tax Bureau, a small and little-publicized group which has had considerable success against organized crime. Each of these units had mounted its own independent twenty-four-hour surveillance of Marcello. They did not coordinate with one another.

One agency did not follow Marcello—the Immigration Service. They knew where he was going. They had summoned Marcello to discuss some technicality, and he was en route to the Immigration Service office. As he and his attorney walked out of the building after the meeting, they were approached by two immigration officers who identified themselves and arrested Marcello.

The lawyer went off to get a federal judge. Marcello was placed in a car and taken to the New Orleans International Airport where a U.S. Border Patrol aircraft, engines already warmed up, awaited him. Carlos was put aboard and told for the first time that he was being deported to Guatemala, "where you have citizenship."

Twelve hundred miles later the plane orbited over the mountains of Guatemala City and received clearance to land at

---

*The scene and dialogue were described by a member of the Kennedy staff. The source of the Okinawa passport remains a mystery, and neither the staff member nor investiations by the author have learned how the Immigration Servvice obtained an Okinawa document or how it was created.

the military airport. There Marcello was dumped, without luggage, without passport, and with very little cash. Although Robert Kennedy would subsequently accept the blame for this kidnapping, it had in fact been engineered without his knowledge by the Immigration Service, anxious to do a favor for the President's brother. Meanwhile, in New Orleans the agents of the FBI, IRS, and Alcohol and Tax Bureau were sending out frantic phone calls from the airport, trying to explain what they had seen.

Marcello was picked up at the airport by Colonel Antonio Batres, second in command of the Guatemalan air force, and taken to a secret hideaway. Batres kept Marcello twenty-four hours, during which time, either through Marcello or other sources, the air force learned the background of the citizenship. The colonel then turned Marcello over to civil authorities and sat back to watch developments. It was a time of great leftist unrest. If the government fell because of the Marcello bribes, the generals would have an excuse to ignore corrupt civil authority and open a military campaign against the left.

Under the watchful eye of the generals, Carlos was installed in a suite at the Biltmore Hotel. He made no protest, confident that the government had an even keener interest in getting him back to the United States than he did. His continued presence would almost certainly lead to inquiries that would unravel his involvement with the two cabinet ministers. It was an election year and a scandal was ardently desired by the generals on the right and by the socialists and Castroites on the left. The government sent urgent messages, official ones to the U.S. State Department and private ones to other officials, asking that Marcello be reclaimed. From all sides the answer was no—he was an alien without papers and could not enter the United States. The Immigration Service's present to Attorney General Valladares had turned into an international incident and threatened to bring down a government that only five years earlier the Central Intelligence Agency had preserved from a Communist coup.

Meanwhile, the central pawn in the chess match was organizing a staff. Marcello's brothers flew in with money and clothes.

A war council was held and they selected a Shreveport attorney, Mike Maroun, to come to Guatemala and remain there as Carlos's aide-de-camp. Marcello's wife and children were flown down and given rooms in the hotel. The government, anxious to keep Carlos quiet, assigned guards and a chauffeur to his entourage. They hoped the storm would blow over.

It didn't. The pressure mounted from right and left. The Guatemalan government informed Washington that it could not survive if it kept Marcello. Washington said he could not be returned. On April 26, three weeks after his arrival, the Guatemalan president ordered Marcello deported. On May 3 his wife and children returned to New Orleans. On May 4 the secret police took Carlos and his attorney, Maroun, to the airport.

The exit, heralded by newspaper headlines, television, and radio, was gloriously loud. There were motorcycles and a long parade of official cars with small flags flying from the fenders. Carlos was amused. "You'd of thought it was the President of the United States coming in instead of me going out. We got to the airport with sirens blowing." Once the airplane was aloft, however, the amusement ceased. He was flown to a little-used jungle field in El Salvador, where he and Maroun were told to get off. For about two hours, Marcello and his attorney wandered in the jungle until they found a small collection of shacks. Police were notified and soon afterward cars arrived. The Americans were gathered up and taken to the city of Santa Ana, where they were interrogated, told nothing by the police, and placed in cells. There they remained five days.

El Salvador did not have the peculiar political problems of Guatemala, but nevertheless had no intention of keeping an American gangster in its midst. On the morning of the sixth day, Carlos and Maroun were taken out of their cells and put onto a bus loaded with a platoon of soldiers. For six hours the bus strained and steamed along dirt roads climbing into the central mountains. Although Marcello did not realize it, the bus crossed the border into Honduras. Some twenty miles inside Honduras, on top of an unnamed mountain, the Americans were put off and the bus sped away, raising great clouds of red dust.

The two men looked after the departing bus long after it couldn't be seen, long after its motor couldn't be heard. Then they began walking. Daylight faded and they walked eight hours and seventeen miles before they reached a village. During this walk, Marcello, an overweight man who had spent his lifetime at sea-level altitude, fainted three times.

In the morning, Maroun bought food and hired *muchachos* to guide them to the nearest seaport or airport. He agreed to pay the guides the equivalent of two dollars per day. He would have paid more, but didn't want the Indians to think he was wealthy. The two Americans had other problems not shared by the usual highlands hiker. Both were wearing silk Shantung suits and, Maroun said later, "the thorns were ripping us apart." Their footwear was alligator shoes, inside of which each man had stuffed some three-thousand dollars in bills, making it almost impossible for them to walk.

They descended in altitude as they walked east to the sea and each hour was hotter and more humid than the last. The tough old Marcello, however, was improving with distance and lower elevation. They spent a night on the trail, another day on the trek. They entered foothills, beyond which lay the Honduras coast. It was there that they noticed a perceptible change in the attitude of the muchachos. The Indians kept whispering among themselves and gesturing toward the Americans. From the beginning Maroun and Marcello had feared that the Indians might get ideas about robbery and murder. Now they were certain.

In the descent from the mountains the trail had become increasingly clogged with jungle growth. As the muchachos walked in front, hacking lightly with their machetes to clear the path, Marcello and Maroun fell farther and farther behind. Finally, at a series of bends in the trail, they were out of sight of the Indians. Seizing their chance, the two dived down a slope, tumbling, rolling, and running, going half a mile into the cover of jungle. Shouts went up from the muchachos. The pair went on, stabbed by bayonet grass, falling on rocks, breathing in great gulps. Then they collapsed in the thick brush and burrowed in like small animals. Carlos, regaining his breath, whispered that his side hurt. He had broken two ribs in the downhill scramble.

They heard the Indians up above them, in close pursuit. The Americans grabbed up big stones in their hands, their only weapons. They could hear the machetes leveling the brush at a terrifying rate. "We could hear them slashing the grass looking for us," said Maroun. "We were scared to death." The swishing machetes came nearer and nearer. Then, about fifty yards from the Americans, the Indians gave up.

Carlos and Maroun spent the night in their burrow. At daybreak they found a trail and continued the descent. At nightfall they arrived in a coastal town* and rented a room. It was then they noticed their shoes. The rocks had worn through the soles and for some time they had been walking on fifty- and hundred-dollar bills, now all chewed through with large holes.

In the morning they bought baths, shaves, shoes, and clothes. Maroun made arrangements to fly out in a rickety old airplane so that he could return to the United States and make arrangements for Carlos's secret reentry. A few days later, Marcello boarded a Louisiana fishing boat and was taken to a dock near Morgan City. He was back home to stay.† But his troubles with the government were not over.

Five years later, in early 1966 the FBI assigned a member of its elite New York Hoodlum Squad, called within the bureau the Cosa Nostra Squad, to obtain intelligence on the Louisiana Cosa Nostra operation and, if legally possible, disrupt it. The agent assigned was Pat Collins, an Irish-American who spoke Sicilian and was one of the twenty or so top experts on Cosa Nostra activities in the country. Collins hit with devastating effect, crippling the Louisiana mob's gambling operations. Within six months Marcello offered ten thousand dollars to cer-

---

*In a discussion of these events with the author, attorney Maroun said he never did learn the name of the town. From his description, however, it appears to be Puerto Cortes on the Gulf of Honduras.
†In a 1972 deportation proceeding, Marcello testified he entered via commercial airline to Miami, where he passed through immigration and customs without being checked. Government investigation tended to corroborate this, but it is the author's opinion that the fishing boat route was used and once in the United States, Marcello, or someone else, passed through the Miami airport to establish a quasi-legal port of entry.

tain politicians in Texas, people in direct communication with the Lyndon Johnson White House, if they could get Collins transferred out of Louisiana. The attempt failed.

In the same summer, intelligence breakthroughs in Louisiana led to government raids on Cosa Nostra gambling operations in Oklahoma, Arkansas, Texas, Louisiana, and Mississippi. In September 1966, Carlos, who had been a boss only three years, was summoned to a commission trial in New York to answer for the series of costly raids. His answers were satisfactory and he was reconfirmed in his position. The happy settlement of the inquiry was celebrated at a dinner in La Stella Restaurant in Queens. Present were New York bosses Carlo Gambino, Thomas Eboli, Joe Colombo, Tampa boss Santo Trafficante, and Marcello. Also attending were Mike Miranda, consigliere of the Genovese family, and several capos and soldiers. The dinner was raided by police and the participants hauled in, with enormous publicity, as "material witnesses."

Released on fifty thousand dollars bail, Marcello flew back to New Orleans. He arrived at the airport shortly before midnight and was met by a huge reception committee of policemen, reporters, and television cameramen. Moving disdainfully through the crowd, he swept toward his waiting car. Suddenly, standing directly in his path, he saw his enemy, the FBI agent Pat Collins. Shouting "I am the boss here," Marcello launched a roundhouse right at Collins's jaw. It missed, flicking the agent's coat, but the next day Marcello was charged with assault on a federal agent. He was eventually tried in a federal court in Texas and convicted. He spent six months in the federal prison hospital at Springfield, Missouri, where he lost forty pounds. (Marcello later said the bed rest he got in the prison hospital, along with the weight loss, added at "least ten years to my life.") The significance of the trial turned out to be not the conviction but rather the effect that Marcello's presence, and the publicity resulting from it, had on some Texans. Entrepreneurs from the underworld and the business world sought out members of the Marcello entourage and asked them to set up new operations in Texas. Areas of the state that were previously unexplored by Cosa Nostra were now brought into the fold. A businessman in San Antonio borrowed twenty-five thousand dollars. Bookies in San Antonio and Laredo joined the syndicate. One of Houston's largest builders began a series of real estate negotiations with Marcello. The wealthy Louisiana Mafiosi, hounded in their home city, spread over Texas like Sooners in the land rush. They bought controlling shares in at least three banks, and their investments reached into towns as small as Denton.

All this was done with the approval and enthusiastic cooperation of Texas's only resident Cosa Nostra group, the small Civello family in Dallas. By November 1971, the penetration of the Louisiana family seemed profound. The state attorney general, Crawford Martin, announced that the syndicate had eight hundred bookmakers in the state, handling gross annual revenues of $700 million and a "profit for the Mafia of $94 million . . . Mafia activities in Texas now include auto theft, extortion, swindling, bribery, loan sharking and other financial ventures."

The *San Antonio Express and News* reported that a profitable enterprise in that area had been partially financed by a Louisiana capo. The *Houston Chronicle* reported the sudden presence of "Mafia-type operations" and described how a U.S. Senate investigator, William Gallinaro, was beaten in his San Antonio hotel room while working on "a Mafia-linked case." A *Chronicle* editorial posed the question: "Mafia is a word associated with New York, New Jersey and Louisiana. Mafia is not a word generally associated with Texas. Or is it?" That was the state of affairs as the Louisiana family closed out its first century of operations.

# BOOK FIVE
UNIONE CORSE

CONTEMPORARY OPERATIONS

In the second half of the twentieth century, the brotherhood entered new phases of growth. Geographical expansion was one kind of growth, as families appeared for the first time in Canada and Australia.

The new Canadian family was located in Montreal and was originally a regime under command of the Buffalo, New York, family. In 1972 the Montreal capo was given boss status by the Cosa Nostra commission. The McClellan subcommittee described the new boss as "head of the largest and most notorious narcotics syndicate on the North American continent. A supplier of major Mafia traffickers in the United States with direct French-Corsican sources of supply."

Three families appeared in Australia, two Calabrian and one Sicilian. The Calabrians are located in the eastern Australian states of New South Wales and Victoria and are headquartered in the state capitals of Sydney and Melbourne. The Sicilian family is located on the other side of the continent, in Perth, capital of the state of Western Australia. According to senior Australian officials, all three families entered the country in the 1930s. Their present stage of development is similar to that of American groups during Prohibition. They are mainly engaged in gambling services, extortions from the Italian community, and the control of certain vegetable monopolies. In 1964 the Sicilian family attempted to move in on the Calabrian family of Melbourne, and a year-long war ensued which involved numerous shootings and bombings.

Another kind of growth in the mid-twentieth century was a change in the function of the American Cosa Nostra. It began to roam further and further from traditional crime services and closer to legitimate business and finance. In accordance with its new interests, around the year 1950 Cosa Nostra invented a new position in its ranks. The position was called "plant," meaning a seed that is carefully buried and nurtured and not touched until it is mature and ready for harvest. Noncriminal "plants" are usually recruited in their youth and are deliberately kept clear of criminal activity so that someday they can take a high place in the business or political world. Their main asset is their anonymity.

An example of a plant is Anthony Scotto, American delegate to the International Labor Organization, an international association of labor unions. A resident of Englewood, New Jersey, he has a college education, is articulate, makes a good appearance, and has never been convicted of a crime. He is a country-club, board-of-directors type, and the sole complaint against him is that he may serve sinister masters. Through electronic surveillance and other means, the Justice Department compiled a considerable dossier on Scotto and officially listed him as a *capodecina* in the Carlo Gambino family. Despite the identification, Scotto was appointed as American delegate to the ILO by two presidents, Lyndon Johnson and Richard Nixon.

As a presidential appointee and an international representative of American labor he has political clout, and his name gets attention in the White House, among senators and congressmen, in unions, and in the business community. In addition, he is president of Local 1814, International Longshoremen's Association, a position of real commercial value. As president of the local he can provide jobs, which means he can influence any company doing business across the New York wharves. He can also provide intelligence on import and export shipments.

Scotto is not unique. Another plant was uncovered in the 1957 Apalachin, New York, raid of a Cosa Nostra bosses' meeting. Besides the bosses who attended, police seized John C. Montana, a prominent Buffalo, New York, businessman who had been named "Man of the Year" in that city. Investigation showed that he was a capo in the Maggadino family and had quietly been a member of Cosa Nostra since at least 1931. Valachi said he had met Montana at Cosa Nostra gatherings several times in the early years "but after that we stayed away from him and he said he didn't want to be seen with any of us other members."

Also in the late 1950s a plant was positioned in Las Vegas. The Moe Dalitz [non-Cosa Nostra] syndicate in Cleveland needed a man to function as an instant banker for the Dalitz-controlled casinos there. The man had to be utterly trustworthy and knowledgeable about organized crime, but at the same time have no police record and be absolutely unknown to Nevada authorities. The Dalitz syndicate lacked a nominee, but the Cleveland Cosa Nostra family offered the services of one of its members, a plant.

The plant moved to Las Vegas, where he openly operated as a heavy construction contractor and secretly operated as Dalitz's instant banker. As banker his job was to maintain a cache of nearly $1 million cash, money that he had immediate access to. If a mob casino ran out of cash after normal banking hours, say at two o'clock in the morning, he provided it. This particular plant was still operating in Las Vegas, successfully and anonymously, as of 1970.

The phenomenon of plants, which began only about twenty-five years ago, is predicated on stability and longevity, and indicates the Cosa Nostra leadership's belief in its own future. It takes fifteen to twenty years of protection and financial subsidy to bring a youth from college to a position of value in the legitimate world. These new Cosa Nostra members, men engaged in legitimate activities but bound by the society's disciplines, are characteristic of Cosa Nostra's overall trend toward disengagement from overt crime. Examples of the disengagement have occurred in the cities of Buffalo and Detroit. For decades those cities had been Cosa Nostra strongholds. But in the past twenty years, the local Cosa Nostra families have lost their underworld dominance to rival organized crime groups.

In both cities, Cosa Nostra had at one time derived the bulk of its revenue, prestige, and political power from its control of illegal services, mostly gambling and narcotics. But beginning around 1950 three long-term changes in the nature of the cities began to accelerate.

The first of these was the sharp incline of Negro population. The second, corollary to the first, was a rise in hostility toward white management. (This change was met temporarily, as it had been in Harlem, by dealing through black employees.) The third phenomenon was the assimilation of the families' bosses and capos by the American middle class. This last factor was the most destructive of the three.

The bosses became increasingly charmed by the profits and pleasant life of legitimate business. They plowed their immense capital into restaurants, banks, and real estate, and became so preoccupied with these new risk-free sources of wealth that they began to ignore their family duties. The soldiers, left on their own, began to drift. Some left organized crime altogether. A few began satellite organizations in other cities, such as Erie, Pennsylvania.

Concurrent with this disintegration, the families were being muscled out of their monopolies on gambling and narcotics, to be replaced by blacks, and in certain instances by Lebanese. This pattern of abandonment and replacement is being repeated in several other cities such as Philadelphia, where the boss Angelo Bruno has sent up signals that he'd like to retire and take up a life in the business world.

CONTEMPORARY OPERATIONS

Cosa Nostra as a national organization seems to be losing its enthusiasm for illegal services. And while gambling remains the financial rock on which the society stands, there is no indication that it is expanding its gambling operations in the United States. Nor is there evidence of expansion in labor racketeering. The policy instead is simply to maintain its dominant position in the old rackets while concentrating its expansion on a new area—the world of finance, which the bosses are entering into with all the zest they once showed for bootlegging. Penetration into legitimate business, bank manipulation, and stock swindles is the wave of the future.

An example of Cosa Nostra penetration is Castro Convertibles, one of the nation's largest furniture makers. In the 1960s, the management of the firm was approached by Ettore Zappi, identified by the McClellan subcommittee as a capodecina in the Carlo Gambino family, who asked to be employed in a minor executive position. He obtained the post and shortly afterward proposed to management that a separate corporation be established to be the exclusive producer of mattresses for Castro. He, Zappi, would be president of the new corporation.

The proposition had several business advantages for Castro. As the sole customer of the Zappi company, Castro would be in a position to dictate matters of price and production, without having to manufacture its own mattresses or pay competitive prices. But the contract that was finally signed was written so tightly that Zappi turned out to have the greater advantage. Castro had to depend *entirely* on Zappi for its mattresses, which is to say for its existence.

And with that hold, the Gambino family, through Zappi, began to expand. The mattresses, for example, had to be transported from the Zappi company to the Castro plant. The exclusive franchise for this was given to another newly organized Gambino company, a trucking firm. The firm in turn aligned itself with Teamsters local 854. The principals in the latter were Zappi's son, Anthony, who was secretary-treasurer, and Steve and Frank Dapolito, respectively the vice-president and the organizer. In this manner the Gambino family, starting with no connections at Castro, created two lucrative franchises in the legitimate business world, direct employment for many members, a further foothold in the Teamsters, and contracts worth several million dollars that could be used as financial collateral.

A second Cosa Nostra activity is bank manipulation. This type of exploitation takes two forms. The first is direct, unsophisticated looting. Cosa Nostra, usually through front men, buys enough shares in an existing bank to control it. Loans are then made to Cosa Nostra appointees. The loans are never repaid, and the bank, or savings and loan company, collapses. Depositors are paid off at anywhere from ten cents to fifty cents on the dollar, depending on how thoroughly the bank has been looted.

In the second form of bank manipulation, the controlled bank is never directly tapped for funds but is instead used as a "character reference," issuing false statements of worth so that a Cosa Nostra man may obtain loans from other banks or purchase stocks on the pledge of nonexisting assets. This form of manipulation is virtually foolproof as long as the controlled bank is not suspected.

A further use for this form is intelligence gathering. A controlled bank can obtain financial information from other banks on virtually any individual or corporation in the United States —information that normally would not be divulged even to confidential financial reporters such as Dun and Bradstreet.

A third Cosa Nostra favorite is stock manipulation. Officials in the Securities and Exchange Commission believe that 90 percent of all stock frauds in the United States are committed by a central group of approximately one hundred and fifty front men, mostly Anglo-Saxon, who are financially backed by the Cosa Nostra families. Said one SEC official in a confidential interview: "Practically every major stock swindle and bank failure in this country links up with Cosa Nostra. The bosses are all over the place. Territorial lines are forgotten. Marcello is in Detroit. Gambino is in California. Salt Lake City is kind of the headquarters for it because there are so many defunct mining companies that can be taken over for nothing, the stock kited and then put up for collateral on loans. These sophisticated swindles are a new thing for Cosa Nostra. The risks are minimal and the money is maximal."

CONTEMPORARY OPERATIONS

In 1972 the McClellan subcommittee prepared confidential summaries showing that Cosa Nostra appointees controlled $10 billion in stolen stocks, bonds, and other securities. They controlled another $15 billion in counterfeit and criminally inflated stocks and bonds. Their manipulations, furthermore, were not confined to the United States but were international, involving stocks in the markets of Canada, Great Britain, France, Italy, and West Germany.

Virtually anyone who owns a stock, bond, or insurance policy can be affected, directly or indirectly, by criminally inflated stock. And the swindle procedure is not particularly complex. Basically, the idea is to take a stock, say the Wombat Gold Mine Company of Ogden, Utah, which is no longer doing business. Although nonoperating, the company still has assets and $50,000 worth of stock. The Cosa Nostra buys it, then builds a history of rising prices by swapping it back and forth among Cosa Nostra appointees. Wombat, therefore, looks like a golden investment to the innocent buyer, be he broker or private citizen. If a broker inquires why Wombat is rising, he is told because of new mineral discoveries, which of course are secret. Wombat sells $10 million of stock to the public. Of this, $1 million (or nothing) is actually used by the company in its operations. As the public money rolls in and the stock price climbs, the Cosa Nostra men can either sell their shares on the market at the inflated price and run, or swap the shares for legitimate stock, or use the shares as collateral for loans.

The Wombat Gold Mine Company is a fictitious example. But such swindles occur frequently, as a legitimate New York computer company found out in 1967.

The company was a reputable one which serviced computers on the U.S.S. *Pueblo* and other top-secret naval intelligence ships. In 1967 the company wanted to expand and needed financing. It eventually ended up talking with Bobby Baker, former clerk of the Senate. Through that contact it was referred to one of Baker's business partners, Seymour Pollock. Pollock agreed to provide financing on condition that three partners be brought into the computer company. This was done, and the three new partners of the computer firm were Aniello Dellacroce, Joseph Riccobono, and Salvatore Battalamenti. They were, respectively, the underboss, consigliere, and capodecina of the Carlo Gambino family. The capo, Battalamenti, was to be the man on the scene and oversee the operations of the front man, Pollock.

Once in control, Pollock began to kite the firm's stock and take his profits. He also used the outfit's reputation to obtain fraudulent loans. For instance, he and Battalamenti went to California and bought a junked and worthless computer for five hundred dollars. They then took the ownership papers, and the legitimate computer company's government contracts, to a bank in a small Mississippi town, where they were given a $300,000 loan, with the junk computer as collateral. Between the stock kiting and the fraudulent bank loans, the money rolled in by the millions.

The operation continued for about a year before it was discovered by the SEC. In the ensuing investigation, a thirty-two-year-old female secretary of the computer company turned government witness and testified on all the maneuvers, including the roles of Pollock, Battalamenti, Riccobono, and Dellacroce. In the spring of 1969, following her testimony, she was found in a motel in the Washington area, dead of "unknown causes."

According to the SEC, the Cosa Nostra team's year of maneuvering with the computer company had netted $4 million profit through stock kiting, fraudulent loans, and fraudulent bankruptcies. In 1970 Pollock was tried and convicted in Alabama. The Gambino men escaped untouched.

As the 1970s began, Cosa Nostra, one of the world's largest holding groups, was making a forceful entry into the legitimate marketplace, armed with billions of dollars in capital and an absolute scorn for ethics. It became, accordingly, more and more of an international conglomerate along the lines of the oil cartels and other vested interest groups, and less of a brotherhood proletarian society.

This is not to say that Cosa Nostra has expired. Far from it. Despite massive federal surveillance and prosecution from 1970 onward, the society has continued to operate with impressive secrecy. For instance, when Joe Colombo, boss of a New

York family, was shot in the head and paralyzed in June 1971, there was much government speculation about who would replace him. The shooting itself was blamed on the Gallo brothers, a dissident group in the Colombo family. It wasn't until 1974, three years later, that the government learned the shooting had been ordered by the Carlo Gambino family, as a disciplinary measure. Colombo had picketed the FBI, held massive Italian-American rallies in New York and in general drawn attention to Cosa Nostra's existence. When Gambino warned him about his flagrant excesses, Colombo spat in Gambino's face. Five weeks later he was shot.

It also took the government three years to learn the identity of the new boss—Thomas Di Bella, a retired tractor foreman from the Brooklyn docks. Di Bella had been a member since 1932, but prior to 1974 his eminence in Cosa Nostra was unsuspected. He had only one conviction, in 1932 for bootlegging. And as recently as 1971 he had been listed as only a low-ranking soldier in the Colombo family. Di Bella was raised up and installed as boss with Gambino's blessings, without the knowledge of the four federal agencies and three local agencies that had maintained twenty-four-hour surveillance, bugs, and taps on the Gambino and Colombo families for three years.

Cosa Nostra reached the apogee of its national power in the period 1931–1951. In 1975, however, despite the federal assault, it is nowhere near defeat. The midwest and western families are virtually untouched. Detroit has disintegrated due to black competition and absorption of its leaders into the American middle class, but Chicago, St. Louis, Cleveland, Dallas, and Kansas City are nearly as powerful as ever. The New Orleans family has even expanded its operations to include Mississippi, northern Louisiana, and southwestern Texas.

Only the eastern families are in a state of siege. There the old bosses are dying or being sent to prison. Angelo DeCarlo, the onetime New Jersey underboss in charge of gambling and loan-sharking, went up for twelve years, but served only thirty-three months before being granted executive clemency by President Nixon. New Jersey boss Sam DeCavalcante, New England's Raymond Patriarca, and Philadelphia's Angelo Bruno all went to prison for a time. The Cosa Nostra commission itself retired boss Joe Bonanno to Tucson and replaced him with Natale Evola. In 1973, Evola died of cancer and Gambino, who has become the most powerful of the New York bosses, installed a successor whose name is still unknown. The old Lucchese family passed in an orderly manner into the hands of Carmine Tramunti, who in turn went to prison for contempt and stock fraud. The family, however, has continued to operate much as before, under unknown leadership.

Of the two remaining New York City families, Gambino's is relatively unimpaired, although the boss himself, seventy-six years old, is under deportation order. The old Luciano-Genovese-Costello organization has weathered a succession of leadership crises, ending with the assassination of boss Tommy Eboli in 1972. The assassination probably was ordered by Gambino because Eboli had grossly mismanaged business, including a $4 million cash loss caused by a narcotics raid. The new boss is a Gambino protégé, Francesco Tieri. Tieri, a longtime power on the waterfront and in the garment district, is regarded as highly competent and was described by a federal agent as "a real first-echelon money-maker, one of the classiest gangsters in the New York area."

Chicago's leadership has passed through numerous hands without apparent disruption to the family's profits, its control of gambling, or its influence in politics, labor, and law enforcement. The titular boss, Sam Giancana, fled arrest warrants and retired to Acapulco in 1966. The acting boss, Tony Accardo, has survived unscathed and is seemingly impervious to all federal efforts. He has been a power on the Chicago scene since the days of Capone, Torrio, and Aiello.

The grand old man of Cosa Nostra, Buffalo boss Stefano Maggadino, died of a heart attack in July 1974, at age eighty-two. He was succeeded by Erie boss Russell Bufalino.

Maggadino was one of the eight original 1931 Cosa Nostra commission members. Of the eight, Lucchese, Profaci, Luciano, and Maggadino died natural deaths. Vincent Mangano was murdered by fellow bosses. As of 1975, Bonanno and Giancana were alive and retired. The remaining boss, Joe Zerilli of Detroit, is still in power.

During the first forty-four years of Cosa Nostra's existence, the leadership has managed to survive law enforcement efforts. In that time period, however, approximately eighteen bosses were stripped of power or assassinated by the society itself. Two bosses—Luciano and New Orleans's Sam Carolla—were effectively removed from power by deportation. One boss, Luciano's successor, Vito Genovese, died in the federal prison at Atlanta.

As the new generation of bosses comes into power in the 1970s, there is little indication they are less competent than their predecessors. Indeed, law enforcement may prove more difficult from now on because many of the new leaders are unknowns, like Colombo's successor, Thomas Di Bella, whose importance in Cosa Nostra went undetected for more than forty years.

In the 1960s and 1970s the government achieved considerable success against the middle management level of Cosa Nostra. But despite announcements in the press of Cosa Nostra's demise, the success of law enforcement agencies has been concentrated on the eastern seaboard and, as of 1975, has not permanently affected the national syndicate.

THE NARCOTICS SERVICE

The brotherhood has always provided services not available in the legal marketplace. Over the decades and centuries, the nature of the services has changed in response to client demand. The Garduna dealt mainly in gambling and crimes for hire. A client who wished to humiliate an enemy could commission a threat, mutilation, or even murder. Another species of client was the Spanish Inquisition, whose priests and officers, disregarding their vow of chastity, commissioned the kidnapping of so many girls that such kidnappings accounted for one-third of all Garduna crimes commissioned over a one-hundred-and-sixty-two-year period. Another service of the Garduna was high-interest loans.

In the Camorra loansharking and gambling continued to be important functions, but the nature of the other services

THE NARCOTICS SERVICE

changed. Crimes for hire virtually vanished. Instead, the Camorra provided policing. It protected individual clients and kept order in the towns and markets. In return it levied a tax and appropriated certain commercial monopolies unto itself.

For the Sicilian Mafia gambling ceased to have a prominent role. Policing became all-important in response to the need for order in government, commerce, and justice. Like the Camorra, the Mafia took payment by levying taxes and acquiring certain monopolies.

One can make a case that each of these societies survived only as long as did a need for its services. The Garduna's demise coincided with the expulsion from Spain of its chief client, the Inquisition. The Camorra's growth and decline was inversely coincident with the improvement of government performance in Naples. The Mafia has flourished in all periods except the Fascist regime, when Prefect Mori replaced Mafia law and order with his own. The elimination of the Mafia's service function was the key to Mori's program. The society returned to power only with the chaos of 1943.

The services of those three societies were simple and direct. Their geographical territory was small and communications could be handled on a face-to-face basis. More complex operations were the innovation of the American societies, the American Mafia and the Cosa Nostra.

Prior to 1909 the American Mafia engaged in no major services to the non-Italian general public, with the exception of keeping order on the public wharves. The families confined their activities to the Italian community, where they provided such services as policing, gambling, job procurement, and illegal alien entry.

The American Mafia did not have nationwide influence until about 1909. That year saw not only the execution of Lieutenant Petrosino and the subsequent lift in brotherhood morale, but the passage of the Opium Exclusion Act, which was followed in quick succession by laws forbidding the casual, i.e., nonprescription, sale of heroin, morphine, cocaine, and other addictive narcotics. These prohibitions presented the American Mafia with its first real opportunity for large-scale public activity. Already adept at smuggling aliens and counterfeit money from the Mediterranean, the Mafiosi easily switched to the narcotics traffic. The society's expansion became a boom in 1920, when the Volstead Act added a nonaddictive narcotic, ethyl alcohol, to the proscribed list. It was that combination of prohibitions, from the Opium Exclusion Act of 1909 to the Volstead Act, which created Cosa Nostra.

It is generally agreed that the use of narcotics is the third most serious social problem in the United States, following poverty and violent crime. But addiction in America is nothing new. In the golden age of 1900 the drug addiction rate in the United States was 1 out of every 400 persons. This is to say that, per capita, there were more Americans addicted to drugs in 1900 than there were in the epidemic years of 1962–1972 when the rate averaged 1 in 475. What has changed is the profile of the drug addict.

In 1900 the most frequently purchased drugs were opium and morphine. These were legally obtainable in drugstores and were as popular with discreet ladies "on dope" in Biloxi, Mississippi, as with hookers in Chicago and New York. Eighty-three percent of the addicts of 1900 were women, and virtually all addicts were white. The remainder were mostly Chinese. Opium dens flourished openly in such cities as San Francisco, Los Angeles, New Orleans, and Chicago. Inside the dens, addicts of all races and both sexes lay in bunks, side by side.

In 1914 heroin was outlawed, and statistics taken in that year showed again that 1 out of every 400 adult Americans was addicted. Again, users were predominantly white women. Army medical examinations of all recruits in 1917–1919 showed 1 man out of every 1,100 being rejected for addiction. This figure once again reflected a national addiction rate, men and women, of 1 in 400. In comparison, World War II military physicals rejected because of addiction only 1 man out of every 10,000 recruits. This figure, accompanied by the declining use of drugs by women, reflected a national addiction rate of 1 out of 6,000—probably the lowest addiction rate in American history.

THE NARCOTICS SERVICE

The statistical curve shows that from the time drugs were made illegal in 1914 through World War II, the number of users fell from 1 out of 400 to 1 out of 6,000. Beginning about 1962, however, drug use again began to climb. The renewed fashion was part of a social liberalization which swept the spectrum from sex to politics to entertainment, religion, and personal attire. In July 1972, when President Nixon placed the addiction rate at a maximum of 1 in every 475 persons, more than 80 percent of the addicts were men and slightly more than 50 percent of all addicts were black.

Early arrest records suggest that the American Mafia began supplying the national appetite for drugs from the first year of their prohibition, 1909. There was a steady rise in Mafia and then Cosa Nostra drug trafficking through the 1930s. The national and global drug network of that era was splintered among many allied groups and individuals. On the East Coast the top man was gambler Arnold Rothstein. In the South the major drug syndicate was in the hands of the New Orleans Mafia family headed by Sam Carolla, who used the ports of New Orleans to supply the interior states. West of the Rockies, the king trafficker was Tony Parmagini, called "Black Tony." He imported his supply from Indochina, mostly aboard the fleet of huge cargo ships he owned. His influence was such that in 1929, when he was convicted and jailed, the price of morphine, opium, heroin, and cocaine tripled in the entire western third of the United States and remained at that inflated price for more than one year before new suppliers were established. These suppliers, lacking Parmagini's fleet, turned to Mexico as a supply base. To this day, heroin, opium, and other narcotics used in the western states continue to come from Mexico, while the rest of the nation is supplied by the Middle East and Indochina.

Virtually all of the Middle East supply in the period 1929–1937 was the monopoly of the brothers George and Elias Eliopoulos. Residing in Greece, they bought up Levantine and Turkish opium crops, processed them into harder drugs, and shipped the product to mostly Jewish gang leaders—Lepke Buchalter, Mandy Weiss, Dutch Schultz, and Meyer Lansky—for distribution. However, the growing war troubles in Europe, coupled with increased border security, weakened the Eliopoulos syndicate,* and from about 1937 onward their operations were absorbed by Cosa Nostra.

Cosa Nostra's own supply routes were cut off in 1940 by the war. From then until 1945, the American syndicate relied on the opium crops of Haiti, Mexico, and Cuba, a product inferior to the high-grade Middle East opium.

Meanwhile, a third organization, small in comparison with the Eliopoulos brothers or with Cosa Nostra, had begun setting up drug routes in the Mediterranean. This was a Marseilles-based organized crime group composed mostly of Corsicans. Originally it was not a brotherhood family but did include Corsican brotherhood members. In 1932 the group established a drug route from Lebanon to Marseilles to supply French clients. A few years later it introduced a second route, running from Turkey to Yugoslavia to France via the Orient Express train.

World War II suspended all drug traffic in the Mediterranean. When peace came, it was not the Greeks or Cosa Nostra who set up new supply routes, but the Corsicans, who had come to rule the Marseilles organization. They constituted a new and distinct brotherhood society. A year later, in 1947, the Sicilian Mafia, encouraged by the deported Lucky Luciano, established its own drug routes, but the Corsicans proved more efficient and emerged dominant. Since then they have created a worldwide network with supply centers (i.e., opium-growing farms) in the Mediterranean, South and Central America, and the Far East. The principal market for all these production centers is the United States.

One reason for the Corsican domination of world narcotics is that since World War II Cosa Nostra had never made drug trafficking a primary enterprise. Cosa Nostra feared involvement in the drug trade because of the wild, unorthodox, and effective enforcement of the old, now defunct federal Bureau of Narcotics under Henry Anslinger. This small agency, with 3

---

*The Eliopoulos brothers fled Greece in 1939 and took sanctuary in the United States where they lived out their lives in wealth and security.

THE NARCOTICS SERVICE 213

percent of the personnel of the FBI, had the highest conviction rate of all federal agencies, and the vast majority of Cosa Nostra members imprisoned in the period 1946–1966 were put there by the Narcotics Bureau.*

As early as 1937 the commission issued a recommendation —not an order—that families disengage from narcotics traffic. In 1948, Frank Costello, as acting boss of the Luciano family, ordered his members to cease dealing in dope. Valachi, a Costello soldier, testified to the McClellan subcommittee about the results.

"In 1948, the rule was laid down. No narcotics. You are in serious trouble if you were arrested for narcotics. You had to prove them—you had another trial after having a trial with the government." In short, a member was not only breaking federal law but Cosa Nostra law and would have to stand trial for both.

Costello's 1948 law was not binding outside his own family, "but after Anastasia died in 1957, all families were notified—no narcotics. It was a rule discussed by the bosses themselves," said Valachi. (Anastasia, shot to death in the Park Sheraton barber shop on October 25, 1957, was one of the biggest dealers in narcotics. With his control of the Brooklyn docks he held a strategic position in the supply lines.)

Although there have been numerous individual cheaters, such as Valachi himself, the 1957 commission order took most Cosa Nostra families out of the narcotics business. The most successful disengagement was that of the Chicago family in 1950.

"They gave their soldiers $200 a week to stop selling narcotics," said Valachi. "The New York soldiers were grumbling about it. In Chicago, they gave you $200 a week. Over here, they wanted you to stop for nothing." The New York soldiers cheated, but "Chicago didn't have any trouble. They didn't try any phoney business. They are pretty honorable." If a Chicago soldier did sell narcotics, "after getting that kind of payment

---

*The Bureau of Narcotics is the only federal agency ever to infiltrate Cosa Nostra directly. One of its legendary agents, Sal Vizzini, actually became a roommate of Lucky Luciano in Naples during the 1950s.

there was no chance at all for them. They paid with their lives."

The major holdout was the Tampa family, which simply ignored the commission's order. The Tampa organization is among the more ancient in the United States and dates certainly from 1914 (or, by inference from New Orleans documents, from about 1903). It is unique in American brotherhood history in that it is the only family to engage in narcotics trafficking as its primary source of revenue throughout its life span. The most powerful of its early bosses was Ignacio Antinori, who was a major narcotics figure during the 1920s. Under Antinori's direction the family became the United States end of an international syndicate that linked up with the Marseilles group and shipped drugs through Cuba for distribution in Florida and the Midwest states.

A 1950 report of the Narcotics Bureau outlined the ties between Marseilles, Cuba, Tampa, and the Midwest:

> The Kansas City Mafia went into narcotics in 1933 after Prohibition. The main personnel were Joseph De Luca, Nicolo Impostato, and James De Simone who were known members of the Mafia. The Kansas City group was closely associated with the organization in St. Louis headed by Thomas Buffa, the known Mafia leader in that city. The major source of supply was the Antinori family of Tampa, long associated with the smuggling of narcotics, aliens, and liquor. It has been ascertained that the source of supply of the Antinoris was a prominent and influential official of the Cuban government named———, who was acting as an intermediary between a group in Marseilles, France, and the organization in the United States.

Antinori leadership ceased in 1940, when Ignacio was murdered. He was succeeded by Santo Trafficante, Senior, a Sicilian born in 1886 who had been a resident of Tampa since 1904. A description of the events of his tenure is provided by a remarkable document which in 1960 came into the hands of Jack De La Llana, a Tampa police intelligence officer. The document was prepared in 1945 by a Florida gambler named Charles Wall and was written as an insurance against his murder.

According to De La Llana, Wall declared that "from 1920

THE NARCOTICS SERVICE

through 1945 he controlled gambling in Tampa and in the Florida counties of Hillsborough, Pinellas, Pasco, Hernando, Polk, and Orange. His rival for control was the local Mafia organization. This was headed, he said, by Santo Trafficante, Senior, the Decidue brothers, James Lumia, Ignacio Antinori, and Salvatore Italiano. Antinori was murdered on October 22, 1940; Lumia was murdered on June 5, 1950; and Italiano fled to Mexico in 1951.

"Wall admitted that he had good reasons for going along with Trafficante in 1945 [when the two became partners in several gambling activities]. Previously the Mafia group had made three attempts on his life."

Wall retired from all criminal activities in 1952. In April 1955 his body was found in his home. He had been brutally beaten and his throat had been slashed. Five years later his "insurance" document was turned over to the police.

Santo Trafficante died in 1954 and was succeeded by his son Santo, Junior, one of the few instances in brotherhood history where a boss was succeeded by his son. The younger Trafficante, born in 1914, had made Cuba his residence since 1946 and operated mob gambling casinos there until Fidel Castro ejected him. He returned to Tampa, where he has maintained his international ties, especially with the Corsicans. In 1969 he traveled to Saigon to make arrangements with the Corsicans for importing Indochinese heroin into the United States.

What the Tampa family has done on a large scale, the rest of Cosa Nostra has done on an individual basis. Members cheat here and there, handling one shipment or maybe two to make a profit and get out. The net result is that Cosa Nostra has never been out of narcotics, despite the 1957 commission's order. The service is too lucrative.

Evidence of the staggering profit involved was given in 1972 by a study group named Policy Sciences Center, Inc., which was funded by the Department of Justice to make a report on underworld revenue in the Bedford-Stuyvesant area of New York. The conclusion of the study was that Cosa Nostra took more money out of the neighborhood in vice services than the federal government took in taxes.

The study showed that during 1970 this slum area of

280,000 people paid $87 million to organized crime operations. In the same year the IRS collected $70 million in taxes from Bedford-Stuyvesant. The highest income came from narcotics, for which the residents, including 6,000 identified addicts (1 in every 47 persons), paid $51 million. (The remaining $36 million was spent on numbers gambling.) A breakdown of this gross revenue was not made, but roughly it would come to one-third for the street salesmen, mostly black; one-third of the narcotics sales to the suppliers, Frenchmen or Corsicans; and the remaining third to the three Cosa Nostra families who control organized crime in the area. Such profits are irresistible.

On August 12, 1972, the Cosa Nostra commission held a meeting on Staten Island to discuss the society's reentry into international drug traffic. The meeting was monitored by federal agents, whose findings were reported in the Los Angeles *Times*. Under discussion was not only Cosa Nostra's position on drugs but also its concern about competitive organized crime groups:

> Since about 1960 the five New York crime families and a majority of the 27 [sic] crime families across the country have had a firm rule against its members dealing in narcotics. . . . When the ban was imposed, blacks and Puerto Ricans rushed into the vacuum. By the mid-sixties, after a massive influx of Cubans to the area, that ethnic group cornered the New York market with a paramilitary organization. Recently, younger Mafia members, eager for the quick, large profits, have agitated for re-entry into the trade. So far they have been held in check, at times violently. These Cuban groups are organized into crime families which operate in New York, New Jersey, and Florida and are structured like the Mafia.* Many of the senior members come from the ranks of former Cuban dictator Fulgencio Batista's army. Many report-

---

*The Cuban crime families do not seem to be a brotherhood society. Despite alleged "Mafia structure," there is no indication that they have brotherhood institutions—pensions, appellate procedures, etc. They appear instead to be a paramilitary group which is bound together by political considerations and engages in crime as a source of income. Another example of this type of group is the Irish Republican Army. Such organizations differ from the brotherhood in that they are impermanent and lack bureaucratic complexity.

edly were trained by the U.S. Central Intelligence Agency for an invasion of Cuba and have used their training in undercover operations to smuggle in drugs from Latin America.

The report said the Cuban groups had been active in gambling, loansharking, and narcotics, primarily among Latin ethnic groups and in ghetto areas. In one instance, in New Jersey, a Cuban group moved into a vacuum caused by the jailing of Bonanno capo Joseph Zicarelli. The Cubans took control of gambling and shylocking and the leaderless Zicarelli soldiers were unable to hold them back.

At the Staten Island meeting, a surprising argument was used to support Cosa Nostra reentry into drugs. "Aside from the profit motive," said the federal sources, "they felt they would be doing a service to the country. They said that narcotics had become a widespread national problem only after Cosa Nostra got out of the business. Cosa Nostra had kept it in the ghetto. Now it is in the suburbs because of other groups, including blacks and Cubans, who are the principal distributors and sellers."

If Cosa Nostra does actively reenter the drug market its main agent would be Santo Trafficante. He, along with the small, newly organized Montreal family, has close connections with the Corsican syndicate. The Corsican organization is a throwback to the old-time brotherhood. Devoid of religious or political motivation, it exists solely for the purpose of crime. It is organized into crime families that are an extension of blood families in Corsica. It has a hierarchy and laws, along with a judicial and appellate procedure. French police call this new society the Unione Corse.

UNIONE CORSE

The existence of the Unione Corse has been rumored for years. The name itself has been used by novelists since the 1950s, although French security agencies did not begin to accept its actual existence until the mid-1960s. This was about the same time that U.S. narcotics agents arrested two Unione Corse members in New York. Since 1967 the U.S. Narcotics Bureau has slowly put together dossiers on the Unione Corse based on reports of narcotics agents in France, Lebanon, Indochina, Canada, and the United States. These dossiers describe the Unione Corse structure and chief personnel and compare in quality to dossiers compiled on Cosa Nostra prior to Joe Valachi. That is to say, they outline the basic structure, but leave many gaps in detail.

The Unione Corse is a product of the island of Corsica,

and the island itself, its topography and political history, played a large role in the shaping of the society.

It is called "the scented isle" because Corsica gives off a bouquet so heady and far-reaching that its most famous son, Napoleon Bonaparte, once said he could be blindfolded, three miles at sea, and be absolutely sure when he was close to home. It is almost exactly the size of Puerto Rico, but with one-tenth the population.* Geologically, Corsica is a mountain that rises abruptly from the Mediterranean and crests in a peak called Monte Cinto. The mountain is forested, and belted at the waist by underbrush called the maquis. Near the sea the maquis gives way to meadows and then white beaches and deep but hazardous harbors. This topography—water's edge, mountain peak, separated by the maquis—has played a determinant role in the island's history.

It was, and is, the maquis that gives off the fragrance Napoleon claimed he could smell three miles away. The maquis stands between five and six feet high, at least as tall as most men on the island. In the maquis one can see but not be seen. Walking through it, one can cross the entire island of Corsica without being observed. For centuries those qualities have made the maquis the natural haven not only of bandits, but of revolutionaries and fugitives from the vendetta. The very word "maquis" came to mean a fugitive rebel. In the maquis arose the Corsican tradition of the bandit of honor, the Robin Hood who steals only when necessary, and only from those who can afford it.

The rise of outlaw bands friendly to and befriended by the general population began in Corsica prior to the eighteenth century and was the direct result of Genovese rule, which was unresponsive and oppressive. Those Robin Hood bands, in alliance with aristocrats like the Bonaparte family, played a significant role in eighteenth-century guerrilla warfare on the island and were responsible for the success of a national revolt in 1755. Some of these maquis outlaws were ordinary citizens; fugitives

---

*Corsica's population in 1970 was approximately 280,000; Puerto Rico's, 2.8 million.

of the vendetta, fathers and sons who hid out from blood feuds to preserve the family line.

The vendetta custom seems to be stronger in Corsica than anywhere else in the world, including Sicily and Montenegro. Feuds lasting more than a century are common rather than rare. Until 1860 the Corsican vendetta followed precise and relatively humane rules. When a serious abuse was committed, the leader of the wronged victim's family was obliged to seek justice. Depending on the offense, they could demand an apology, money, a marriage, a whipping, or a death. If, as frequently happened, the punishment matched the crime, the vendetta was then ended to the satisfaction of both families.

Sometimes, however, the penalty demanded was considered excessive by the offender. Then the killing began. By strict custom, the hunter and the hunted families alternated. The hunted hid out in the maquis for one, five, ten years, maybe more. If he died naturally, he was replaced by the successor to family leadership. If he was caught and killed, then the other family became the hunted. Tradition forbade preemptive strikes or preventive shootings. If one family attempted to eliminate its enemy in a massive spate of killings, it became the vendetta target of all families—a mad-dog menace to society.

Under the system, participating families might expect a vendetta killing every five or ten years, and there was no significant attrition in the population. At the same time, the vendetta performed its sociological function. It provided law and order, a system of justice.

All this changed in 1860 when the rifle arrived in Corsica. This technological advance over the knife, blunderbuss, and musket so stepped up the hunters' accuracy that vendetta families began to exchange killings every month. Family lines that had endured vendettas for centuries vanished entirely within a few years.

Never inclined to emigration, even to mainland France during the Napoleonic era, Corsican families suddenly found it imperative to send at least one son abroad. The usual destinations were, in order of preference, Marseilles, Paris, Beirut, and Algiers. In those various cities the islanders' cultural emphasis on manliness and courage soon gave them an advantage in certain occupations. By the 1920s Corsica was providing France with a disproportionately large number of gangsters as well as the best policemen.

In the 1920s the underworld—a most energetic purveyor of legends, folklore, and myths—came to view the Corsicans as something special. The European underworld has a belief or superstition that nationalities have specific talents. Italians are the best safecrackers. English are best for climbing jobs. Scots are best for explosives. The best triggermen in Europe are by far the French, and the best of the French are the Corsicans.

Thus arose the Corsican reputation. Their advantage in foreign cities was further enhanced by an informal solidarity arising from their common island heritage—back in Corsica, their families surely knew each other or someone in between. A final important factor was the Corsican language.* Like Sicilian, it was incomprehensible to outsiders and could be used as a secret tongue.

The first big-city Corsican gangster was Paul Carbone, the vice lord of Marseilles from about 1914 onward. In the early 1920s Carbone's power was challenged by not one but two new organized crime groups. One of these was European, led by the Neapolitan Antoine La Rocca and his Marseillais partner François Spirito. The other was an African group called the Ratons, comprised of Arabs from Algeria, Morocco, and Tunisia.

The Corsican Carbone shut down his brothels and sat back to let the other two syndicates kick each other to death. Although outnumbered by the Ratons, the Europeans prevailed by introducing American techniques. While the Ratons were still wiring their victims to concrete and throwing them into the bay, La Rocca's men were ambushing Raton leaders from speeding automobiles and using Thompson submachine guns. When it appeared that the Europeans might be too successful, Carbone stepped back in and provided police with some evidence against La Rocca. The Neapolitan fled

---

*The linguistic status of Corsican is uncertain. Non-Corsican authorities regard it as an Italian dialect, while Corsican scholars classify it as a distinct language.

France,* and Carbone made a partner of the Marseillais survivor, Spirito.

Between them, they ended the African challenge, and by 1928 had established a crime syndicate in Paris and Marseilles based on prostitution, gambling, and the protection rackets. In terms of political control, immunity from the law, and swagger their organization had no counterpart in the world except for the Capone syndicate in Chicago. In Marseilles, roaring around in twin Hispano-Suiza tourers, Carbone and Spirito took precedence over city councillors. They went to sports events, and were greatly in demand to present prizes. Their cars were waved through the thickest traffic by police.

In 1930 Carbone and Spirito expanded into narcotics and organized the Mediterranean supply-transport-processing network that has survived into contemporary times. The system was put together by Spirito, who, accompanied by two Marseilles girls, went to Alexandria, Egypt, the center of eastern Mediterranean drug supply at that time. There he arranged for large quantities of raw opium to be sent to Marseilles, where his own chemists would process the opium into morphine and heroin.

Shortly afterward, Carbone retired from crime, more or less to clip coupons. The leadership was left to Spirito, but Carbone assigned two Corsicans to protect his interests. They were Jean Paul Stefani, called the "Corsican Captain," the first of that title, and Ange Foata. Stefani and Foata are the world's first identifiable members of the Unione Corse.

At this time (in the 1930s) the island of Corsica was divided into crime families based entirely on blood relationship. Virtually every village and town had a criminal family, presided over by the oldest male, that monopolized the stealing of sheep, the allotting of public pastures, and the maintenance of order. The family did not prey on fellow villagers but on the estates of absentee landlords. This primitive form of Unione Corse is identical to the primitive form of the Sicilian societies.

---

*La Rocca fled with millions but went downhill fast. He tried to set himself up first in Egypt, then in South America, then in Spain. At each turn he was first robbed by the authorities and then booted out. He sneaked back into France and ended up in Lyons, where a few years later he killed his mistress and was sent to prison for fifteen years.

The similarities go further. The New York police investigations of 1903 showed that Mafia organizations in the United States were first formed as outposts of the respective village and town Mafias of Sicily. The same pattern was followed by the Unione Corse. As sons of the village families emigrated to France and to the colonies of Lebanon and Indochina, they organized themselves according to island origins. Thus, those from the town of Bastia would group together, while those from Aleria, Calvi, or Ajaccio formed other groups.

Territorial groupings are still the basis of Unione Corse organization. The two dominant families in France are those of Bastia and Ajaccio, which are linked by many intermarriages. All five families meet, irregularly, in Ajaccio or Marseilles. At these meetings a confederation of families settles disputes, fixes responsibilities for financial losses, assesses levies for operating expenses, and allots new enterprises.

The title of boss exists but families are ruled by elders. The bosses function in the field and make all immediate decisions, but ultimate power and prestige remain on the island of Corsica with the remote, simple-living elders. The relationship of boss to elder may be compared to a company president and a powerful chairman of the board.

Judicial proceedings are conducted by a council of advisors, akin to a council of consiglieri. Decisions can be appealed by a member to his family's elder. If the elder agrees, a commission of two or more elders is summoned to sit as a supreme court. As in other brotherhoods, members are regularly taxed and funds are set aside for widows' pensions, legal fees, and other costs. These characteristics place the Unione Corse at approximately the same stage of development as the Palermo Mafia of 1900.

As an organization, the Unione Corse crossed into France in the 1930s in the persons of the "Corsican Captain" Stefani and his lieutenant, Foata. Through them other Corsicans were brought into power positions, and within a few years the Unione became the dominant organized crime group in France.

The Corsicans attacked their rivals directly. In the mid-1930s Paris witnessed the kind of conflict that previously had been restricted to Marseilles and Chicago—machine-gun war. During the fighting the Corsicans opened a second drug transport route, from Yugoslavia direct to Paris via the Orient Express. Profits were used to finance the war. By 1938 the Corsicans had won. Their first act was to order Spirito, the old Marseilles boss, into retirement. There was no place for him in the Unione.*

But the Corsicans had little time to consolidate their victory. Two years later the German army invaded and conquered France in three weeks. The entire French underworld entered the employ of the Gestapo, with the exception of the Corsicans. Almost to a man they joined the Resistance, and were among the first and the best of the Resistance guerrillas. The Gestapo retaliated by dismantling the Corsican crime syndicate and was enthusiastically aided by French police and the underworld. Corsican franchises in gambling, narcotics, and prostitution were redistributed to collaborationists. But prisons could not contain the Corsicans. The walls of the Nimes jail were dynamited and thirty-three Unione Corse members fled into the countryside where they established a maquis of legendary deadliness.

After the war the Corsicans set about repairing the old organization, but not without a struggle. In Paris and Marseilles machine guns rattled and Citroens sped away from daylight ambushes. The wars between French gangsters and their rivals in the Unione even carried into the small Corsican capital of Ajaccio, which witnessed machine-gun battles and gun duels in the streets at high noon. By 1950 the Corsicans had won, settled the rivalries that had existed among themselves, and commenced to reestablish their worldwide drug network.

United States authorities first felt the direct impact of the expanding Corsican network in the 1960s, when Corsicans were caught supervising deliveries in New York. In the late 1960s, New York police, on separate occasions, arrested four Unione Corse members who proved so obdurate during interrogation that, as one officer put it, "they make the Mafia look

---

*In 1948 Spirito showed up in Marseilles and asked to be let back in. When the Unione refused, he traveled to New York, where he landed in 1948, penniless, homesick, and with a fake passport. His efforts to establish himself with Cosa Nostra were pathetically futile, and in order to eat, he was reduced to naively peddling small packets of heroin from bar to bar. Quickly arrested, he was sentenced to a long term in a U.S. prison in 1951.

like blabber-mouths. These guys won't even tell you their names. They go to jail without telling you their names."

In 1972 the French government for the first time began to move against the Unione Corse. The cause was the spiraling rate of French drug addiction, with twenty thousand addicts in Paris alone. In the area between Marseilles and Aix-en-Provence French police raided five laboratories. Their biggest bag was Etienne Mosca, a key figure in international traffic, who was shipping 1,763 pounds of heroin first to Spain, then to Mexico, then to the United States.

Nevertheless, Unione Corse, the most rapidly growing crime syndicate in the world, remains protected by its group integrity. A senior U.S. intelligence officer said, "Despite 10 years of investigation in France itself, we don't know who Mister Big is. We do know many of the key individuals. There is no question that Unione Corse dominates the world narcotics traffic. Beirut *was* the key, but it is no longer needed. The Unione now deals directly with the Turks and it has always dealt directly with the Indo-Chinese.

"Although it has entered French Canada it has not come, as an organization, into the United States because there is no cover here. They would stand out too much as foreigners. Crime groups always work primarily under the cover of their own population and prey on their own population. Italians on Italians, blacks on blacks, Puerto Ricans on Puerto Ricans. It is due to this lack of cover in the United States that the Unione deals with Cosa Nostra. They'd come in directly if they thought they could get away with it. They have no fear of Cosa Nostra."

Brotherhood societies, once limited to the neighborhood of Seville, have traveled from the Mediterranean basin to America, Canada, and Australia. The main conduit of flow has been the movement of Spanish, Italian, and American populations. Now the rising Unione Corse opens new avenues—the French populations of Europe, the Middle East, Africa, Indochina, and French Canada.

CONCLUSION

Originating in fifteenth-century Spain, the brotherhood is a relatively recent historical phenomenon, but it has been on the scene long enough to allow some generalizations about its nature.

Every brotherhood society has been basically feudal in structure, and the major societies have all been long-lived. The Garduna and the Camorra both lasted approximately four hundred years. The Sicilian Mafia is already more than a century old and, according to the 1972 Italian Parliamentary investigation, is more powerful than ever. The American Mafia, which evolved into Cosa Nostra, has been operating for more than a century, despite its location in the United States where sociological change tends to be greatly accelerated. It is among the oldest institutions in America and its extinction is far from imminent.

CONCLUSION 227

The brotherhood's role in the human community has always been essentially governmental. It can survive only in nontotalitarian political climates, but at the same time the brotherhood itself is totalitarian. Its presence is a direct threat to the liberty and physical safety of the individual citizen. Where the brotherhood has reigned supreme, as it has in Sicily and at intervals in neighborhoods of New York, New Orleans, and Chicago, the citizen must unquestioningly obey the dictates of the lowest ranking brotherhood member. He has no court of appeal save to go hat-in-hand to the local capo. Conversely, the brotherhood represents an indirect threat to liberty because only the most totalitarian law enforcement methods have ever suppressed a brotherhood. Such measures, by their nature, affect the liberties of the general population. Totalitarianism has kept the brotherhood out of communist nations, although as countries like Yugoslavia increase their liberties, brotherhood activities are beginning to enter. Law enforcement that is legal in America, such as federal agencies have attempted over the past twenty years, can keep the societies in check without disturbing civil rights; it cannot stamp them out.

The presence of a brotherhood society is a symptom of inadequacy in the legal government. The brotherhoods have survived only as long as they could provide services. The Garduna's function was to provide a livelihood for its members, people who were alienated from and ignored by the larger Spanish community, and to provide the members with a form of law and justice. As the brotherhood evolved, it extended its services to the general population, but only when and if the population agreed to pay for them. For a price, the society would police a neighborhood in Naples, sell the Sicilian farmer a stall in the marketplace in Palermo, get the immigrant a job on the New Orleans docks, manufacture whiskey in Chicago, smuggle narcotics from Marseilles, or loan money to any individual, politician, or corporation.

So the question arises, why did the brotherhood not come into existence prior to the fifteenth century? Nontotalitarian societies were numerous before 1400, and all of them had inadequacies. What happened in the fifteenth century that spawned the new phenomenon?

The answer may be an impersonalization of government, caused by two related factors: population growth and the demise of feudalism.

Most historians agree that an increase in world population set off a chain of fifteenth-century migrations that extended from the Gobi desert to the Americas. This movement of population caused much of the disorder of the times. In reaction, ambitious leaders like King Ferdinand seized the opportunity to incorporate new people and large hunks of new territory under a single governmental umbrella. A small number of trained civil servants, using democratic and monarchical political forms designed for small populations, suddenly had to administer to large numbers of widely dispersed people. One result was inadequate protection of the marketplace and the public safety. A second consequence was the demise of feudalism. For centuries, the people had been accustomed to buying protection from local lords whom they could see and hear. As feudalism slowly gave way to large, impersonal national governments, the people looked increasingly for a local authority to fill the gap. The self-appointed replacement was the brotherhood.

The elimination of local government was a mistake that Rome, for instance, had avoided. While Rome did have a large, impersonal national government, it ruled its empire through existing local governments and institutions.

The experience of American cities tends to support the theory that the brotherhood cannot establish itself in communities where local government is responsive. San Francisco in 1878, with all its faults, paid attention to its Italian people and the Mafia was unable to survive. Size of the city does not seem to be a factor. Janesville, Wisconsin, population 35,000, is near Chicago, but has no organized crime. Panama City, Florida, with an identical population, is four hundred miles from the nearest Cosa Nostra family, but has numbers rackets and bookies. Quality of government seems to be the test. When local governments become too big, too impersonal, or too corrupt to serve people, the brotherhoods thrive.

CONCLUSION 229

That, then, may be the ultimate significance of the brotherhood. It is, above all, a symptom of modern western society's failure to provide a system of government scaled to human size and human needs.

APPENDIX A
EARLIER SOCIETIES

Three criminal societies functioned like the brotherhood, but worked toward different goals: the Assassins, the Thugs, and the Chauffeurs.

The Assassins, the most ancient of the criminal societies, were politically motivated. The group was founded in eleventh-century Persia by Hassan Sabbah, known in European legend as "the Old Man of the Mountain." Even European kings were terrified of him, because it was well known that Assassins were often dispatched long distances to carry out the instructions of their master.

Tradition has it that the society took its name from the word hashishim, derived from hashish, which was the chief intoxicant used by Hassan's followers.

The Assassins were a secret order of the Ismaili sect of

APPENDIX A: EARLIER SOCIETIES   ○ 231

Islam. It began around A.D. 1090 in the mountain fortress of Alamut (in present-day Iran south of the Caspian Sea) and spread over Persia and Syria, winning many strongholds and inspiring terror throughout Islam. The Crusaders came into contact with the Assassins in the twelfth century and spread their reputation to Christendom.

Despite the political motivation of its leaders, the society was organized like a religious sect, and many of the rank-and-file were religious fanatics. The order had a Grand Master, called the Sheikh al-Jabal, and under him members were organized into strict classes, according to degree of initiation into the secrets of the order. The most colorful was the "devotee" class, whose members sought martyrdom and were the instruments of assassination. It is believed that devotees were rewarded for their acts with admittance into the fortress of the Grand Masters, where they could indulge in hashish and "the most exquisite forms of sensual pleasure."

The first Grand Master, Hassan, and his next six successors wielded great political power throughout Islam. The coming of the Mongols destroyed that power. In 1256 Hulagu Khan destroyed the Assassins' fortresses in Persia and massacred thousands of followers. Pockets of the sect survived, however; they remained active in Persia and Syria in the nineteenth century and are believed to exist today.

The heir to the title of Old Man of the Mountain is the present-day Aga Khan, hereditary ruler of the Muslim Ismaili sect with followers in India, Pakistan, East Africa, and Central Asia. The Aga Khan's claim to the title was confirmed in a rather singular civil suit heard in a British court at Bombay in 1866. The plaintiff was the Aga Khan II, who contended he was owed an annual tribute of £10,000, approximately $250,000 in modern currency, from a community of merchants known as the Khodjas. The tribute was owed, said the Aga Khan, because the Khodjas were members of the Assassins sect and he, the Aga Khan, was the direct descendant of the last Old Man of the Mountain and therefore the present-day Grand Master of Assassins. The British court investigated the pedigree, declared it proved, and awarded the judgment to the Aga Khan.

The term assassin is used today to mean murderer, particularly one who kills for political motive.

The Thugs of India were a quasi-religious order founded in the thirteenth century, but unknown to the western world until the nineteenth century, when they were discovered by the British. The Thugs were Hindus and Muslims who declared themselves to be followers of the goddess Kali. According to Thug interpretation, Kali desired extinction of the human race on grounds that the gods had made a mistake in creating man. She therefore endowed her followers with the right to commit murder in her name.

The Thugs' specialty was the strangulation and robbery of travelers. Victims were buried with a peculiar pickaxe which represented the tooth of Kali. One Thug, hanged at Lucknow in 1825, was convicted by a British court of having strangled six hundred persons. Another confessed to 999 murders and declared that only respect for the profession had prevented him from making it a full thousand. Among the Thugs, he said, a round number was considered vulgar.

Unlike membership in the Assassins, being a Thug was not a full-time occupation. For most of the year, members followed ordinary pursuits. But each fall they gathered in huge congregations, then split up into small bands, and traveled the countryside disguised as merchants or religious beggars. When they encountered wealthy travelers, they would ingratiate themselves and await an opportunity to kill their victims, usually by strangling them with a special scarf carried for the purpose. Women and members of lower castes were, for some reason, exempted from attack.

A British investigation showed that the sultan of Delhi had first reported their existence in the thirteenth century, when he arrested a thousand Thugs. For the next six centuries they were protected by strong organizational secrecy and by local officials with whom they divided their loot.

The Thugs had several ranks, based on proficiency. Lowest was apprentice, one who gave information on travelers. Next was journeyman, one who was allowed to hold the arms and legs of struggling victims. The top rank was master, the strangler.

APPENDIX A: EARLIER SOCIETIES

The society as a whole was divided into smaller territorial groups. "They divided up their territories and the areas in which they operated, never overlapping without some exceptional reason, and thus ensured that each group could work on its own tract of country without disturbance."

When the British discovered them in 1799, there was a general disbelief that such a society could exist. Sir William Sleeman, the man placed in charge of eradicating the Thugs, said: "If any man had then told me that a gang of assassins by profession resided in a village not 400 yards from my door . . . I should have thought him a fool or a madman; and yet nothing could have been more true. The bodies of a hundred travelers lay buried in the grove and a gang of assassins lived in and about the village while I was magistrate of the district."

The primary difficulty facing Sleeman "after he had fully grasped the extent and secret horror of Thuggee, was the utter indifference of a large proportion of Indian rulers themselves: they had no serious wish to see the end of them and, in a certain minority, there was the most active hostility to any tampering" with this source of revenue.

In the beginning the Thugs were amused by the British attack, but their mood changed to horror at Sleeman's success and there were numerous attempts to kill him. Surprisingly quickly, however, Sleeman cracked the Thugs' discipline of secrecy and by 1833 hundreds of them came forth with confessions. In one arrest of seventy-six Thugs, seventeen made full confessions implicating not only themselves but a score of colleagues. Some three hundred Thugs were hanged, with Sleeman presiding at each execution. Sleeman followed up the executions with efforts at rehabilitation. In 1838 the British established a school for children of the Thugs and taught them "a trade or craft by which they might earn an honest livelihood. At first their parents were opposed to the idea, but soon joyfully acquiesced." By 1847 the school had an enrollment of 850.

The Chauffeurs, or Burners, were a satanic sect located in northern France and northwestern Germany. Formed during the thirteenth-century religious wars, the Chauffeurs were exterminated in Napoleonic times, although small enclaves may still survive.

The Chauffeurs constitute an intermediary stage between the nonproletarian criminal societies and the modern brotherhood, incorporating aspects of both. They had satanic rites, manifested in black masses and marriage and funeral ceremonies that mocked the Roman Catholic Church. But they also had proletarian characteristics—they were outcasts who organized to protect themselves against the lawlessness of the larger society.

The Chauffeurs seldom numbered more than a few hundred at any one time. Their laws and rituals were passed down through five centuries, via the blood-family clans that were their basic unit of organization. Great priority was given to the education of Chauffeur children, who were taught at a young age how to spy and how to commit small thefts.

Some of their laws were identical to those of the brotherhood. Theft from a fellow member was forbidden. The honor of wives of members was to be strictly respected. And there was provision for trials of offending members. There was an important difference, however. The Chauffeurs lacked any institution for the systematic bribery of public officials, a circumstance which partially explains their limited success.

The Chauffeurs prospered as a subterranean community, conducting their own religious and marriage rites, running their own schools, and living off the proceeds of their crimes. When the French Revolution took place, however, they overreached themselves. Under the cover of patriotism, large Chauffeur bands invaded houses and castles to murder and rob. It was in this period they acquired the name the Burners. The government reacted quickly and decimated them with two purges in the late eighteenth century. The last known Chauffeurs were executed at Mayence in 1803, after which time they seem to have disappeared.

The Assassins, the Thugs, and the Chauffeurs shared characteristics which contributed directly to their survival. Each kept its activities and membership secret from the outside

APPENDIX A: EARLIER SOCIETIES

world. Each had a complex structure of laws and institutions which were distinct from and hostile to those of the larger society. And, most important, each was organized in the dimensions of space and time. Their organizational and training structures extended not only geographically but also across the generations. The laws and traditions were passed on from father to son, from veteran practitioner to novice recruit.

This organization was successfully combatted only by the British, when they established schools for the offspring of the Thugs. This cut off the supply of new recruits and made the sons part of a world different from their fathers'.

APPENDIX B
MINOR BROTHERHOODS OF THE NINETEENTH CENTURY

During the careers of Leone and Esposito, the Mafia triggered the creation of country Mafias throughout Sicily. These country societies used the Palermo organization as a model and accepted Palermo as the keystone of an islandwide confederation. At the same time, the Palermo Mafia inspired the creation of competing criminal societies. In the period 1870–1890 at least eight distinct brotherhood societies sprang up in Sicily and mainland Italy. A ninth brotherhood society, composed of Greeks and Italians, came into existence in Turkey.

Each of these societies had a short life span. Only one of them, the Stoppaglieri of Sicily, had any influence beyond its provincial borders. It had a hierarchical authority: the head of the entire organization was a boss of bosses, called capo. Each district, including the various neighborhoods of Monreale and the affiliate villages, was under the direct jurisdiction of a sot-

APPENDIX B: MINOR BROTHERHOODS ○ 237

tocapo. These in turn each had an elder advisor, designated consiglio directtivo. A council of these leaders met to judge infractions. This structure is a highly evolved version of the Camorra, with a boss of bosses at the top and with districts presided over by captains who are advised by counsellors. The leaders constituted a commission which acted as a judiciary body.

In its structure the Stoppaglieri was more complex than the nineteenth-century Mafia, which was a loose confederation of families and which lacked the institution of a boss of bosses, a standing commission, or the post of consigliere. The post of consigliere, or advisor, was also absent in the Camorra.

This society was eventually absorbed by the Palermo Mafia, a few years prior to 1900, but even today it retains a certain independence and prestige, and is known as the "Monreale Mafia." The chief instrument of the Monreale society's demise was a six-year feud with the Fratuzzi, a brotherhood group centered in the nearby town of Bagheria. It was also attacked by the Palermo Mafia, which did not look kindly on independent groups. Most writers have regarded these two groups as part of the Sicilian Mafia and not as individual societies. But the Stoppaglieri had a different structure than the Mafia and was distinct from that organization.

The Mafia and the Stoppaglieri were the only significant brotherhood societies created in Europe during the nineteenth century. Other societies, however, did appear and they illustrate various forms the brotherhood has taken:

The Accoltellatori, described as a "criminal club," was discovered in 1874 in Ravenna, on the north Adriatic coast of Italy, and seems to have been confined to that city. It was the most northern of the nineteenth-century brotherhoods. The novice member was called *giovanotto onorato* and a journeyman member *picciotto di sgarro*. Both titles came directly from the Neapolitan Camorra.

The society was founded in 1865, probably by Mazzinists, for the members are described as "remnants of an old political secret society" in a context which can only refer to Mazzini. The Accoltellatori was secret, had a hierarchy, its own laws, and a judicial procedure for its members—all of which are brotherhood characteristics. Its main motive for existence was criminal profit, and it provided services which allowed it a place in the community. The primary service of the Accoltellatori was to be an instrument of arbitrary justice and to assassinate those members of the community who had, in the eyes of the brotherhood, behaved badly toward the popular interest. Typical victims were a magistrate who took bribes, a rapacious banker, a surgeon who cornered the grain market, created a false scarcity, and then sold dear. These men and others were murdered publicly in front of the Ravenna courthouse as a demonstration of Accoltellatori power.

In October 1874, this small society was put out of business with one blow. Twenty-three of its members, including all of the leaders, were convicted of killing thirteen public officials.

The Mano Fraterna, an eastern Sicilian society, was discovered in 1883. C. W. Heckethorn described it, in 1897, as "an offshoot of the Mafia, though its members repudiated the idea of being robbers and extortioners. They called themselves the instruments of universal vendetta." Like the Accoltellatori, they provided a sort of vigilante justice, "making the roads safe for travelers" and executing predatory bankers, lawyers, and landlords.

The Mala Vita, on the other hand, made no pretense of keeping the roads safe or performing other admirable acts. Its members were full sworn to pursue the Evil Life, a name taken from the title of a popular novel of the era.

Mala Vita was headquartered in the Adriatic city of Bari. Once the major port of embarkation for the Crusaders, Bari was the heart of a province which, like Sicily, had a vendetta tradition and a Greek-Muslim-Norman culture. Mala Vita first came to public attention in 1884, when a Bari newspaper publisher, the Chevalier Gaetano Rodavio, obtained information on the society and published it in his paper to attract the attention of the government. By Rodavio's account, the society was presided over by a boss of bosses, called the "Wise Master." Beneath him was the captain (called Camorrist), followed in

APPENDIX B: MINOR BROTHERHOODS

rank by picciotto (comparable to a Cosa Nostra soldier), and giovanotto (a novice). Structurally the Mala Vita, numbering some five hundred members, was organized like a Camorra *paranza* ("family").

As in other brotherhood societies, a Mala Vita nominee had to be sponsored by a member in good standing, and he was presented to the family chief, who alone had the authority to approve him. If accepted, he took a most elaborate oath. He stood with one foot placed in a hole, representing an open grave, and the other foot attached to a chain. He swore to abandon father, mother, wife, and children in favor of the Mala Vita. This latter provision is curious, for it is contrary to the main line of brotherhood societies, which are designed to exploit blood family ties rather than negate them.

The novice concluded his oath by swearing he had never done business with the police, gendarmerie, or the customs house and "in the name of humility, I belong to the Evil Life."

All proceeds from the various crimes were turned over to a society cashier whose duty it was to apportion it among all members within eight days. A large share was set aside for the chief's administration. It was his responsibility to dispense funds for pensions, legal costs, and bribes.

The judicial procedure of the Mala Vita was primitive. Defendants were tried by the entire society membership rather than by a council or tribunal.

In 1891, 179 members were brought to trial in Bari on charges that included robbery, assault, and murder. Of these, all but 14 were convicted and received terms averaging fifteen years. The government pointed out, however, that none of the leaders had been caught. A year later another 159 members were convicted. This meant that two-thirds of the membership had been imprisoned by 1893. Nevertheless, the Mala Vita continued to be a force in the Apulia province until about 1900, when reports about it cease.

An unnamed society in Turkey was first reported in the 1880s as "a branch of the Camorra . . . an organized band of assassins who infest Constantinople and the provinces." This Turkish group, however, was not a small operation. According to the Levant *Herald,* it extended throughout the Turkish empire. "The members," reported the *Herald,* "are almost entirely Italian and Greek—chiefly from Naples, Sicily, and Cephalonia; but they differ in rank, some being mere workingmen, while others are men of fashion, who arrange the matters of business, and carry out the better class of work which requires something more than a strong arm and a bludgeon."

Internal details of the organization are unknown. The society was headquartered in Pera, the European suburb of Constantinople. Like the Garduna and the Camorra, it committed assassinations, mutilations, and kidnappings for clients on a fee basis. It also engaged heavily in usury, and was inventive about conceiving profitable low-risk crimes. The first year fire insurance was introduced in Turkey, the incidence of arson rose 3,000 percent in Constantinople. The *St. James Gazette* took notice of these activities in 1889: "The method of procedure in this very profitable class of business is as follows. Either a member of the band is installed in a well-furnished house or shop, or a man already established is induced to join the band by the offer of a share in the spoils. The place is insured, generally by one of the many foreign offices, as English agents are too particular as to whom they insure; and a month or two after, preparations for incendiarism are made. The goods are first removed, and the walls and floors smeared with petroleum. The place is then fired. Should the insurance agent be too curious about the circumstances, he is promptly waited upon by a member of the band who gives him plainly to understand that the affair is in the hands of the Camorra . . . the agent pays the money without demur. He cannot fight the band single-handed; the police will do nothing unless they are bought."

Due to Turkish censorship, no report seems to have been made on the society later than 1890. But the Turkish "Camorra" survived until the period 1920–1923, vanishing with the dissolution of the Ottoman government and the establishment of the Turkish republic under Ataturk.

INDEX

Acapulco, Mexico, 180, 206
Accardo, Tony, 206
Accoltellatori, 237–238
Adonis, Joe, 136, 138, 153, 157
Aiello, Joey, 136, 149, 151, 152, 176, 206
Ajaccio, Corsica, 223, 224
Ajnello, Ralph, 77, 78, 100
Alcohol and Tax Bureau, 188–189
Alfano, Enrico, 24, 117, 122
Algeria, 41, 220, 221
Allen, Matt, 175
Alongi, 19–20
Amite, Louisiana, 175
Anastasia, Albert, 153, 165, 166, 213
Anslinger, Henry, 212
Antinori, Ignacio, 214–215
Argentina, 13, 57
assassination, *see* gang warfare and assassination
assassins, 2, 230–232, 234–235
Atlanta, Georgia, 123, 131, 169
Atlantic City, New Jersey, 138, 176
Australia, 57, 197–198, 225

Bailey, William, 176, 177
Baker, Bobby, 203
Baltimore, Maryland, 176
bank manipulation, 202
Barcelona, Spain, 12
Bari, Italy, 238–239
"barrel murder," 111, 112, 113–116
Basile, Tobia, 20–21
Bastia, Corsica, 223
Batres, Antonio, 189
Battalamenti, Salvatore, 203–204
Battista, Fulgencio, 216
Bedford-Styvestant, 214–215

Beirut, Lebanon, 220, 223, 225
Bender, Tony, 163, 167, 168
Berger, Meyer, 165
Bertin, L., 83–84
Beverly Club, 183
Bianchi, Giuseppe, 101, 103
Bingham, Theodore, 119, 123
Bisacquino, Sicily, 120, 121–122
Black Hand, 67–72, 106, 135
Boland, Dan, 46, 49
Bonanno, Joe, 19, 57, 135, 136, 149, 150, 156, 206, 217
bootlegging, 130, 131, 138, 176
Boston, Mass., 138
Boylan, Tom, 45–46, 50
Brazil, 13
brigata, 16
Bronx, N.Y., 130, 133, 140, 143, 147, 151, 154
Brooklyn, N. Y., 71, 106, 110, 111, 114–115, 124, 129, 131, 133, 134, 135, 136, 137, 142, 153, 162, 165, 166, 170, 205, 213
Bruno, Angelo, 200, 205
Buchalter, Lepke, 134, 162, 165, 166, 211
Bufalino, Russell, 206
Buffalo, N. Y., 57, 112, 114, 115, 136, 138, 150, 156, 162, 197, 199, 200, 206
Buffa, Thomas, 214
Bureau of Narcotics, *see* Narcotics Bureau, U.S.
Burners, *see* Chauffeurs
"Buster," 146, 147, 148, 151, 152, 158
Byrnes, Thomas, 72, 81, 108–111

INDEX

Camorra, 1, 13–24, 25–26, 28, 29, 30, 31, 35, 36, 60, 80, 117, 118, 119, 121, 122, 124–126, 131, 144, 169, 208–209, 226, 237, 239, 240
   and Italian revolution, 22
   origins of, 14–16
   vs. Mafia, 108, 110–111, 124–126, 131
Campanillo, Giovanni, 117, 121
Canada, 197, 203, 218, 225
Cantone, Vincenzo, 118
capataze, 13
capo, def. of, 13, 17
Capone, Al, 42, 126, 137, 138, 149, 151, 153, 157, 162, 176–177, 206, 222
caporegima, see capo
Capuzzi, Nick, 147
Carbonari, 25
Carbone, Paul, 221–222
Carolla, Sam, 97, 175–180, 182, 184, 207, 211
Carolla, Sylvester, 61
Caruso, Angelo, 156, 159
Caruso, Enrico, 123
Caruso, Jim, 82, 87, 91
Cascioferro, Vito, 122
casseta, 56
Castellammarese War, 136, 144
Catania, Joe (Jr.), 141, 142, 151–152, 158
Catania, Joe (Sr.), 114–115
Central Intelligence Agency, 61, 189, 217
Cervantes, Miguel, 6, 7, 9, 12, 13, 18
Chauffeurs, 2, 230, 233–235
Chicago, Ill., 87, 88, 114, 115, 117, 122, 135, 136, 137, 138, 149, 151, 156, 160, 162, 163, 165, 176, 177, 179, 205, 206, 210, 213, 222, 223, 227, 228
Cincinnati, Ohio, 72, 130
Civello family, 194
Clancy, Frank, 182–184
Cleveland, Ohio, 88, 137, 138, 149, 162, 199, 205
Cleveland Plain Dealer, 19
Coll, Vincent "Mad Dog," 160
Collins, Pat, 192–193

Colombo, Joe, 193, 204–205, 207
"Combination, The," 165
Connolly, Richard, 108
Coppola, Frank, 61, 62, 182
Coppola, Mike, 57, 135, 136, 142–143, 149, 154
Cordova, Spain, 12
Corleone, Sicily, 62, 112, 113, 118
Corsica, 217, 219–223
Corte, Pasquale, 84
Cortina, Francisco, 12
Cosa Nostra, 1, 6, 13, 15, 17, 18, 19, 26, 57, 61–62, 91, 97, 100, 113, 118, 126, 131, 135, 154–156, 159, 160, 161–162, 163, 165, 166, 168, 169, 172–174, 179, 185, 193, 194, 197–217, 218, 225, 226, 228
   and Murder Incorporated, 164–167
   consolidation of, 161–163
   first organizational meeting, 154–156
   international expansion, 197–198
   leadership struggle in, 159–161
   move to legitimate business, 199–200
   present-day, 205–207
   Purge Day, 160–161, 162, 165
   structure and rules of, 155–156, 163–164
   see also Mafia (American)
Cosa Nostra Squad, 192
Costabili, Enrico, 117
Costello, Frank, 136, 157, 167, 169, 178–179, 180, 181–182, 206, 213
Cuba, 167, 212, 214, 215
Cuban groups in U.S., 216–217
Cuccia, Don Ciccio, 53–54

Dalitz, Moe, 162, 199
Dallas, Texas, 194, 205
D'Amato, Gaetano, 69
Daniello, Ralph, 124–126
Dapolito, Steve and Frank, 201
Davis, Jimmie, 183–184
DeCalvacante, Sam, 164, 205
DeCarlo, Angelo, 205
Decidue brothers, 215

INDEX   243

De La Llana, Jack, 214
Dellacroce, Aniello, 203–204
De Luca, Joseph, 214
De Simone, James, 214
Detroit, Michigan, 57, 136, 138, 162, 176, 179, 200, 202, 205
Devereaux, Thomas, 50
Dewey, Thomas, 59, 60, 167
Diamond, Legs, 134
Di Bella, Thomas, 205, 207
Dimaio, Frank, 86, 88–89, 92
Dio, Johnny and Tommy, 168
Diodati, Antonio, 71
Di Palermo, Joe, 169
Domingo, Francisco, 69–70
Donaldsville, Louisiana, 116
Donatelli, Crocco, 29
Don Quixote, 6, 10
Doto, Joe, *see* Adonis, Joe
Doyle, Bobby, 144–145, 146–147
Dwyer, William Vincent, 130

Eboli, Thomas, 193, 206
Edinburgh Review, 18
Eliopoulos, George and Elias, 211–212
El Paso, Texas, 171
El Salvador, 190
Emmanuel II, King, 22, 27, 40, 53–54
Erie, Penn., 200, 206
Esposito, Giuseppe, 40–51, 67, 79, 80, 81, 83, 86, 99, 100, 108, 110, 134, 236
Evola, Natale, 206

Federal Bureau of Investigation, 164, 181, 183, 188–189, 192, 205, 213
Ferdinand, King, 1, 7–8, 16, 228
Ferrigno, Stefano, 134, 136, 147–149, 153, 156, 158
Ferro, Don Vito Cascio, 56–57, 114, 117, 118–119, 120–122, 136, 137, 157
Five Points gangs, 42, 105–106
Flaccomio, Antonio, 109
Florida, 57, 130, 138, 165, 192, 193, 214, 215, 216, 228
Foata, Ange, 222, 223

Forty Thieves, 105
France, 2, 167, 185, 203, 212, 218, 221–225, 233, 234
  see also Paris, Marseilles
Franks, Mr., 186–187
Fratuzzi, 80, 237

Gagliano, Gaetano (Tom), 136, 145–147, 149, 150, 156, 162, 163
Gallenga, Antonio, 26
Gallinaro, William, 194
Gallo brothers, 205
Gambino, Carlo, 57, 135, 136, 193, 198, 201, 202, 204, 205, 206
gang warfare and assassination, 80–82, 108, 110–111, 131–133, 136–141, 144–154, 157, 159–161, 177, 198
Garabaldi, 22, 27, 28, 29
Garduna, 1–13, 15, 17, 18, 24, 208, 209, 226, 227, 240
Genna family, 135
Genovese, Vito, 60–61, 113, 126, 136, 153, 154, 156, 157, 159, 160, 163, 167, 168, 169, 174, 193, 206, 207
Geraci, Rocco, 49, 81, 82, 85, 86, 87, 91
Germany, 203, 233
Getty, J. Paul, III, 39
Giancana, Sam, 206
Goff, John, 110
Gordon, Waxey, 138
Granada, Spain, 2, 7, 8
Grand Council, 16, 18, 19, 138
Grand Master, 16, 24, 26, 117, 231
Greece, 211, 212
Griscom, Lloyd, 119
Guatemala, 185–190

Haiti, 212
Heckethorn, C. W., 13, 18–19, 22, 23, 30, 68, 238
Hennessey, David, 44–47, 49, 50, 51, 79, 81–87
Hines, Jimmy, 143
Hoffa, Jimmy, 187
Honduras, 190–192
Hoover, J. Edgar, 173

Houston, Texas, 50, 74, 194
Houston Chronicle, 194

Iamascia, Danny, 141, 142
Immigration Service, U.S., 161, 180, 187–189
Impostato, Nicolo, 214
Incardona, Bastian, 91, 92, 96
India, 2, 231, 232–233
Indochina, 211, 215, 218, 223, 225
Inquisition, Spanish, 7–9, 12, 208, 209
Internal Revenue Service, 172, 173, 188–189, 216
International Labor Organization, 198
International Longshoremen's Association, 42, 199
Italiano, Salvatore, 215
Italian, anti-, demonstrations, 88, 89–90, 175
Italian Squad, 116–117, 123
Italy, 6, 35, 52, 53, 60, 90, 106, 107, 111, 135, 167, 175, 203, 236, 237–239
 parliament of, 84, 107, 117, 118, 120, 185, 226
 see also Rome, Naples, Sicily

Janesville, Wisconsin, 228
Jersey City, N.J., 165
Johnson, Art. 140–142
Johnson, Lyndon B., 170, 193, 198
Justice, Dept. of, U.S., 19, 61, 170, 172, 174, 187, 198, 215

Kansas City, Missouri, 122, 138, 162, 176, 179, 205, 214
Kefauver, Estes, 183
Kefauver hearings, 103, 183, 184
Kelly, Paul and Jim, 42
Kennedy, Robert, 170, 187–189
Kerryonians, 105
Khan, Aga, 231
Khodjas, 231
kidnapping, 36–37, 39–40, 106–108
kiss of death, 16, 169

Labruzzo, Tony, 46–49
La Guardia, Fiorello, 143, 179

Lamonti, Charles, 131
Lansky, Meyer, 134, 138, 149, 153, 160, 162, 174, 179, 181–182, 211
Laredo, Texas, 194
La Rocca, Antoine, 221–222
Las Vegas, Nevada, 162, 199
Lebanon, 212, 218, 220, 223, 225
Lecca, Giulio, 29
Leone, 37, 38–41, 43, 134, 236
Lercarda Friddi, Sicily, 134
Levant *Herald*, 240
Levine, Red, 160
Lewis, Norman, 58–59
Life, 165
Liggio, Luciano, 62
Lincoln, Abraham, 24–25
Livorsi, Pete, 153, 154
Lombroso, Cesare, 16, 18
Long, Huey, 178–179
Los Angeles, 100, 103, 165, 210
Los Angeles *Times*, 216
Louisiana, 116, 174, 175, 178–185, 188, 192–194, 205
 see also New Orleans
Lucania, Salvatore, *see* Luciano, Lucky
Lucchese, Thomas, 136, 146, 156, 163, 206
Luciano, Lucky, 42, 59, 60–61, 62, 113, 133, 134–135, 136, 138–139, 143, 151, 153, 154, 156, 157, 158, 159, 160, 161–162, 163, 164, 165, 166–167, 178, 180, 182, 206, 207, 212, 213
Lumia, Domiano, 59
Lumia, James, 215
lupara, 77, 91
Lupo, Ignatius, 111, 113, 115, 116, 118–119, 121, 122, 123–124, 130, 131, 141
Luzenberg, Charles, 90–92, 97
Lyons, France, 222

Maas, Peter, 170
Macheco, Joe, 49, 50, 73–75, 76, 77–85, 89, 91, 92, 95, 97, 100
Macino, Joseph, 107
Madden, Owney, 130, 138
Madonia, Benedetto, 115–116

INDEX   245

Mafia (American), 15, 24, 209, 223, 226
  and Black Hand, 67–72
  and Prohibition, 130
  and protection by government, 99, 105, 108, 125–126
  and Sicilian Mafia, 100, 103, 104
  arrival in America, 57–58, 80–81
  beginning of, in New Orleans, 73–98
  beginning of, in New York, 105–126
  beginning of, in San Francisco, 99–103
  growth in New York, 129–157
  in Louisiana, 73–98, 174–194
  vs. Camorra, 108, 110–111, 124–126, 131
  see also Cosa Nostra, gang warfare and assassination
Mafia (Sicilian), 1, 2, 6, 14, 24–31, 35–41, 52–63, 117, 118, 122, 135, 136, 197–198, 209, 212, 223, 226, 236–237
  aid to Allies, 58, 59–61
  and Cosa Nostra, 61–62
  origin of term, 28–31, 89
  origins of, 24–31, 37–41
  vs. American Mafia, 77–78
  vs. Fascists, 53–61
Maggadino, Antonio, 135
Maggadino, Stefano, 135, 136, 149, 150, 157, 162, 199, 206
Magliocco, Joe, 57, 135, 136, 138, 149
Mala Vita, 238–239
Mangano, Vincent, 57, 138, 156, 206
Mano Fraterna, 238
Manzella, Cesare, 62
Maranzano, Salvatore, 19, 57, 100, 135, 136–139, 142–143, 146–147, 149–157, 158–160
Marcello, Carlos, 174, 180–194, 202
Marcello, Joseph, 186
Marchese, Francesco Paola, 116
Marchesi, Antonio, 91
Marchesi, Aspari, 85, 91, 96
Maroun, Mike, 190–192
Marseilles, France, 41, 57, 111, 212, 214, 220, 221, 222, 223–225, 227
Masotto, Constantine, 181
Masseria, Joe, 113, 130–139, 143, 145–149, 151, 152–154, 156, 157, 158
Matranga, Charles, 76, 80, 81–83, 85, 87, 88, 89, 91, 96, 97, 98, 174, 175, 176, 184
Matranga, Tony, 82
Mazzini, Giuseppe, 15, 22, 24–31, 237
McClellan committee, 62, 144, 155, 158, 170, 197, 201, 203, 213
McClellan, George, 123
Mealli, Michael, 125–126
Meli, Francesco, 111
Meli, Rosario, 100–103
Messino, Salvatore, 101, 103
Mexico, 13, 167, 180, 206, 211, 212, 215, 225
Miami, Florida, 57, 130, 192
Middle East, 211, 212, 225
  see also Lebanon, Syria, Turkey
Mineo, Alfred, 134, 136, 148, 149, 153, 156, 158
Miranda, Mike, 136, 193
Mistretto, Salvatore, 123
Monasterio, Pietro, 85, 86, 91, 92, 95
Monia, Sam, 161
Monipodio, Señor, 10–12
Monnier, Marc, 15–18
Monreale, Sicily, 80, 120, 236–237
Montana, John C., 199
Monte Carlo, 167
Montreal, Canada, 130, 197, 217
Mooney, James, 46, 49
Moore, Cecil, 177–178
Morano, Pellagrino, 124, 125, 126
Morello, Antonio, 111, 112
Morello, Joe (Peter), 113, 116, 118, 122, 123–124, 130–131, 132, 133, 137, 141, 146, 158
Morello, Nicholas, 113, 124, 126, 130, 131, 144
Morello, Vincent, 113, 124, 130, 131
Moretti, Willie, 144
Morgan City, Louisiana, 192
Mori, Cesare, 53–57, 209

Morocco, 221
Morrison, Chep, 182
Morrison, Jimmy, 180
Mosca, Etienne, 225
Motto, Vincenzo, 107
Murder Incorporated, 162, 164–167
"Murder Stable," 113
Mussolini, Benito, 29, 53–54, 58, 60, 135, 157
Mussomeli, 59, 60

Naples, 14, 21–24, 28, 29, 36, 107, 108, 111, 119, 120, 121, 122, 126, 167, 209, 227
Narcissus, Quervada, 186
narcotics, 130, 143, 167–168, 197, 209–217, 218, 222, 224–225, 226, 228
Narcotics Bureau, U.S., 19, 184, 218, 212–213, 214
Nassau County, N.Y., 132
Natara, Antonio, 124–126
National Fascist Party, 53, 58, 60
Navarra, Dr. Michele, 62, 118
Navarra, Paola, 117–118
Newark, N.J., 161, 165
New Jersey, 102, 110, 113, 138, 161, 162, 164, 165, 194, 205, 216, 217
New Orleans, 31, 41, 42–51, 57, 67, 69–71, 73–98, 99, 100, 102, 103, 104, 107–108, 110, 114, 115, 116, 121, 122, 123, 138, 156, 162, 174–190, 193, 205, 207, 210, 211, 218, 227
 beginning of Mafia in, 73–98
 Innocents, 75, 76
 twentieth century, Mafia in, 174–190
 White League, 78–79
New Orleans *Daily Picayune*, 31, 43, 45, 47, 75, 78, 87
New Orleans *Daily States*, 51
New Orleans *True Delta*, 69, 70, 75–77, 108
New York City, 41–42, 45, 48–50, 57, 59, 69, 71, 72, 81, 87, 88, 99, 102, 103, 104, 105–126, 129–157, 158–167, 170, 178, 181, 182, 183, 193, 194, 199, 202, 203, 204–205, 213, 215, 216, 217, 223, 224, 227
 beginning of Mafia in, 105–126
 growth of Mafia in, 129–157
 Port of, 173, 199
 see also Bronx, Brooklyn, Queens, Staten Island
New York Herald, 48
New York Times, The, 29, 37, 38, 39, 50, 60, 71, 96, 102, 106, 109, 110, 111, 114, 129, 148, 159–160
Nimes, France, 224
Nixon, Richard, 173, 198, 205, 211
Nola, Italy, 60
Norfolk, Virginia, 57

Oblonica, 30
O'Dwyer, Bill, 166
Ogden, Utah, 203
Opium Exclusion Act, 209–210
Orient Express, 212, 224
Ottumvo, Vincenzo, 81

Padami, Steve, 156, 161
Palermo, Sicily, 24, 27–28, 31, 35–41, 46, 53, 54, 60, 61, 75, 78, 80, 100, 102, 103, 104, 106, 109, 111, 114, 115, 116, 117, 118, 119, 120, 121, 122, 134, 136, 180, 223, 236, 237
Panama City, Florida, 228
Pantaleone, Michele, 58–60
paranze, 17
Paretti, Tony, 125
Paris, France, 220, 222, 224, 225
Parisi, Alessandro, 39
Parkerson, W. S., 93, 96
Parmagini, Tony, 211
Partinico, Sicily, 120, 122
Pascanante, Antonio, 122
Patriarca, Raymond, 205
Pearson, Drew, 180
Pellegrini, Nick, 86
Pelletieri brothers, 118
Peraza, Luis de, 9
Persia, 2, 230–232
Persico, Michele, 17
Peru, 13

INDEX

Perugia, 35
Petrelli, Dominick "the Gap," 144, 145
Petrosino, Joseph, 111–123, 129, 130, 136, 209
Philadelphia, Pa., 72, 102, 124, 138, 162, 200, 205
Piani dei Greci, 53–54
Pinkerton, William, 79, 86, 88–89
Pino, Rosalino, 27
Pinzolo, Joseph, 145, 146, 153
Pittsburg, Pa., 114, 115
pizzu, 56
"plants," 198–204
Polizi, Joe, 31, 89, 91–92, 95
Polizzolo, Raffaele, 117
Polizzoti, Francesco, 121
Pollack, Seymour, 203–204
ponteadores, 10, 11
Poretto, Charles, 178
Profaci, Joe, 135, 136, 138, 146, 147–148, 149, 156, 162, 206
Prohibition, 97, 126, 129–131, 135, 162, 176, 198, 214
Provenzano, Joe, 49, 80–83, 85–88, 97, 98
Provenzano, Pete, 86

Quateraro, Carlo and Vincenzo, 109, 110
Queens, N.Y., 193

Ratons, 221
Ravenna, Italy, 237–238
Reina, Gaetano, 134, 136, 142–146, 147, 154
Reles, Abe, 166
Reno, Nevada, 124
Riccobono, Joseph, 203–204
Riis, Jacob, 109
Rinconete and Cortadillo, 9–12
Rizzoti, Giuseppe, 28
Rocco, Joseph, 106–107
Rodavio, Gaetano, 238
Rome, Italy, 26, 41, 49, 50, 53, 58, 83–84, 119, 120, 121, 122, 185, 228
Romero, Frank, 81, 91
Roosevelt, Franklin D., 143, 178
Roosevelt, Theodore, 111, 112

Rose, John Forester and George, 36–37, 38, 39–40, 45, 134
Rossi, Count Pellegrino, 26
Rothstein, Arnold, 138, 143, 211
Russo, Giuseppe Genco, 59, 60, 118
Russo, Luigi, 161
Rynders, Captain Isaiah, 105

Sabbah, Hassan, 230–231
Saccaro, Frank, 77
Saccarona, Louis and Frank, 143
Saietta, Ignazio, *see* Lupo, Ignatius
Saigon, Vietnam, 215
St. James Gazette, 240
St. Louis, Missouri, 47, 72, 87, 88, 89, 165, 176, 205, 214
Salerno, Italy, 111
Salt Lake City, Utah, 202
San Antonio, Texas, 194
San Antonio Express and News, 194
San Francisco, Cal., 72, 87, 88, 99–103, 210, 228
San Francisco *Examiner*, 100, 101
Santuccio, James, *see* Doyle, Bobby
Saupp, John, 148, 169
Sausolito, Cal., 101
Savino, John, 141, 142
Scaffidi, Antonio, 91, 92
Scalise, Frank, 156
Schultz, Dutch, 134, 141, 144, 149, 153, 157, 162, 211
Scotto, Anthony, 198–199
Seabury investigations, 143
secrecy, code of, 2, 18
Secret Service, 112, 113, 115, 123
Secret Societies of All Ages, 13, 18–19, 22
Securities and Exchange Commission, 202, 204
Semmes, Thomas J., 90–91
Senate investigations, U.S., 13, 118, 150, 158, 168, 187
 see also McClellan committee
Seville, Spain, 2, 5, 9, 10, 12, 13, 225
Seymour, Horatio, 74, 75
Shapiro, Jacob "Gurrah," 134
Sicily, 7, 14, 24, 27–31, 35–41, 52–63, 80, 100, 102, 103, 107, 108, 111, 112, 113, 115, 117, 118, 120–122, 130, 134, 135, 167, 174,

175, 180, 209, 220, 222, 226, 227, 236–237, 238
Allied invasion of, 58–61
see also Palermo
Siegel, Buggsy, 134, 138, 149, 153, 160, 162
slavery, Italian, 106–108
Sleeman, Sir William, 233
Solomon, Charles "King," 138
Spain, 1, 2, 5, 7, 8, 9, 10, 12, 13, 68–69, 209, 222, 225, 226
Spirito, François, 221–222, 224
Staten Island, N.Y., 138–139, 216–217
Stefani, Jean Paul, 222, 223
Steffens, Lincoln, 109, 111
stock, manipulation of, 202–204
Stone, Captain, 101, 102, 103
Stoppaglieri, 52–53, 80–83, 87, 88, 98, 126, 236–237
Strolle, Tony, 117
Strollo, Tony, *see* Bender, Tony
Strong, Seleh, 132
Suffolk County, N.Y., 132
Syracuse, Sicily, 102
Syria, 231

T. Leoluca, 184–185
Talese, Gay, 150, 156
Tammany Hall, 42, 105–106, 108, 123, 141, 143
Tampa, Florida, 57, 138, 193, 214, 215
Teamsters Union, 201, 202
Tedaro, Frank, 177–178, 180, 181
Terranova, Ciro, 113, 124, 130, 131, 133, 136, 139–144, 146, 149, 151, 153–154, 156
"Theory of the Dagger," 27
Thompson submachine gun, 137
Thugs, 2, 230, 232–233, 234–235
Tieri, Francesco, 206
Times, The, London, 35, 36, 96
Toledo, Spain, 12
Torrio, Johnny, 42, 117, 126, 162, 206
Trafficante, Santo (Jr.), 193, 215, 217
Trafficante, Santo (Sr.), 214–215
Tramunti, Carmine, 206
Trapani, Sicily, 53, 54, 120

Trapani brothers, 101, 102, 103
Tucson, Arizona, 206
Tunisia, 52, 57, 181, 185, 221
Turkey, 212, 225, 236, 239–240
Turkus, Burton, 166
Tweed Ring, 41
Tweed, William Marcy, 108
Twenties Group, 135–136, 142, 149

Uale, Frank, *see* Yale, Frank
Union Corse, 1, 2, 217, 218, 222–225
Unione Siciliana, 135–136

Valachi, Joe, 18, 19, 137, 144–152, 153, 154–155, 156, 157, 158–160, 162–163, 166, 167–171, 172, 174, 199, 213, 218
Valachi Papers, The, 170
Valenti, Rocco, 132–134
Valladares, Antonio, 186–187, 189
Vallero, Alessandro, 144
Vanderwoort, George, 81
vendetta, 219–221
Venezuela, 167
Villalba, Sicily, 59, 60
Vitale, Albert, 140–143
Viterbo trial, 117, 169
Vizzini, A., 30
Vizzini, Don Calo, 58–61
Vizzini, Sal, 213
Vollero, Alessandro, 124
Volstead Act, 129–130, 210

Wall, Charles, 214–215
Walsh, Thomas "Paddy," 138
Washington, D.C., 176
Weiss, Manny, 211
Whyos, 42
Williams, Alexander S., 42

Yale, Frank, 133, 135, 137, 142
Yonkers, N.Y., 151
"Young Italy Society," 25–26, 30
Yugoslavia, 212, 224, 227

Zapata, 6, 7
Zappi, Ettore and Anthony, 201
Zerilli, Joe, 136, 206
Zicarelli, Joseph, 217
Zwillman, Longy, 138, 162